MW00975765

The Business of Captivity

Plan of U.S Military Prison, Elmira N.Y.

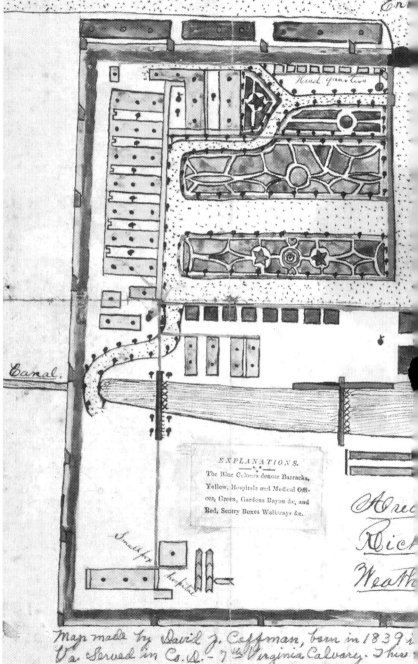

Head quarters

Canal.

EXPLANATIONS.

The Blue Colours denote Barracks,
Yellow, Hospitals and Medical Offi-
ces, Green, Gardens Bayou &c, and
Red, Sentry Boxes Walkways &c.

Map made by David J. Coffman, born in 1839 i—
Va Served in Co. D. - 7 th Virginia Calvary. This

Observatory

Road to Elmira

Pump

17

guard

guard house

yard
50 to El. Bride

nclosure about 49 Acres.

Sands, Exposed to freshets.
mmer, mild & pleasant.
er, very cold, Snow all winter.

while he was a prisoner of war at Elmira N.Y. Military
Prison
mmon or Hood River

The Business of Captivity

Elmira and Its Civil War Prison

MICHAEL P. GRAY

THE KENT STATE UNIVERSITY PRESS

KENT AND LONDON

To Sandy, m.j., and the memory of all American soldiers
who sacrificed mind, body, and spirit while in captivity.

Frontispiece: Virginian David Coffman mapped out his confines while a prisoner at Elmira. He added the watercolors and the printed key after his release on June 27, 1865. Notice the observatory at the upper right corner, the Foster home in front of the prison gates, and his "explanations" inside the enclosure. Courtesy of the Library of Virginia.

© 2001 by The Kent State University Press, Kent, Ohio 44242
All rights reserved
Library of Congress Catalog Card Number 2001029594
ISBN 0-87338-708-2 (cloth)
ISBN 978-1-60635-266-3 (paper)
Manufactured in the United States of America

Library of Congress Cataloging-in-Publication Data
Gray, Michael P., 1968–
    The business of captivity : Elmira and its Civil War prison/Michael P. Gray.
        p. cm.
    Includes bibliographical references (p.   ) and index.
    ISBN 0-87338-708-2 (alk. paper) ∞
        1. Elmira Prison (Elmira, N.Y.) 2. New York (State)—History—Civil War, 1861–1865— Prisoners and prisons. 3. United States—History—Civil War, 1861–1865—Prisoners and prisons. 4. Elmira (N.Y.)—History, Military—19th century. 5. Chemung county (N.Y.)—History, Military—19th century. 6. Prisoners of war—New York (State)—Elmira—History— 19th century. I. Title.

E616.E4 G73 2001
973.7′72—dc21   2001029594

Contents

Illustrations

Acknowledgments

Academic pursuits have left me indebted to many individuals and institutions. First, I thank Jeff, Marcy, Mandy, and Tess Wingo for their hospitality; since they courteously provided me with accommodations in the Elmira and Washington areas, I was able to keep travel expenses to a minimum.

I would like to thank the library staff at Kent State University, particularly the Inter-Library Loan and Reference departments, for making every effort to assist me. Also, the library staffs at Ohio State University, Columbus; Cornell University, Ithaca; Steele Memorial Library in Elmira; the New York Public Library, Manhattan; the New York State Library, Albany; the Alabama State Archives, Montgomery; and the public libraries in Honesdale, Pennsylvania, Port Jervis, New York; and Portland, Maine. Academic institutions providing holdings from their special collections were just as crucial in my research, including Emory University, Atlanta; Duke University, Durham, North Carolina; the University of North Carolina, Chapel Hill; and the University of Missouri, Rolla.

I spent many hours at local historical societies, notably the Chemung County Historical Society in Elmira—I am very grateful to its director, Connie Barone, along with its entire research staff, for their cordial and professional assistance in directing me through the historical society's voluminous resources. I would also like to thank the *Chemung Historical Journal* for giving me permission to have a June 1998 article "Uncovering a Ring Leader," published for this work.

I extend great appreciation for the information gathered from the Shohola Railroad Museum in Pike County, Pennsylvania, and for the help of George J.

Fluhr. Dr. John M. Coski of the Museum of the Confederacy in Richmond, Virginia, assisted me with that institution's holdings, as did Dr. Richard Sommers and David Keogh at the Army War College, Carlisle Barracks, Pennsylvania. A large majority of my research was conducted in Washington, D.C., at the National Archives; and to staff members Michael Musick, David Wallace, and Michael Hoover, I am very grateful.

In addition, I need to thank the Kent State University History Department, especially members of my dissertation committee for their suggestions. Of course my advisor, Dr. Frank L. Byrne, deserves the most credit—his advice, encouragement, and guidance will never be forgotten. Dr. Byrne not only encouraged me to investigate the economics at Elmira Prison, but he helped me by sharing his own experiences while researching Civil War prisons—moreover, the work of his doctoral advisor, William B. Hesseltine, has undoubtedly inspired us both.

As the dissertation had moved into the publication stage, Director John T. Hubbell became instrumental in its progression, from his editing to his valuable suggestions, for which I am truly grateful. I am indebted, too, to the anonymous readers who reviewed this work at an early stage, encouraged its publication, and offered thoughtful comments for its improvement. Thanks, too, to copyeditor Leigh Johnsen, for his crucial close, careful attention to detail. Moreover, the proofreading and copyediting of Managing Editor Erin Holman has made my first experience in writing a book extremely positive, something that I hope will be the case in future endeavors. I am grateful, also, to each of the other individuals at the Kent State University Press who in some way contributed to this book. I also gratefully acknowledge the Kent State University Press for allowing me permission to include in this work my article "Elmira, a City on a Prison Camp Contract," first published in *Civil War History* 45.4 (December 1999).

I must mention that in a recent work on Andersonville Prison the author expressed dissatisfaction with competing historians who failed to assist him in his research, something that could be attributed to the controversial nature of Civil War prisons. Fortunately, I never experienced that situation; Carl Morrell, J. Michael Horigan, George Fluhr, and George Levy, all of whom are currently working or have worked on facets of Elmira Prison, deserve especial commendation.

I am also fortunate in having supportive family members who have helped me in some way during this project, including my mother, Ronnie; sister, Katie; and father, Richard. My father deserves special credit because he was able to procure for me the invaluable personal papers of John S. Kidder, through his relatives Carlton Pike and Jerry Reed. I cannot forget to mention my two sons, Matthew and Joshua, who occasionally and not regrettably took me away from this study, each of them serving as a reminder of the more important things in life. Finally, with all the help, guidance, and encouragement that I have received, one person comes to the forefront for her unending patience, support, and love—words especially exemplified in the determination of a wife putting her husband through graduate school, not to mention in the hours spent proofreading, typing, and providing companionship on research trips. This book would not be possible without my wife, Sandy, and therefore it is dedicated to her, and for every sacrifice she made for me to see to its comple-

The Chemung Valley Prior to Civil War

Long before the American Civil War, the Chemung River Valley had served as a gathering place for people. Native American tribes, particularly Senecas from the Iroquois Confederacy, created villages along the river and set up markets for trade. During the American Revolution, British soldiers and Indian warriors combined their forces in the valley before their bloody attack down into Pennsylvania, which culminated in the Wyoming Massacre of 1778. The following year, Continental troops under Gen. John Sullivan won a decisive battle in the heart of Chemung Valley, established a base there, then proceeded with five thousand soldiers on an expansive expedition through the New York frontier. After pillaging the countryside, broken parties rendezvoused at Chemung fort about three weeks later. Their objective in stripping the Chemung, Genesee, and Finger Lakes region to keep the enemy from foraging was so complete that natives abandoned the area altogether, leaving settlement open for the taking.[1]

Mathias Hollenback recognized the favorable environment of the Chemung Valley, notably for businessmen. Fortunate in being a survivor of the Wyoming attack, Hollenback organized a profitable trading post in 1783 near the site of the fort by the confluence of Newton Creek and Chemung River. In addition to Hollenback's agents, other early pioneers included Revolutionary War veterans that had participated in the Sullivan expedition. Many of these men returned, this time to till the soil and make their home.[2]

From early settlement, the Chemung Valley's topography was conducive to being a hub of economic or military activity. The terrain and river act as a natural corridor from west to east and gradually slopes southward. The valley could also be reached from the north by the Finger Lakes and further east as the Susquehanna bent toward its headwaters. From the west, the Chemung River began at a fork where the Tioga and Cohocton Rivers empty, flowing into a valley some forty miles long. As the Chemung winds through a wooded landscape, the valley widens to about five miles in its middle, while the river runs at the base of nearby hills and mountains typical of the Northern Appalachians. Still meandering southeasterly, the valley tapers, reopening again so that the river can catch the stronger current produced by the main trunk of the Susquehanna in Pennsylvania. By design of Mother Nature, travel in and out of Chemung Valley was easy.[3]

Early in the nineteenth century, hamlets, and settlements were organized throughout the river valley. Three such hamlets established near Hollenback's trading post united to form the village of Newtown in 1815. In 1828, the name of Newtown was formally changed to Elmira, allegedly after a local pub owner's daughter. Elmira numbered just under three thousand individuals and consisted of a courthouse, jail, post office, schools, churches, taverns, and inns. Blacksmiths, coopers, carpenters, tanners and distillers began setting up shop. Bridges and roads were constructed, while creeks and rivers were dammed for grist, flour, and saw mills. Farmers raised wheat, grain, corn, and oats, and corralled horses, cattle, chicken, sheep, and other livestock.[4]

When the Valley's first canal was completed in 1833, farmers and craftsmen expanded their markets. That same year a bank was chartered in Elmira that bore the name of the canal, indicating its financial value to the community. The Chemung Canal was built with fifty-three locks and extended twenty-three miles from Elmira north to the waters of Seneca, one of the Finger Lakes. The lumber industry improved markedly due to the canal and indigenous trees, especially pine, which were felled and brought to sawmills for manufacturing. Grain was another local product, while cargoes of coal and salt were transported inward from outlying regions. It took almost a quarter of a century to increase trade further south via the Junction Canal, which linked the Chemung and Susquehanna systems. By that time, however, a new technological innovation had made commerce a year-round endeavor, with speed and practicality the canal could not match.[5]

In the fall of 1849, the New York and Erie Railroad was ready for business at Elmira. This railway became a main line connecting New York City and the East Coast with the western and southern parts of the state. Later that year, the Chemung Railroad was completed so that a route could parallel the canal to the Finger Lakes. In the 1850s, more lines merged and rail service expanded north from Canandaigua to Williamsport, Pennsylvania, and south, and subsequently consolidated under the Northern Central Railroad. With the north-south tracks of the Northern Central, which intersected the east-west path of the New York and Erie, the Chemung Valley was accessible from all four directions with the best vehicles of the day. Elmira became an important railroad terminus that would change the composition of the town as it adjusted again to its later purpose as a military rendezvous.[6]

On the eve of the Civil War, Elmira was keeping pace with nineteenth-century development, but city status proved evasive. Its population stagnated from 1850 to 1860, increasing by only 516 persons to an ending total of 8,682. Businesses, churches, schools, and even a women's college had been founded, but a folksy attitude prevailed. No police department existed, nor was one necessary to guard over the town's people and property. Most residents of Chemung County were primarily engaged in agriculture. The community was simply a rural town that lacked the hustle and bustle associated with cities. On April 14, 1861, when a Union garrison surrendered at a far away fort in South Carolina, the pace of ordinary country living in Elmira changed forever.[7]

I

The Elmira Depot

On April 15, 1861, reporters at the state capital in Albany were informed that Governor Edwin G. Morgan could recruit as many as 25,000 men in response to a presidential call for 75,000 volunteers to suppress the rebellion. Morgan's public appeal for volunteers was not authorized until April 18, and with the approval of the New York legislature, he asked for 13,280 troops to fill the Empire State's quota. Governor Morgan also announced that the military bases where soldiers would be mustered and trained should "be at New York, Albany, and Elmira."[1]

Two of the three selections seemed obvious. Albany not only was the capital, but was also the state's military headquarters. New York City, a major commercial center with a population over a million, could easily support large numbers of troops. The selection of Elmira, however, must have come as a surprise to many, especially the mayors of Buffalo, Rochester, and Syracuse. Evidently, Governor Morgan was pressured enough by Secretary of War Simon Cameron to take special notice of Elmira's geographic location and the various railroad lines leading into and out of town, particularly that of the Northern Central—which ran through Cameron's home state and in which he had money interests—so Cameron would make sure it received more than its fair share of use. These decisions confirmed Elmira's place in history as a military hub, serving as a gathering place for Union troops from western New York and beyond, sending them down the valley to the south and to the battlefields of civil war.[2]

Elmira became consumed with its newfound military assignment. On April 20, the *Elmira Daily Advertiser* predicted that up to seventeen thousand soldiers would be raised, which "will make for stirring times in Elmira, for some time."[3] On April 21, Mayor Steven Arnot signed a contract with the assistant quartermaster for the lease of a barrel factory to house troops at fifty dollars a month. On the same day, a local merchant leased two rooms in his brick store for five dollars a month to keep munitions. By the end of the week, T. Post and H. H. Purdy had secured a contract to provide daily rations for soldiers at forty-two cents a man. They would be busy since 5,000 men would consume 6,500 pounds of beef, 600 pounds of sugar, 300 pounds of coffee, 4 bushels of salt, and 13 bushels of beans. Such appetites required appropriate eating utensils, so orders were filled by Riggs Watrous and Elisha Cook. Knives and forks sold for three and one-half cents, spoons two and one-half cents, while 2,500 tin cups and plates were bought at seven cents apiece. Elmira was full of financial opportunities, but an even more lucrative contract was available.[4]

As volunteers arrived in Elmira, officials realized that more than a barrel factory was necessary for their shelter. On April 29, a contract was drawn between Jervis Langdon and the New York state military to build seventy barracks for recruits. They were to be made from pine and measured about ninety feet long and eighteen feet wide, have sloped roofs double boarded with vents, doors at each end, and windows every ten feet. The work was to "commence immediately and to be finished at the least possible time."[5] If the Quartermaster's Department felt the project was not being carried out under the negotiated terms, it could void the agreement and hire workers to finish the job at Langdon's expense. It was well worth the risk, since the builder would be paid two hundred dollars for each unit finished, amounting to a fourteen-thousand-dollar contract.[6]

One month after Governor Morgan designated Elmira as a state rendezvous, more than six thousand soldiers occupied the depot. Those unable to stay in barracks had to be content with sleeping in buildings not usually associated with the army. If needed, churches, warehouses, and public halls were utilized. Schiller Hall, for example, was rented out at eighteen dollars a month. Most soldiers found themselves at one of the four main military installations set up in town during May and June. Officially designated as the Arnot Barracks, Post Barracks, Camp Robinson, and Camp Rathbun, they could accommodate more than ten thousand men altogether.[7]

Arnot Barracks were constructed on a three-hundred-yard square plot, fenced in on three sides, about a mile northeast of Newtown Creek. A road led directly to the camp on its open side, where one might see its ten barracks, mess hall, guardhouse, and two officer buildings. Each barrack, 88-by-18 feet, was intended to hold from 100 to 150 men, whereas the entire camp was outfitted to provide for no more than fifteen hundred troops. A little northwest of this facility were the Post Barracks, situated closer to the Chemung Canal. This camp was more rectangular than the Arnot camp, containing twenty barracks, one mess hall, two guardhouses, and officer quarters. Two public roads ran through camp, so Post Barracks could be fenced only on the north and west sides. Post Barracks could house two thousand troops, and with some adjustments could accommodate another thousand. Camp Robinson, a mile and a half southwest of downtown on the opposite side of the Chemung River, resembled Post Barracks in size and shape. If needed, it could also hold up to three thousand soldiers.[8]

Camp Rathbun deserves special attention because it eventually became the stockade known as Elmira Prison. William Foster of Elmira had leased out some of his farmland to the state of New York for the purpose of establishing a military encampment. Terms of the lease were elastic and the land could be occupied from one month to a year, or perhaps longer. The cost was fixed at $375 annually. The ground under contract, a portion of it once used as a racecourse, encompassed a field from the Chemung River to a road that passed the Foster house. In addition, the army had the right to use an elongated pond owned by Foster, located back by the river. Foster was promised that his land would be returned to him in its original condition, other than wear on the soil and vegetation.[9]

Camp Rathbun was built along Water Street, a good road that made travel easy to downtown Elmira, approximately a mile to the east. Between the road and river was the 300-by-500-yard campground. The rectangular area was fenced on the west, north, and east; Foster's Pond formed the southern boundary. A camp road divided the grounds, with ten barracks on each half, constructed under the specifications given to Jervis Langdon. The twenty units, 88-by-18 feet, had two rows of wooden bunks running down the sides. Behind the barracks were officer's quarters, a sutler's storehouse, and sinks. Further back were two mess halls containing tables and benches that could seat a thousand men each, and each hall was separated by a kitchen equipped with boilers, ranges, furnaces, and a steam engine, with the capability of cooking for two thousand persons at a time. Foster's Pond, twelve yards wide and extending nearly the entire length of the camp, provided water for washing and bathing. Camp Rathbun was originally designed to support two thousand soldiers, although with some remodeling it could house another thousand.[10]

Companies were assigned to the four main bases after senior officers reported to the commander of the Elmira Depot. Requisitions had to be submitted for rations, uniforms, and arms. In the meantime, here in the Chemung Valley hundreds of miles away from the war, men were supposed to be made into soldiers. A terse order from the adjutant general's office stated what was expected of them during their stay: "Officers and men will use all diligence acquiring a knowledge of the duties which will be required of them when in the field."[11] During war, 20,796 soldiers trained in Elmira. By the end of June, not even three months after the depot opened, 9,500 had already gone through that process.[12]

This movement of soldiers typified Elmira throughout much of the Civil War. Men arrived for basic training; citizens gathered for their dress parades; then the soldiers marched away. On July 6, the *Elmira Weekly Advertiser* reported that "all the regiments of this depot have received their uniforms, and now will be forwarded to the seat of war. . . . By the close of next week," the newspaper predicted, "Elmira will be 'itself again.'"[13] The *Advertiser* could not have been more wrong, although for at least a while its prediction may have seemed correct. Toward the end of August, only two thousand soldiers occupied the depot. By New Year, 1862, most of the barracks were uninhabited.[14]

In late June 1862, Capt. Henry M. Lazelle inspected the Elmira Depot for Commissary General of Prisons William Hoffman, who was looking for new places to confine captured Southerners. Lazelle found hardly any troops in the barracks except fifty at Camp Rathbun. In fact, Camp Robinson and Post Barracks would never be used again. As for Hoffman's dilemma, by next month the belligerents had worked out a prisoner exchange system. In addition, President Abraham Lincoln would soon make a call for another 300,000 men, making barracks space once again at a premium.[15]

At the beginning of 1863, the federal government organized the Department of the East, which controlled all camps, forts, and barracks within New England and New York. Elmira was named headquarters for the western part of the Empire State, and when conscription was implemented the War Department designated it as a draft rendezvous. Since Post Barracks and Camp Robinson were disbanded, more facilities were erected at the remaining camps. Arnot Barracks and Camp Rathbun, also identified as Barracks Number 1 and Barracks Number 3, were the two active rendezvous bases in Elmira. The Elmira Depot would also consist of hospitals, storehouses, corral stables, and eventually, a prison camp.[16]

Events in 1863 had important implications for the Elmira Depot. By the end of summer, the agreement for exchanging prisoners had come to a halt. The exchange cartel had significantly lessened prisoners of war, and therefore reduced the number of places needed for their confinement.[17] The system worked by swapping men of the same rank or trading a number of common soldiers for officers—a general, for example, was valued at sixty privates, a colonel at fifteen, and a captain at six. No later than ten days after being captured, men were to be placed on parole and usually sent to camps behind their lines as they awaited orders. Paroled men were not to serve until officially exchanged.[18]

The cartel was doomed for a variety of reasons. Men might readily surrender, preferring a safer life as a prisoner to duty at the front. There were also instances when parolees had been sent back into service before being formally exchanged. Add African Americans fighting for the Union and the Confederacy's unwillingness to exchange them, along with Southern threats to execute the white officers of these African American soldiers, and the system proved unworkable. A year later, when the manpower of the South was highly valued, Ulysses S. Grant balked at reconciling differences: "Every man we hold, when released on parole or otherwise, becomes an active soldier against us at once either directly or indirectly."[19]

Grant's policy of total war could not be burdened with an exchange system.[20] "We have got to fight until the military power of the South is exhausted," he believed, "and if we release or exchange prisoners captured it simply becomes a war of extermination." Henry W. Halleck, concurred: "It is much cheaper to feed an enemy in prison than to fight him in the field." The system would operate sparingly throughout the war's remainder, used only in such special circumstances as exchanging inmates too ill to bear further suffering in prison.[21] Unfortunately, many captives fell under that category, but their appeals to return home fell on deaf ears. For all practical purposes, federal leaders considered the cartel dead, theorizing that it was better to sacrifice men in prison instead of on the battlefield, thus hoping to bring the war to a quicker end.

Throughout the first quarter of 1864 Elmira grew as more draftees and recruits arrived in the Chemung Valley. The transient military personnel led to a steady rise in the population, to over twelve thousand individuals. On April 7, 1864, the state legislature incorporated Elmira, which was divided into five wards, as a city. Businesses were prospering and locals signing contracts not possible without the military post.[22]

May 1864 was one of those relatively idle times at Elmira. Six companies of the 179th New York Volunteers had recently departed, and barracks were emptying at Camp Rathbun.[23] On May 14, Asst. Adj. Gen. Edward D. Townsend informed Commissary General Hoffman, who wanted to establish a new stockade due to the congested state of his prisons, that "there are quite a number of barracks at Elmira, N.Y., which are not occupied, and are fit to hold rebel prisoners. Quite a large number of those lately captured could be accommodated at this place."[24] Hoffman did not hesitate to act on this recommendation.

2

Preparations, Arrivals, and Disaster

The Inauguration of Elmira Prison

On May 19, 1864, Commissary General William Hoffman ordered Rendezvous Commander Seth Eastman "to set apart the barracks on the Chemung River at Elmira as a depot for prisoners of war."[1] Lieutenant Colonel Eastman, who had prior experience managing prisoners at the McLean Barracks in Cincinnati, was directed to secure Elmira's Barracks Number 3 with a stockade wall twelve feet high, framed on the exterior and far away enough from buildings to deter escapes. For additional protection, a sentry walk was to be attached to the wall so guards could view from above those inside and outside the enclosure. Hoffman expected the number of prisoners to be around ten thousand because he had been told that Barracks Number 3 once held a similar number. Eastman was properly concerned about the numbers and even more concerned when Hoffman told him that the prison might be needed in ten days.[2]

On the same day that Hoffman wrote to Eastman, he also explained the situation to Secretary of War Edwin M. Stanton. There were ten thousand Rebels confined at Point Lookout Prison in Maryland and Hoffman thought it should accept five thousand more. The exchange cartel's suspension was made worse by recent battles that produced a multitude of prisoners. Hoffman believed that Elmira could solve the dilemma of overcrowded Union stockades in an economical manner. Hoffman, who throughout his military career demonstrated a penchant for thrift, interjected, "By fencing them in at a cost of about $2,000 they may be relied on to receive 8,000 or possibly 10,000 prisoners."[3] It was a low price that should have even pleased the war secretary.

On May 23, Eastman responded to Hoffman. After all, Hoffman was proposing a population inside Barracks Number 3 close to the holding capacity

Wartime bust of Lt. Col. Seth Eastman, the commander of the Elmira Depot. Courtesy of the Massachusetts Commandery, Military Order of the Loyal Legion, USAMHI.

for all four original camps that comprised the Elmira Depot. Although ten more barracks had been erected recently, Eastman thought the camp could hold only about half the men his superior had hoped. The quarters, which had double bunks and good ventilation, were in excellent shape. Four thousand men could be housed in them while another thousand could live in tents. A kitchen and bakery could feed five thousand a day and the mess room could accommodate fifteen hundred per sitting. The camp had no hospital because facilities were provided in the city, so again tents could be used. Eastman seemed more concerned that the size of his garrison, two hundred members of the Veterans Reserve Corps, was not sufficient for guarding the numbers either he or Hoffman had presented. In closing, Eastman reported that construction of the stockade wall had begun and should be finished by the first week of June, so he hoped that no Southerners would be delivered until then.[4]

The conversion from a training base for Northerners to a prison camp for Southerners caused Elmira's Quartermaster's Department to become very busy. Barracks Number 3, erected by the state of New York and then transferred to the federal government, would undergo another transition. The provost general had to relinquish control to the adjutant general when the camp was modified into a stockade. Buildings inside Barracks Number 3 were consigned to Elmira's quartermaster, Capt. John J. Elwell, and land leases paid by his assistant, Capt. Simon P. Suydam. The $375 contract awarded to William Foster for just the stockade area had to be extended another year. Favored by their close proximity to the camp, the Foster family continued to lease or rent its real estate to the military at annual rates. A. S. Foster leased 25 acres of his property for $375 and Jesse Foster rented 40 acres at $840, both contracts necessitated by the introduction of the prison garrison.[5]

In addition to taking care of buildings, property, and leases, the Elmira Quartermaster Department was responsible for hiring persons to help construct the stockade. For a monthly wage of forty dollars, John Blastock, Ure Deck, M. A. Kenneday, V. Johnson, and Lorenzo Shaffer were employed as teamsters to deliver lumber to the construction site. Some thirty carpenters earned up to $2.50 daily. A water carrier was paid a dollar per day.[6] In accordance with Hoffman's specifications, the twelve-foot-high fence extended 5,610 feet around a rough rectangular plot. Sunken about eighteen inches into the soil, the planked wall had sills nailed together along the exterior bracing slats, which were further buttressed by posts leaning into the facade. A main gate faced the Foster residence across from Water Street, while a smaller doorway for officers was built next to it. The wooden walkway above, eight feet up and four feet wide, had sentry boxes set at intervals. Altogether forty-seven sentry boxes existed, each with diamond-shaped windows so that the entire area could be seen even in foul weather. Stairways outside the enclosure led guards up to an elevated position where railings guided them along, which proved especially helpful during night watch. On the inside of the fence, water wells were dug, while soldiers still stationed there prepared for their relocation across town to Barracks Number 1.[7]

On June 22, a perturbed Hoffman wrote to Eastman: "By direction of the Secretary of War the barracks (No. 3) at Elmira will be prepared to receive prisoners of war according to the instructions contained in my letter of May 19. In establishing the fence it is advisable, if practicable, to inclose ground enough to accommodate in barracks and tents 10,000 prisoners."[8] All supplies, such as tents or cooking items, were to be estimated for those numbers. On June 30, Capt. Elwell wired the quartermaster general that the pen was ready for ten thousand, but Eastman complained to the adjutant general about his lack of staff. If fifty companies of two hundred prisoners each were expected, and if according to prison regulations one officer had to be in charge of each company, then the twelve men Eastman had for this purpose would be inadequate. More officers were required, as was housing, because no barracks were planned for them; wall tents would have to suffice during the interim. Eastman also requested permission to pay soldiers and civilians to work at prison jobs that ranged from clerks to bakers to laborers. Meanwhile, on the day that Elmira Prison was finished, Hoffman ordered the commander at Point Lookout to prepare two thousand enlisted prisoners for removal. They were to be divided up into groups of four hundred, each detachment escorted by one hundred guards, and all men were to be given two days of cooked rations. These Rebels were the first of many to leave the lower Maryland shore for the valley of the Chemung and embark on the arduous journey north.[9]

The prisoners assembled by the main gate; some left their possessions behind, unaware of their impending trip. They marched to the dock to board steamers, among them the *Favorite, Continental,* and *Victor.*[10] Some passengers referred to the vessels in uncomplimentary terms, one claiming his to be "a narrow log of a propeller," another, "a miserable old government transport only fitted to carry cattle."[11] Their course took the prisoners down the Chesapeake Bay, past Hampton Roads and into the Atlantic Ocean, then up the Delmarva Peninsula and Jersey Shore for New York Harbor. The voyage at sea could take two days, but for many it seemed to last much longer.[12]

The ships had limited space and no sleeping arrangements.[13] Private Walter D. Addison, captured in the Wilderness campaign, wrote that the men, who numbered about a thousand, were crammed together "in the sweltering heat of July." "The sight of these holds was sickening in the extreme . . . the voyage can be imagined better than described."[14] A number of men were already ill before they boarded, and the bread and fatty pork ration, combined with ocean waves, did not quell their queasy stomachs. The poor ventilation and lack of equipment to clean the ships resulted in a putrid odor that hung over the vessel, provoking even more bellies to churn. The filthy floors were so crowded that some men slept upright.[15] One recalled, "We had not been on the ocean long until one after another became sick and we numbered thousands."[16] A North Carolinian seemed proud because "a great many of our boys were seasick, but not I."[17] However, a witty Virginian was "consummately miserable" until reaching the harbor. His sickness was due to "that infernal stomach pump, known as the 'ground swell,'" an undulation of the sea which, in his opinion, Mother Nature produced "to prevent her children from the folly of navigation."[18]

The overland trip to the Chemung Valley was generally a more pleasurable experience. At Jersey City the prisoners were loaded onto cars of the Erie Railway for the three-hundred-mile trip to Elmira. Delays were frequent because trains had to stop to take on fuel or yield the track to other locomotives traveling the same route. Guards ordered the men not to converse with civilians as they awaited departure, yet if the chance arose Southerners might persuade civilians, especially women, to slip crackers or tobacco past the guards. Men would more often yell insults at the captives. In spite of inhospitable Yankees, whatever could be had was worth the trouble because Confederates would soon lose contact with much of the outside world.[19]

At daybreak July 6, the train carrying the first contingent of four hundred prisoners chugged into Elmira's Erie Station. Arrival marked not only the beginning of a new day, but also the dawning of Chemung Valley's newest enterprise. Guards marched the prisoners in double column for about a mile, south on Main Street, and then turned west onto Water Street. The stockade gates swung open, the prisoners entered, and the business of captivity began. Prisoners were counted, separated into companies of one hundred, and shown to their quarters. A commissioned officer was in charge of each company, while an enlisted man served as an orderly sergeant. Special Order No. 251, issued four days earlier by Lieutenant Colonel Eastman, designated the officers in charge, and each was expected to report to the new prison commandant, Major Henry V. Colt, 104th New York Volunteers.[20]

Like many detailed to Civil War prisons, Henry Colt was given his position because he was unable to serve in the field. Colt, whose brother gained fame from pistol making, was born in Portland at the western corner of New York. He had been a farmer before enlisting in 1861 for three years in the cavalry. On May 10, 1862, while on a forced march from Alexandria to Yorktown, Colt

Maj. Henry V. Colt, the first commandant of Elmira Prison. Colt was generally well liked by his Confederate prisoners. Courtesy of the Chemung County Historical Society.

attempted to jump over a ditch. He landed awkwardly, his momentum forcing the point of his saber into the ground, and the saber rammed its handle into a delicate area. Suffering now from an inguinal hernia made worse by lifting and bouts with rheumatism, he returned home to New York.[21]

In 1863, Colt was assigned to detached duty at the Elmira Rendezvous. He supervised Barracks Number 1, and in the following year was appointed head of the prison. Colt had just turned thirty-one when given command of the pen. He stood five feet nine inches tall, and had a portly frame, brown hair, blue eyes, and a light complexion. He wore his hat cocked stylishly to the side when in uniform, and his bearing suggested the personification of the officer and gentleman class. His only fault, besides being a poor hurdler, seemed to be an addiction to cigars. His demeanor and temperament made him popular with Union and Confederate soldiers alike, a trait not shared by many of his counterparts, North or South.[22]

Five days after the first Confederates arrived another detachment of 249 was led to the stockade. Their arrival at 5:00 A.M. was too early for citizens to meet them at the station, but the local newspaper supplied details. "They were ragged and dirty as usual, but withy, enduring looking fellows, and seemed docile and contented."[23] On the next day, two hours after the preceding group arrived, 502 weary Rebels from Spotsylvania and Cold Harbor were dropped off. Their later arrival prompted a number of onlookers to help escort them to prison. The prison population had risen to 1,150 just a week into its operation.[24]

The twelve-foot wall could not conceal the Chemung Valley's vivid green panoramic slopes, which were preferable to a drab sky and endless sea at Point Lookout. Grass and sod comprised the forty-acre prison yard, but more important to the prisoners was the fresh and plentiful water supply, something that their old confines lacked. Elmira Prison's topography was uneven because the prison had been erected on the north bank of the Chemung River, so the camp was divided. The upper portion was level with the city and comprised two-thirds of the enclosure. This high ground contained most of the camp buildings, including headquarters near the main gate, the twenty original barracks or wards, plus the ten more recent units. Tree-lined roads helped give order to the compound. A thoroughfare ran south from the gate until it intersected a macadamized street that led to the mess rooms, a cookhouse and bakery, and supply buildings. The lower half of the camp dropped 20 feet toward the pond and river, where weeds grew in loose, sandy soil. Foster's Pond, 12 yards wide and 580 yards in length, dominated this portion of the prison. The pond came within twenty feet of the western wall, and on its opposite side a bridge crossed over the water, while the pond narrowed underneath the eastern fence and connected to the river.[25]

Five days after the prison opened, Surgeon Charles T. Alexander inspected the pen at Hoffman's request. He found two major concerns. First was the camp's sanitary condition, caused by inferior sinks located near Foster's Pond. They contained stagnant water and if not cleaned might quickly "become offensive and a source of disease."[26] Alexander recommended either building new sinks or flushing the old ones by running a conduit from the river. Hoffman did not immediately heed the suggestions, thereby worsening the problem. The other warning dealt with poor hospital organization. William C. Wey, a local civilian, was the only physician to visit the pen.[27] Alexander told Hoffman that it was imperative for "a competent surgeon to take charge." Furthermore, the notion of using tents for a hospital was inappropriate, so an area on the upper side of the pen was selected for three pavilion wards, each of which cost five hundred dollars. The expenditures of Hoffman's prison were increasing, but it was good that a hospital was being planned because one would soon be needed.[28]

The fourth group of Point Lookout prisoners transferred to Elmira was the largest yet, numbering 833, along with 125 guards and 3 officers of the 11th and 20th Veterans Reserve Corps. On Tuesday evening, July 12, they embarked on the *Crescent*, reaching New York on Thursday at 3:00 in the afternoon. Before sunrise the next day they climbed into cars of the Erie Railway in Jersey City. The captors soon realized that three Confederates had hidden onboard the vessel, which delayed the entourage more than an hour until the prisoners were found, but eventually the party left around 6:00 A.M. An opened drawbridge prolonged its stay for another two hours. Locomotive 171, operated by William Ingram and assisted by fireman Daniel Tuttle, pulled eighteen cars behind its tender, three of the boxed type carrying thirty to forty men, five of whom were guards. Successive coaches accommodated more than sixty passengers each. The officer in charge, Capt. Morris H. Church of the 11th Veterans Reserve Corps, posted guards at the front and back platforms of each car. The last three cars conveyed Union soldiers not on detail, plus their equipment. Upon reaching Port Jervis, New York, at 1:00 in the early afternoon, the train took on water and wood before steaming ahead.[29]

For twenty-three miles after Port Jervis the Erie Railway's dual tracks merged into a single road. As the train proceeded behind schedule into the mountainous Upper Delaware Valley, it crossed to the Pennsylvania side and followed the Delaware River's twisting course. Riding precariously along ledges of the scenic Poconos, passengers were confined on one side by jutting bluffs, while a steep bank dropped on the other side to a gliding Delaware River below. Travelers could do little but admire the beauty, brace for curves, and rely on the skill of those who worked the iron horse. Trying to make up for the nearly three hours they had lost, Ingram and Tuttle pushed on at a pace of twenty-five miles per hour until they reached the station at Shohola.

There, they were given possession of the lone track, not having to pull off for oncoming traffic, which would have caused further delay.[30]

Chugging from Shohola toward Lackawaxen on the sun-filled midafternoon of July 15, the train approached King and Fuller's Cut, a halfway point between the junctions. The cut was named after contractors who had hollowed out rocky ground around a ridge for rails, which resulted in a tricky bend that could limit vision to fifty feet when cornering. In this turn another locomotive suddenly appeared. For some reason, at the Hawley connection in Lackawaxen a heavily loaded coal train pulling fifty cars had been admitted to the occupied rails. The coal train rolled downhill at twelve miles per hour, each swaying car loaded with twelve tons. Ingram frantically reversed his engine, while the engineer in the coal train dove out of his cab. A tremendous crash shook the ground on this warm summer day, the screech of tearing metal and crack of buckling wood resonating over the natural quietude of the upper valley. An eerie, silent moment preceded the heartrending cries, moans, shouts, and screams of the wounded and dying.[31]

The smoke and debris cleared to reveal a grim spectacle. Both locomotives were elevated high against each other, and cars down the line were crushed, overturned, ripped in half, or on top of each other. All but one man in the first car perished, thrown clear before the impact smashed the car to a length less than six feet. Soldiers in the leading cars, the majority prisoners, bore the brunt of the accident. Many of the detailed guards also lay injured or dead, especially those riding on outside decks. Captain Church called together reserves in the last cars, which felt the effects of the collision less, and had them promptly encircle the wreck to foil plans of escape. About five Rebels, however, managed to slip away during the confusion.[32]

One guard, Frank Evans, rushed ahead to find the cause of the mishap and saw the locomotives embracing "like giants grappling."[33] Ingram and Tuttle were wedged between a ruptured boiler, which emitted scorching steam, and firewood, thrown on them when their tender toppled. Ingram was still alive, but warned others to stay clear, afraid that the boiler might blow up at any second. Then his words faded as he slowly roasted. Engineer Samuel Hoitt, who jumped from the coal train, also feared an explosion. He gathered his thoughts and ran for his engine to release the steam and look for survivors. It took him three minutes to find his fireman and drag him out of the wreckage. Shortly thereafter, the fireman died. The impact had also killed the brakeman.[34]

Almost two miles away villagers in Shohola heard the collision and followed the noise to the scene. Bodies were strewn on or around the track; victims still living pleaded for help. The force of the collision maimed and mangled men; body parts were tossed about.[35] As afternoon passed into night, more than one hundred injured soldiers were taken to the village. A relief train came from Port Jervis with doctors and railroad employees. Union guards, Confederate prisoners, and local citizens were already helping to clean up, a morbid job that continued into the next morning. Corpses were moved closer to the river, the owner of the land where the crash occurred preferring a mass grave off of his property. Discarded arms, legs, and trunks were collected, and at least two bodies were found decapitated. Some corpses were so severely disfigured as to be unrecognizable. By 11:00 P.M. the digging of a trench, seventy-six feet long, eight feet wide, and the customary six feet deep, had begun on the south bank. Men were identified as well as possible and placed in hastily built coffins, wood from the battered boxcars providing material until pine coffins could be brought to the scene. The majority of dead Confederates, totaling forty-nine, were put four in a box and interred at one end of the grave. Each of the seventeen Union guards was placed in a single casket and similarly buried on the opposite end of the trench. At this spot, between the rails and river, they would rest for almost six decades.[36]

A jury quickly met in Lackawaxen to investigate the cause of the crash. Engineer Hoitt and his conductor, John Martin, both testified that the dispatcher in Lackawaxen, Douglas Kent, had made a fatal mistake giving them the rails. Earlier that morning, a train had displayed flags indicating that an "extra" followed. Although tardy, this first-class extra was the train that held the prisoners. The policy of the Erie Railway was that all first-class trains westward bound superseded other first-class trains traveling east, as well as second-class trains hauling coal. Kent should have given the right-of-way to the locomotive pulling the prisoners, and he realized this because he had previously questioned its whereabouts. Moreover, upon reaching the Erie main line from the Hawley Branch, Conductor Martin had asked Kent outright if he could proceed, and the telegrapher had consented. It was uncertain whether Kent had even recorded a coal train passing his Lackawaxen station, although he definitely did not wire Shohola to warn the dispatcher there to expect one. Had Kent done so, one of the engineers may have been alerted in time.[37]

The jury blamed Douglas Kent, whose imperfections most notably included well-publicized "intemperate habits."[38] Evidently, he had been drinking at a dance in nearby Hawley the night before the accident and was still feeling the effects of a binge. Inexplicably, the jury ruled the crash unavoidable, but so strong was public feeling against Kent that another inquest was ordered.

The second jury alluded to the larger issue of why the railroad company even employed such individuals, but did nothing other than find Kent guilty. This provided small consolation to families that lost loved ones unnecessarily. Douglas Kent fled on a westward train the morning after the wreck, his station log, written proof of his dereliction, vanishing with him.[39]

The same Saturday that Kent made his getaway, the Erie line was cleared so prisoners could be taken to Elmira. The injured were cared for as well as possible during their stay in Shohola. Untiring locals converted their village into a temporary hospital, and men were laid up at the railroad depot and village hotel. Captain Church ordered amputations not to be conducted there, even when injured patients urged it on their own. Area doctors treated flesh wounds, contusions, and fractures through the next morning. Around 11:00 A.M., July 16, survivors boarded a twenty-car train, the injured placed in the front with hay on the floor to ease their pain and nursed by attendants. Twenty men considered unable to travel were left under guard. Despite these efforts, injured men died anyway.[40]

Elmira already buzzed because of a visit and speech by celebrated cavalry general, Hugh Judson Kilpatrick, who was staying with a cousin while recovering from his own bruises. The city was further thrown into a frenzy upon hearing the news of the crash and the imminent arrival of its victims. At 9:30 P.M., the prisoner train finally reached Elmira. Seth Eastman made preparations hours before, meeting it at the station with a special force of guards, helpers, stretchers, and a caravan of twelve wagons.[41]

A torchlight procession guided the party to Barracks Number 3, some members riding, some walking. An ambulance moved ten disabled sentries to a depot hospital. Inside the prison, one of the barracks served as a hospital for eighty-five injured Southerners. William Wey toiled throughout the night, surgical saw in hand, tending immediately to the men who required amputation. The doctor got little rest those days; he was short in staff and lacked the simplest supplies, including bandages. Wey and the Ladies Hospital Aid Society petitioned for donations, but it was hard to meet the demands required in the emergency. Three days after their arrival, many Southerners remained unattended, blood clotting on their clothes from lack of proper dressing.[42] In Shohola, further consequences of Kent's negligence were being felt as another guard died, leaving a wife and three children in Ohio. The crash was one of the worse railroad disasters of its day. Generations later, persons tracing family histories were still finding its effects, discovering the tragic truth behind missing ancestors from the Civil War.[43]

3

The August Buildup

Commissary General Hoffman personally examined Elmira Prison the week after the Shohola accident, after which he ordered the first transfer of prisoners other than those from Point Lookout. On July 25, 625 men arrived from the Old Capitol Prison in Washington via the Northern Central Railroad. Notwithstanding Hoffman's approval of accommodations at Elmira, many occupants did not share his satisfaction. Rumors were common that prisoners were plotting to break through the twelve-foot fence. In response, forty-one kerosene lamps with big reflectors were hung on the inside wall to enhance visibility at night. Sentinels were ordered to be especially vigilant during nighttime watch. The dissatisfaction intensified when black troops were placed on guard, something that did not sit well with Southerners. Heckling escalated into stone throwing, and everything finally came to a crescendo on the evening of July 31.[1]

Granville Garland, an African American, was posted between the mess rooms and Foster's Pond with instructions not to let anyone pass. Around 10:00 P.M., prisoner A. P. Potts decided to test the guard. After four warnings to halt, Garland fired. Potts scurried back to his ward crying "Oh, God, I am shot."[2] The incident was neither fatal nor critical, but newspapers circulated more reports that prisoners were on the verge of breaking out. One story went so far as to claim that Rebels had already escaped, seized a nearby arsenal for weapons, and headed on to Canada.[3] The *New York World* suggested that the recent Confederate raid into Pennsylvania, led by Gen. Jubal Early, might culminate in a northward push onto Elmira to liberate prisoners.[4] The *New York Times* reported "a very serious outbreak was feared among rebel prisoners at Elmira," but the paper later commented "the danger was not so great as was first represented."[5]

Officials in Washington were more concerned with Early's actions closer to home, especially the precarious position of Point Lookout Prison. The prison commissary began to funnel inmates through to Elmira. Hoffman believed that if he could move about half the men at Point Lookout his peninsula stockade would become less of a target by land or sea. In mid-August he informed General Grant that six thousand Confederate prisoners remained at Point Lookout, whereas more than fourteen thousand had resided there prior to the opening of Elmira Prison.[6]

New York governor Horatio Seymour was well aware of the large numbers of prisoners being delivered to the Chemung Valley; their numbers more than doubled from the end of July to August 18, when the fifteenth detachment of arrivals brought the prison rolls to 9,262. Tents had to be pitched on the old racecourse to meet demands for housing. Claims by the *Rochester Daily Union and Advertiser* that citizens were impressed for guard duty were untrue, but a larger force was nevertheless necessary. About 350 members of the 16th Veterans Reserve Corps were the original guards. Governor Seymour sent the 54th New York National Guard from Rochester at the end of July, which increased the prison guard to seven hundred men. On August 1, the governor ordered batteries A and B of the Rochester Union Grays to Elmira with their sixty-six men and four pieces of artillery. The next day, Seymour added the 77th and 99th State Militia from New York City.[7] By the middle of August, the 28th, 56th, 58th, 98th, 102nd, and 103rd New York Militia had been included among the prison guard.[8] The reinforced garrison should have comforted Elmirans, but if not, the *Elmira Daily Advertiser* reassured them on August 22, the "number of guards here at present, armed and equipped, is over three thousand, and a thousand more could be on duty in an emergency."[9] A byproduct of the increased security was a distinct military atmosphere in which the total number of soldiers associated with the prison camp outnumbered the civilian population. The economic value of these soldiers to the community was also beginning to rise.

Lieutenant Colonel Eastman found himself in a quandary trying to provide room and shelter for the increasing number of guards. On August 1, forty more acres had to be rented from A. S. Foster at $1,000. Campground for guards, combined with land leased for prisoners, afforded the Foster family $2,590 annually. On August 7, Eastman informed Hoffman that he had run out of tents not only for prisoners, but also for their keepers. He asked for five hundred more tents and sent tentless sentries to Barracks Number 1. The regular guard force, however, set up camp around Barracks Number 3, their location designated as Camp Chemung and commanded by Col. Charles M. Prevost, 16th Veterans Reserve Corps.[10]

Camp Chemung's sole purpose was to support the prison. The 16th Veterans Reserve Corps bivouacked closest to the western wall, and the 54th next to them. To the west, A and B Batteries of the Rochester Union Gray's Artillery were stationed with four six-pound Napoleon cannon and caissons; the batteries would later be equipped with two ten-pound Parrot guns, two twelve-pound Howitzer cannon, sixty Smith carbine rifles, plus ninety artillery sabers. More regiments encamped off the north wall on the old state fair grounds and others east of the pen, all of which enclosed it on three sides, while the river sealed off the last. Four men were assigned to each tent. Meals were prepared close to quarters, where fires warmed kettles that filled the air with aromas familiar to camp life. A parade ground allowed public ceremonies and entertainments. A three-horse omnibus ran on the hour to the camps from downtown; it could carry officers who rented rooms at hotels, off-duty guards who visited the city, or workers and merchants who had business in the camp.[11] By August 10, the local newspaper had noted "a large number of visitors about the camps." There were no indications of letting up, the paper continued, where "attractions must increase by the accession of more troops, until the grounds embracing Camp Chemung will resemble the thronged aspect which has marked our State Fairs."[12]

As with Elmira Prison, Camp Chemung had an inauspicious debut. On the night of August 13, two guards of the 56th Brooklyn Militia were engrossed in an amusing argument about their city's best fire engines. The amicable debate grew more vigorous, and louder, so someone in jest summoned a corporal of the guard to break it up. Corporal Crummell, a close friend of both men and an officer in their company, had just been relieved at the prison and decided to play along. He barged into their tent and facetiously raised his Enfield Rifle at his fellow Brooklynites, hammer and cap still dangerously set from his prior duty. Cheerful laughter abruptly ended with the crack of Crummell's weapon, which accidentally fired in the direction of his companions, one positioned behind the other. The ball passed into the right chest and lung of Pvt. Thomas Conauton and exited his shoulder blade. Still traveling with deadly force, the projectile entered the second man, Burtis, penetrated his body, and hit a third soldier's knapsack.[13]

Conauton and Burtis were rushed to a nearby hospital and treated; Crummell was arrested. For almost a week, Conauton coughed up eight ounces of blood daily, but the nineteen-year-old private would survive. Burtis's condition

steadily worsened. The wounded men called for Crummell and the corporal was taken to the hospital, where charges against him were dropped, all
deeming the incident unintentional. Not long after seeing his friend set free,
Burtis lay dead. His father took the body back to Brooklyn, leaving behind
a dispirited camp.[14]

In the meantime, medical organization inside the stockade was improving.
Prison officials decided that not three, but six hospital wards would be built.
In addition to the thirty carpenters working at the prescribed rates, another
work force assisted for lower compensation. Prisoners experienced in carpentry were allowed to work, lending their skilled hands in the construction of
wards that measured 25-by-136-by-12-feet, each of which had sixty-two beds
apiece. Instead of earning up to $2.50 daily pay, as their free counterparts did,
captive carpenters were credited ten cents toward the prison sutler and given
extra rations. This development was an early intimation that a prison class
structure would develop at Elmira.[15]

The person who supervised construction of the hospitals and other buildings was forty-year-old Capt. John J. Elwell, formerly quartermaster at Port
Royal, South Carolina. On March 31, 1863, his horse had caved through a
bridge, causing the captain to break both bones below the right knee. Temporarily recovering, Elwell went to Elmira a year later in hopes of reforming
and reviving the quartermaster's department, which had been poorly managed due in part to debts incurred by the previous chief. As a result, it had
become hard to contract for lumber because dealers fixed high prices. Unlike
his predecessor, Elwell tried to spend more sensibly, purchasing wood cheaper
outside the area until local lumbermen agreed on fair prices.[16]

Elwell's job became more demanding when he became head quartermaster
in August. Seven civilian clerks hired to assist him were incapable of handling
all the paperwork, so two more were added, which altogether cost the department eight hundred dollars a month. As soldiers flooded in, more money had
to be spent on storehouses for the Quartermaster and Commissary Departments, estimated at twenty-eight hundred dollars each.[17] A related issue arose
in moving supplies from storage to the camps. Elwell requested more army
wagons and horse ambulances, since the "*large* number of prisoners of war
confined at this post and the *large* number to come require additional land
transportation."[18] When the requisitions remained unfilled, he complained
to Quartermaster General Montgomery C. Meigs that the "work at this
post is immense," especially hauling food, lumber, wood, and forage for
troops and prisoners which "amount to about 15,000 men."[19] Meanwhile, at

Left: Capt. John J. Elwell, quartermaster at Elmira. Courtesy of the Massachusetts Commandery, Military Order of the Loyal legion, USAMHI.

Below: Capt. Simon P. Suydam, assistant quartermaster at Elmira. Courtesy of the USAMHI.

Barracks Number 3, Elwell had his army of carpenters build a large officer mess room, supervised completion of the hospitals, and had the workers extend the guard walk.[20] These and other improvements around the camps, reported the *Elmira Daily Advertiser*, gave "employment to quite a number who know how to shove the plane."[21] Moreover, the building around Elmira Prison was not exclusively conducted by those contracted with the government.

Toward the end of July, a Mr. Nichols acquired a plot of land outside the northeast corner of the enclosure on the opposite side of Water Street. He bought some lumber and constructed a building more than twice the height of the wall. The structure consisted of two large decks one above the other, separated by almost ten feet. At the building's christening Nichols attached a placard to his edifice that read "an observation tower from which to view the prisoners—admission 15¢, refreshments served below."[22]

Up to that point, citizens had not had many opportunities to see the Rebels in prison. Military regulations kept most people outside the wooden barricade, and small openings, either between slats or through knotholes, offered only limited views.[23] Not long after the "Upper Observatory" opened, the *Elmira Daily Advertiser* reported that it was "often crowded with sightseers and must prove a paying institution."[24] Apparently it was, one insider claiming that "the concern paid for itself in two weeks."[25] People came in droves, handed over the fee, and headed up the stairway. The first level was advantageous because its roof could keep patrons dry; but the higher open deck had a superior view. From that position one could see the entire prison yard and much of Camp Chemung. Nichols had spy glasses available at no extra charge, so patrons could "see the vermin which are said to be so plenty upon the bodies of the prisoners."[26] One observer found Confederates to "have a rough appearance, wearing as they do, clothing of as many hues as the rainbow but none so brilliant. The men are generally of good size, and what would be called fair specimens of the race, if they were not Rebels."[27] Of course the viewing period was restricted, and generally each person was limited to no more than an hour or two. However, for a nominal fee customers could long remember their visit by purchasing photographs that Nichols made available to them. Nichols's Upper Observatory was quite popular in Elmira—for locals, strangers, and its architect.[28]

In one of the more perverse episodes of Yankee capitalism at Elmira, only a few weeks passed before another tower emerged a little west of the original. The rival tower had been built by W. and W. Mears, who took out weekly newspaper advertisements at the end of August to promote their structure. The tower was twenty feet higher and cost five cents less than the competition. It

The observatory, right forefront; Water Street separated the observatory and the stockade. Courtesy of the Chemung County Historical Society.

was a three-deck affair "built at considerable expense." Wooden stands soon popped up beside the towers, where visitors could buy food and drink—cakes, peanuts, and crackers, lemonade, beer, and liquor. Indeed, Water Street was becoming more reminiscent of fairs that once took place not far away; however, that land was now occupied by guards who got to see the show for free.[29]

Newspaper correspondents seemed to endorse the observatories. The *Rochester Daily Union and Advertiser* called Nichols "an enterprising Elmira Yankee" who "hit upon a happy expedient for making a pile and serving the public at the same time."[30] He was "a man of genius," professed the *New York Evening Post,* not only because he outwitted the military authorities, but also for being "determined that the rebels should make his fortune."[31] In early August, the *Elmira Daily Advertiser* advised "all our friends who have not gone up there to go at once. It will amply repay the small expense of getting there." About a month later, the paper observed that the "two observatories . . . in operation . . . are both doing a rushing business."[32]

Prisoners were less enthusiastic about money being made at their expense. A Tennessee sergeant, G. W. D. Porter, remembered how "hundreds would crowd daily to get a view of the prisoners—many to gloat, perhaps, on their sufferings; some to gaze in wonder and awe upon the ragged, bob-tailed crew who had on many fields conquered their best armies; and some, no doubt, to sigh for an exchange of these men for fathers, sons and brothers who were suffering kindred miseries at Libby, Salisbury and Andersonville."[33] James Huffman blamed the Northern press for sending "a constant stream of people winding their way to the top of these observatories to get a glimpse of the Rebs, as they supposed us to be like some kind of curious, monkey-shaped animals."[34] Anthony Keiley was "surprised that Barnum has not taken the prisoners off the hands of Abe, divided them in companies, and carried them in caravans through the country . . . turning an honest penny by the show."[35] Captives went beyond written retorts, some gathering close to the tower so that spectators could not miss them derisively perform routines of tumbling and somersaults, as if it were a circus.[36] Even a Union guard conceded "some enterprising Yankees . . . made a profitable show of the Confederate prisoners."[37] On September 10, Hoffman ordered Eastman to "take possession of the whole field, including the visitors stand opposite of Barracks No. 3."[38] The show was over for the refreshment booths and Mears's tower, which were dismantled and removed.[39]

Evidently, there was more to the story of Nichols's Upper Observatory because it endured as long as the prison. At least one Southerner asserted that a Union officer had invested in the tower; another noticed that officers frequented it. Such reports might explain why Nichols was allowed to stay when other merchants had to vacate.[40] Anthony Keiley shed some light on the issue because of personal contact he had with administrators due to his job as clerk in the prison. He reported that one of the original tower's proprietors, who may have received a share before but probably after Hoffman's confiscatory order, "was part of the management in our pen."[41] As a newspaper editor, Keiley knew enough to leave the person virtually anonymous, more than twenty officers falling in that category.[42] He also wrote about the observatory's heyday with flair hard to equal: "So profitable was this peculiarly Yankee 'institooshun,' that a week or two there after a rival establishment, taller by a score of feet, sprang up, and a grand 'sight-seeing-and-sprucebeer' Warfare began, which shook Elmira to its uttermost depths. One building was Radical, the Other Copperhead; one was taller, the other older and more original. . . . Heaven knows where It all would have ended, but the Government confiscated the 'Democratic platform,' under the plea of military necessity, and its abolition brother remained master of the situation."[43]

Keiley, who would one day serve as mayor of Richmond, Virginia, concluded "the shin-plasters rolled in, the lemon pop and ginger cakes rolled out of the orthodox observatory, to the great pecuniary comfort to the true-believers who owned it. Patriotism is spelled with a 'y' at the end of the first syllable up here."[44]

When temperatures fell with the approach of colder months business declined at the Upper Observatory. Family and friends still might have ascended the tower in hopes of spotting a familiar figure or face, but for many the climate became too chilly from such a high point.[45] Regardless of the weather, some onlookers were also beginning to understand that the harsh reality of war—and its prison camps—should not be commercialized in that manner. One individual climbed up the observatory with some country friends anticipating a good time. Unexpectedly, the group took notice of two men carrying a stretcher covered by a tarp that concealed a dead inmate. In half an hour they counted five trips that these pallbearers made. The onlooker self-consciously remarked that he and his friends all "speedily grew melancholy over the spectacle and cut our visit to the top of the tower very short."[46]

While the observatories flourished, more serious matters attended the prison hospital. On August 6, Eugene F. Sanger was designated head surgeon at the pen. Born in Maine and a descendant of Revolutionary War hero Anthony Wayne, Sanger had earned degrees from Dartmouth College and Jefferson Medical College by the age of twenty-three, then studied in Europe. Returning to Maine, he had married in 1857 and settled in Bangor.[47]

Shortly after the outbreak of war, the governor appointed Sanger a major and surgeon in the 6th Maine, despite his somewhat awkward, unmilitary appearance. Sanger's diminutive body did not match his head, which seemed enlarged by partial balding, tired because of droopy eyes, and long from a protruding goatee. His intellectual ability compensated for any physical inadequacies, which evidently included a clubbed foot. He received a promotion to brigade surgeon on Gen. Winfield Scott Hancock's staff, then in the spring of 1862 was assigned to the Department of the Gulf under Benjamin F. Butler. With the fall of New Orleans, Sanger was named medical purveyor of the Gulf Department and head surgeon at St. James Hospital. In 1863, he became a medical director in New Orleans and served as a chief surgeon at Port Hudson. The following year he headed the medical staff of Gen. William B. Franklin and the 19th Corps. In 1864, after participating in the Red River Campaign, Sanger waited in Baltimore to be sent elsewhere. His next assignment was explained to him in Special Order No. 253, making the thirty-four-year-old New Englander the "competent surgeon to take charge" of Elmira Prison's hospital. Unfortunately for Sanger and others, he never wanted to be in the

Chemung Valley. It eventually showed in this tour of duty, not the doctor's longest or last, but his most controversial.[48]

One week after Sanger assumed his position at Elmira, he gave a foreboding diagnosis of the prison. The excremental buildup from so many men confined in such a small space inhibited drainage. Sanger was not so much concerned by what was already in the pond or the sickening smell it produced in the August heat as about how much of the filth accumulated there every day. He reported that Foster's Pond "receives its fecal matter hourly," and calculated that seven thousand prisoners would "pass 2,600 gallons of urine daily, which is highly loaded with nitrogenous material."[49] Deeper vaults were replacing the sinks, yet seepage into the pond was inevitable. Chemical disinfectants could negate the odor as the waste slowly decomposed, but the costs in barrels and human labor outweighed the benefits. A drought precluded the idea of flushing out Foster's Pond by drawing from the city waterworks since supplies had to be regulated for Elmirans. Sanger's advice for cleaning the pen of the "putrid matter" had a familiar tone: He urged administrators to open a channel between the pond and river.[50]

Warned a month earlier about Foster Pond's stagnant water, Hoffman received a reminder. On August 17, Eastman wrote that the filth was becoming "very offensive, and may occasion sickness unless the evil is remedied shortly."[51] Disease was spreading, specifically infectious gangrene. Steps were immediately taken to survey a mile-long ditch from the Chemung River, but from the outset there were snags in the plan. The projected ditch would infringe upon Foster's land and three other farms. Two property owners objected to having their valuable land torn up by a six-foot trench. Another obstruction was the project's cost; Eastman wrote to Hoffman on August 21, that it would total almost five thousand dollars; the prison commissary preferred a much lower price.[52] Prior correspondence to Hoffman alluded to another measure, something that did not include any digging. "Should heavy rains come on shortly this work would not be required," said Eastman; the rain would wash Foster's Pond naturally.[53] Hence, it did not matter that farmers and Eastman could not agree on a feasible ditch, or whether Hoffman was unhappy with the price. So Eastman hoped for rain during a severe drought, while 553 patients lay ill in the hospital and 558 awaited admission. The rain never came, but the number of deaths rose, jumping from 11 in July to 115 at the end of August. Months passed before any ground was broken for the drainage sluice and Seth Eastman would not be around to see its completion.[54]

4

Ingredients for Survival

Food as a Necessity of Prison Life

In September 1864, no more Confederate prisoners were sent to the Chemung Valley. This brought some relief because 5,195 men had already arrived during the August buildup, thus joining 4,411 men already at the prison. Those numbers combined were twice that initially recommended by Depot Commander Eastman. Prisoners had no choice but to live with overcrowding, exemplified in September by their eating arrangements. It took the entire lot of captives three hours to eat its meals, and to accomplish that cumbersome exercise the group had to be broken down into smaller clusters of eighteen hundred individuals each sitting.[1] Eastman hoped to construct another mess hall, since the existing facility was "too small to accommodate 10,000 men."[2] When Camp Inspector Benjamin Munger reported to Hoffman that mess rooms were poorly kept, Hoffman requested an explanation. Eastman replied, "Over 9,000 prisoners are fed daily in this mess room, which leaves but a short time after meals to police it thoroughly."[3] Prospects of more eating facilities were dashed soon after when Hoffman told Eastman that if the men "can get through their breakfast by 11 A.M. and their dinner by 6 P.M., nothing more is necessary."[4]

More distressing was quality of the food—or lack thereof—in the mess hall. An outbreak of scurvy prompted Surgeon Sanger to go through the ranks near the end of August, when he counted 793 cases. By September 11, fears of an epidemic arose when the cases more than doubled.[5] The vitamin deficiency caused assorted spots and irritations on the body, but was principally remembered, as one victim from Elmira put it, for the way it "attacked the mouths and gums, becoming so spongy and sore that portions could be removed with the fingers."[6] In addition to losing their teeth, victims frequently saw their hair fall out and felt their stomachs cramp, leaving some men too weak to walk. Sanger attributed the scurvy to the soldiers' irregular eating habits. He conveniently forgot to mention Secretary Stanton's effort to reduce prison rations in the North, which was becoming more than a retaliatory gesture for Union men deprived of food in Southern pens.[7]

Throughout the war each side charged the other with improper treatment of prisoners, but in early 1864 Northern leaders decided to take a firmer stand. Reports circulated that Rebels were intentionally starving Union prisoners, and those claims seemed confirmed by the emaciated condition of many Northern prisoners after being exchanged in March and April. Consequently, in May, Stanton permitted Hoffman to reduce rations for Southern prisoners, including much-needed vegetables. In August, Stanton and Hoffman also decided to curtail articles that sutlers sold.[8] By the end of that month, these retaliatory measures were becoming particularly effective at Elmira, to the point that Sanger had to ask for increased supplies of vegetables.[9]

Eastman planned to dip into the prison fund to provide necessary vegetables to supplement the prison diet. This financial repository compared to a large slush fund created to purchase such articles as extra food not required by regulations. The hospital department also kept a separate account, although it was not so large. Hoffman modeled the fund on his earlier experiences managing posts for regular soldiers, and reintroduced it to his prison camps. Savings came primarily from sales of what were deemed oversupplies of uncooked rations, which allowed other needed items to be purchased. For example, instead of apportioning every inmate with the mandated eighteen ounces of flour each day, he would be given eighteen ounces of baked bread, the leftover flour being sold back to the Commissary Department and the money placed in the fund. In addition, the fund grew from taxes imposed on sutlerships. It also relied on money generated by sales of valuables that deceased prisoners left behind, including gifts sent posthumously. This money made from dead Southerners was a constant source of revenue at Elmira Prison, where nearly one out of four proved to be a benefactor. Besides utilizing the prison fund, Eastman was also given permission to allow inmates to buy vegetables from sutlers, if the prisoners could afford them.[10]

These efforts were among Eastman's last as depot commander, for his health was failing. Bedridden throughout much of September, his thirty-five years in the military were apparently catching up with him, and juggling the pressures of his current post surely did not bring any relief. On September 19, his successor arrived to assume command. Colonel Benjamin F. Tracy of the 127th U.S. Colored Troops would not have to travel far for his new assignment, for he awaited orders at his home in nearby Owego, between Elmira and Binghamton. Unlike Eastman, the thirty-five-year-old colonel did not bring a record of long service with him, being a lawyer by trade, but he exhibited vigor his predecessor was physically unable to match. Tracy had been restless ever since being forced, due to heat exhaustion, to leave a field command in Virginia, where he had served commendably during the Wilderness campaign. However, along with the Owego barrister's enthusiasm came a firm personality that interpreted military instructions as Tracy viewed the law: rigidly. Whereas Major Colt could be flexible at his headquarters, which carried only the single responsibility of the prison, Tracy could get bogged down trying to balance his other duties at the depot, especially the task of sending draftees off from Barracks Number 1. However, Tracy's recruiting interests, a product of the recent draft, quickly turned to the welfare of prisoners after Tracy was introduced to Captain Munger and his weekly inspection reports.[11] During the new commander's first week in the city, Munger's Sunday report listed 112 deaths among inmates, 29 on a single day. "There seems little doubt," the inspector warranted, "numbers have died both in quarters and hospital for want of proper food."[12]

On paper, the standard ration for prisoners under the articles of war was impressive. Bread comprised eighteen ounces, corn meal the same, beef fourteen ounces, and pork or bacon ten ounces, plus it included beans, tea or coffee, sugar, salt, potatoes, soap, and candles.[13] One *New York Evening Post* correspondent who visited Elmira after the war secretary's alteration found the "new rations not so large," but still "abundant," with fourteen ounces of beef or ten ounces of pork, sixteen ounces of fresh bread or ten ounces of hard bread, and soup.[14] The *Elmira Daily Advertiser* perused the prison camp menu, as well, finding that each prisoner "receive[d] one pound of meat per day, onions, potatoes, and other vegetables [were] provided for them three times a week." The soup, the local paper continued, "looked rich and savory," and the bread "is as good as can be found in any bakery of our city."[15] Newspapermen from the "Flour City" were also impressed by the bread, the *Rochester Daily Union and Advertiser* deeming it "as good as we saw or care to find, under any circumstances."[16] Colonel Tracy described the meal of inmates more succinctly—"For breakfast, eight ounces of bread, eight ounces of meat; for dinner, eight ounces of bread, one pint and a half of soup of excellent quality, made from the meat, potatoes, onions and beans."[17]

A second school of thought concerning food emerged from inside the prison walls. John Brunsan wrote his sister that he was starving: "I only get two meals a day, breakfast and supper. For breakfast I get one-third of a pound of bread and a small piece of meat; for supper the same quantity of bread and not any meat, but a small plate of warm water called soup."[18] Anthony Keiley recalled how rations were "characterized by disappointed 'rebs' in language not to be found in the prayer-book." As for Keiley's own opinion, the meat portion "was invariably scanty," but the bread plentiful.[19] However, even the bakers had detractors, some inmates swearing that the bread "was so thin that they could read the *New York Herald* through it."[20] More detested was the soup. One Rebel called it "quasi soup," another "tasteless," a third found it "nothing more than hot salty water," and a fourth was able to see clear through it "to the bottom of the pan."[21] One Union medical officer agreed, claiming that prisoners washed down bread with "a poor hatched-up, concocted cup of soup."[22] Vegetables mixed into the broth were very scarce, and Marcus Toney once heard "the boys" joke about the supposed ratio of "four beans to a gallon of water."[23] Other prisoners were less inclined to have anything added to the broth, since often roots, hulls, and dirt were cooked among unpeeled potatoes and spoiled onions, which made the soup more memorable for its odor than its taste.[24]

Hardships that prisoners faced during the Civil War lured many to fixate on food because it was obviously a vital ingredient for survival. This was evident at many confines, Elmira included, which has resulted in arguments over the reliability of accounts and is echoed in protests that camp apologists have made. Those who dismiss allegations of inferior rations at Elmira, however, should not overlook documentation by Union officials, who substantiated claims of hunger.[25] A sample from other venues also suggests that food served elsewhere was preferable to the fare at Elmira. At Point Lookout, prisoner John King felt "they gave us barely enough to keep body and soul together," but that food there was "a little more satisfactory" than at Elmira.[26] John Opie soon realized he had become spoiled by rations at the Old Capitol Prison, especially after he measured his meat portion in "Helmira" to be half an inch wide and three inches long.[27] Additional accounts indicate genuine suffering from the quantity and quality of the rations. Astute captives understood that the fault did not entirely stem from indifference by the federal government, but that other factors contributed to the meager provisions prepared for them in the bakery and cookhouse.[28]

Food for prisoners was baked and cooked inside the compound. Elisha H. Cook and Henry C. Covell received a protracted contract, undoubtedly to their liking, for furnishing cooking hardware at the Elmira Depot. Their store was located off Water Street, making it easy for them to deliver to the prison, where they sold stoves, kitchen scales, numerous pots, fifteen hundred tin cups, two thousand forks and knives, two thousand plates, and five brick bake ovens. Each day, Cook and Covell's bake ovens could produce one thousand loaves, each of which were sliced up and served in breadbaskets by inmates who worked as waiters. The prison camp employed two citizen bakers, a head chef, whose salary was sixty-four dollars a month, and his underling, who received fifty-six dollars. Next to the bakery was the cookhouse, with massive iron cauldrons, nineteen fitted to hold 90 gallons and sixteen with a capacity of 120 gallons. These were the principal cooking vessels that occupied the kitchen, while scales precisely weighed portions before the cooks added them to pots warming under the stoves. When the water came to a boil, meat and vegetables were dropped in, cooked, and removed, and the essence converted into soup. Captain George L. Whiton ran the cookhouse and made sure his kitchen operated to his liking each day. Whiton also supervised the prison waiters, who set and cleared tables and were credited ten cents daily and tipped an extra ration for their good service.[29]

The procedures for serving meals resembled those in a factory. Roll call was taken, then a Confederate ward sergeant had his men fall in for breakfast between 8:00 and 9:00 A.M. Inmates marched into the 41-by-396-by-8-foot dining hall in two lines, then they systematically divided as they filed down the tables, facing one another as they took their seats. Food was set on the tables for them, along with their utensils. When eating implements ran out, the prisoners used whatever else they could find as replacements.[30] As they ate, two gigantic American flags dangled high above, their purpose obvious to a defiant South Carolinian—"Since we couldn't be made to fight under the stars and stripes, we were made to eat under them."[31] Due to the influx of new prisoners, the mess hall eventually proved inadequate, so Eastman and Colt, pressed for time and space, decided that the Rebels could eat at their wards. Guards served as mess room monitors, watching closely for any conspicuous characters who might "flank" a ration. This selfish maneuver, despised by guards and most inmates, consisted of either smuggling an extra ration off the table or sneaking back into the mess hall with another eating party. More elaborate schemes existed and inside jobs were common. For example, Mississippi infantryman James M. Gilmore, entrusted with a job as a waiter, stole twenty-five to thirty rations during his daily shifts. His escapades, along with other types of "flanking," resulted in the same outcome: depriving a comrade of a meal.[32]

After all the wards had eaten breakfast, the routine of filing through the mess hall was conducted again around 3:00 P.M. Certain luxuries were afforded to Elmira Prison's "early settlers" during the afternoon session. At dinnertime, inmates were allowed to take seconds, if they chose.[33] Anthony Keiley quipped that all "would ask for more. . . . Not that we were hungry, but merely to satisfy ourselves that the thing was real."[34] Sometimes after dinner, about 5:00, guards escorted prisoners to the Chemung River so they could bathe. One "Johnny" whimsically petitioned his captain for "Windsor soap and towels."[35] Any notion of a pleasurable life in captivity was premature as more men accumulated, testified Keiley, who lamented "gone were our tin plates; gone the knives and forks; gone the seats at the tables; gone the encouragement to cry out for more; gone the ablutions in the placid Chemung."[36] Going, too, were the cattle within proximity of Elmira.

On July 11, the Elmira Commissary Department contracted with local meat dealer Jonathan H. Rogers to supply fresh beef for inmates. Rogers, nicknamed "Mutton," owned the main meat shop in Elmira and won the competitive contract primarily for his price of seven and three-quarters cents per pound.[37] According to the head commissary, Nicholas J. Sappington, the bid was "a very low figure but I think the parties are responsible."[38] Rogers was to supply fresh beef of "good and marketable quality" for a six-month period. Written into the agreement was a provision that if the commanding officer judged the fresh beef inferior on any occasion, the government could appoint a panel to investigate the matter, reserving the right to reject meat considered "unfit for issue."[39] If that were the case, the Commissary Department might obtain beef under the agreed upon terms from another dealer, while Rogers would have to assume the cost.[40]

Rogers's meat market, located downtown, needed thirty head a day. After Rogers signed the contract he began to purchase animals in Elmira and throughout the outlying region, visiting farms miles away. When the cattle were acquired, they were corralled in pastures closer to town. Each morning the animals were rounded up, then driven to a slaughterhouse where they were sectioned. The summertime drought, already having a negative impact on inmates, led to problems further up the food chain. Many farmers were content to sell weakening cattle stocks, the lack of fodder influencing their size and productivity. This held especially true for dairy farmers and those who had extensive herds; with no feed, they were happy to sell what they could. Rogers was happy to accommodate them, one local observing "he bought everything in sight."[41] By early October, the repercussions were being noticed.

On October 3, Colt and Moore were empaneled to survey the fresh beef.[42] Depot Commander Tracy personally found Rogers's meat "inferior in quality." An unfavorable inspection report mentioning the "reprehensible practice" of issuing "beef the same day as killed" did not endear Commissary Sappington to men with fragile appetites.[43] Tracy went directly up the chain of command, updating Secretary of War Stanton, who prodded Commissary General of Subsistence Amos B. Eaton to contact Sappington in the middle of the month. A long debate ensued over the definition of what constituted marketable qualities in Elmira's shrinking cattle market. In the end of October, Sappington blamed camp officers for accepting the beef, yet defended himself for allowing it to be eaten the same day it was slaughtered, terming the practice "unavoidable."[44] The Elmira commissary would hire an "expert" to inspect future meat to determine its quality before and after slaughter so that the beef could "meet with the approval of all concerned."[45]

Amos Eaton preferred that the individual chiefly responsible for the misconduct own up to his negligence. On November 5, he reprimanded Captain Sappington, believing him to be solely at fault, regardless of whether any claims made against him or his department were "precisely accurate." After the rebuke, Eaton calmly reminded Sappington that he was "counted a good officer and a honest man; now let this matter pass and take good care that in the future your beef shall be of 'good and marketable quality.'"[46] That was easier said than done. On December 4, prison inspector Benjamin Munger reported that "a portion of the beef is very lean. Cows milked through the season and too poor for a respectable farmer to winter, are slaughtered and the beef issued to prisoners."[47] To the chagrin of Sappington, Munger took matters—and the beef—into his own hands. He decided to test a piece by boiling a ninety-two-pound forequarter cut, which after it was cooked and "carefully taken off the bone," weighed half the original amount.[48]

When the results of Munger's experiment crossed Eaton's desk, Sappington was better prepared to respond. He replied that the beef distributed to prisoners had the same quality as that given to Union soldiers, and the prison cookhouse head, Captain Whiton, testified in writing to the good quality of the beef, despite Munger's objection.[49] The Elmira Commissary also wrote that when Rogers's contract ended, his next fresh beef contract would stipulate that the cattle weigh no less than five hundred pounds. The commissary conceded that this standard would drive up the price, but it would also mollify "the dispute here, as to what constituted good quality beef."[50] Finally, Sappington enclosed a timely article published in the *Elmira Daily Advertiser* that noted beef quarters were frequently substituted for larger cuts due to contractual obligations. The paper alluded to the fact that the discarded meat "is readily sold in our market and at full rates to our citizens for use in their families."[51] The favorable review brought more than a smile from the Elmira commissary. The next day Jonathan Rogers sent the paper's owner, Charles G. Fairman, "a choice roasting piece." It was eaten that evening with "kind and sincere thanks" to Rogers and his company, "who seem to know what is fit and proper—for loyal editors' table as well as for Government Inspector's examination."[52]

Throughout Rogers's six-month agreement, Sappington had to deal with other difficulties regarding subsistence contracts. Andrew Hawthorne had been providing potatoes for the depot at ninety-seven and one-half cents per bushel, but supplies began to dwindle. In July, Captain Sappington reported that potatoes were scarce and that, although the vegetable restriction made their issue momentarily moot, he was concerned that no bids had been submitted from previous contractors. Sappington correctly anticipated that he would have plenty of potatoes after farmers harvested their crops, but in the meantime asked officials in Buffalo if they could spare any. Vegetables were woefully needed by the time Hoffman lifted their ban because scurvy was so widespread. In October, prison administrators procured 206 bushels of potatoes and 160 bushels of onions, which brought some relief to the prisoners. Officials divided the purchases into allotments of fifteen pounds of potatoes and eight pounds of onions for every one hundred rations, three days out of five. Selected patients under the care of Dr. Sanger received more with the aid of the hospital fund, which incurred more than two thousand dollars in expenses in October.[53]

As the vegetable shortage eased, minor troubles appeared in the bakery. Flour was always abundant, but occasionally the bread was not of good quality. When proper mixing ingredients, such as yeast and hops, could not be obtained, "dark and heavy loaves" resulted.[54] In the last week of November, Inspector Munger found half of the flour that dealers supplied to be of poor quality. In December, a number of barrels bought from William Halliday and Co. were filled with mold.[55] Sappington had the merchant exchange the spoiled batches for good meal, and by the end of the month the captain received reports that bread was once again "light and sweet."[56]

Notwithstanding these difficulties, Sappington executed every subsistence contract for the prison camp. The captain, thirty-three years old and five feet ten inches tall with dark hair, eyes, and complexion, had to adjust from serving marching rations with the Army of the Potomac to more sedentary

Wartime bust of Capt. Nicholas J. Sappington, Commissary of Subsistence at Elmira. Courtesy of the Gil Barrett Collection, USAMHI.

duties at Elmira. Similar to his partner in the Quartermaster's Department, Sappington was assigned to Elmira because he had fractured a leg when his horse fell on him in action, although that accident was preferable to what many of his comrades experienced at Antietam.[57] Again like Elwell, the commissary's work load never slowed after the Southerners arrived. This was even more true with Sappington, whose primary responsibilities at Elmira, he wrote, were "confined almost exclusively to providing subsistence for a large depot of prisoners of war."[58] A week after the pen opened, he requested permission to employ three laborers for forty dollars a month in the department and gradually hired more men. By the end of July, two locals were keeping the books for him, at one hundred dollars and seventy-five dollars per month. Soon, he hired another citizen, then in October a fourth, both of whom received seventy-five dollars. Much of the department's business relied on acquiring food contracts.[59]

Subsistence contracts at Elmira Prison were awarded to the lowest bidder, typically a local merchant, because both parties found this arrangement convenient. Interested vendors, many of whom existed, attached bids in duplicate to a government proposal document for the specific contract they sought, having already been informed by advertisements in the city papers. Written guarantees were mandatory so that contractors could be legally bound to their agreement. Merchants often had to back their proposals with a bond. Each bid would be drafted to a specific order, such as a proposal for meat, flour, or salt. After the bid sheet was entered with the bidder's full name, business, and address, the person submitting the bid needed to be present at the opening to personally answer any questions. From there, bidders could only hope to be part of the military's expanding business.[60]

Elmira's profit-making potential from food contracts did not go unnoticed among other communities, and at least one seemed envious of the new prison camp enterprise. Elmira and Binghamton, connected to each other by the Erie Railroad and both growing in size, were commercial rivals.[61] Near the end of July, the *Binghamton Times* observed that "with so many rebel prisoners to feed, the Elmira bakers must have lively times." The *Elmira Daily Advertiser,* defensively and erroneously fired back: "The Elmira bakers have nothing to do with the matter," because the captives "do their own baking and cooking and washing and scrubbing."[62] Although the prison did employ civilian chefs, it was specifically the merchants who provided food for the camp who were having the "lively times."

Sealed proposals for flour were to be in the Elmira Commissary Department on July 22, by 2:00 P.M. George B. McGrath acquired one of the first flour contracts, which started within twenty days of his endorsement. The contract guidelines called for Double "X" flour at six cents per pound, in quantities desired by Sappington for three months. William Halliday, despite once bringing some moldy batches into the pen, also provided better loads of the finely ground meal, as did B. M. Watts. All the flour procured for the prisoners was of Double "X" quality, except for 197 barrels of a lower grade used for mixing. Later in the year, Robert Covell signed a notable contract for himself, which would start "as soon as the said flour can be delivered." The "said flour" amounted to sixteen thousand barrels, and added up to more than seventeen thousand dollars.[63]

A variety of other food items had to be purchased for captives. Salt was needed for preserving food and adding flavor, so on October 22, Virgil B. Read of Elmira came in at a low enough bid to ensure himself more business that fall. His salt was to be furnished "clean and dry packed in good strong barrels and delivered at a rate of 60 pounds to the bushel," commencing within ten days. He guaranteed at least five hundred bushels and charged seventy cents for each. George McGrath dabbled in the salt trade, as well, while Elmira's local market provided other foods and drink. Whiskey sold at prices that ranged from $2.25 to $2.75 per gallon, J. H. Loring and the Lomore Brothers both being main suppliers. Potatoes and onions were purchased with money from the prison fund when they were in the market, and Andrew Hawthorne, D. D. Reynolds, Levi Coke, F. J. Bundy, Jackson Goldsmith, L. B. Gardener, and Noah Turner each sold a share.[64] Also, the government contracted for pork at prices that ranged from about thirteen to twenty cents per pound, beans three to four and one-half cents, hominy five cents, rice from eight to sixteen and one-half cents, sugar twelve to twenty-five cents, vinegar twenty-three to forty-five cents, and coffee from forty to seventy cents, while tea cost over a dollar a pound. Obviously, the captors did not serve all these items to common prisoners, but portions were allotted to patients in the hospitals and employees on work details.[65]

The amount of food eaten inside the prison yard steadily increased with the number of prisoners. During Elmira Prison's first month, 13,957½ pounds of pork, 21,808 pounds of fresh beef, 35,693 pounds of flour, 3,766 pounds of beans, 1,197 pounds of rice, 1,444 pounds of potatoes, and 1,762¾ pounds of salt were all included among the regular issuance. After Rogers's meat contract, the prison camp became more of a beef eating community: 113,959 pounds of fresh beef were eaten, but only 62,784 pounds of pork. The August buildup also saw a dramatic increase in other food purchases: flour increased to 178,641½ pounds, rice to 7,036 pounds, beans to 17,840 pounds, and salt to 8,601 pounds. By October, the prison required 123,734 pounds of fresh beef, 63,530½ pounds of pork, 242,535 pounds of flour, 17,665 pounds of beans, 8,152½ of rice, and 7,322 pounds of salt. In November, after an exchange of inmates, consumption of pork dropped to 45,305 pounds, whereas beef remained steady at 127,326 pounds, while flour, beans, rice, and salt all changed to 217,390, 20,078, 4,513, and 8,071 pounds, respectively. Pork dropped more in December, to 28,084½ pounds, while beef and flour jumped to 161,513 and 228,926½ pounds, respectively; the poundage of beans (22,848), rice (3,725½), and salt (8,488), remained fairly static.[66]

The contracts that Captain Sappington negotiated also applied to troops at Camp Chemung. Although no discrimination was supposedly permitted as to quality, certainly guards were given more variety and increased quantity. In addition, they had the option of purchasing food. Furthermore, confided one guard, "prisoners, it was alleged, were allowed the same rations, excepting coffee and sugar, that their guards received. They did not get it."[67] In contrast, guards could receive pork or fresh beef, bread, beans or rice, coffee or tea, sugar, vinegar, candles, soap, salt, and pepper. Sappington had to total all expenditures on food for soldiers at the end of each month into one flat rate, which was approved by the commissary general of subsistence. In July, for example, the small number of Union troops at the depot subsisted on the fairly low cost per ration of 24.14 cents. By August, with a buildup in guards, it began to increase, up to 25.74 cents, and more so in September, when it rose to 28.91 cents. In October, it stayed at 28 cents, and remained around that price until the prison camp was dissolved. Sappington had to make sure he appropriated enough money for sentinels, as well as ten thousand principal consumers.[68]

Spending by the Subsistence Department pumped additional income into Elmira's economy. At the end of April, when military activity was relatively slow, the Elmira Commissary Department was granted $2,234 in subsistence funds. On May 7, it received $3,000. In July, income was boosted to compensate for the arrival of inmates to about $15,036. Coinciding with the surge in prison and guard population, expenditures for August more than doubled to about $36,816. In September they were $41,883, and in October, $66,628. The month of November saw funds drop to $60,577. A December disbursement, however, made up for the previous month, when Sappington was granted $100,000 for his department. To the local vendors' delight, food contracts had to be renewed or consummated after the new year.[69]

Even with impressive expenditures on food, rations for prisoners were not sufficient from the outset, and whether the cause could be traced to overpopulation, shoddy contracts, flankers, or insufficient supplies, the prisoners turned elsewhere to satisfy themselves. Self-sufficient groups evolved throughout the prison camp, whereas others supplemented their diets by living off the land. A good number of these "hunters and gatherers" were uneducated by formal standards, unskilled in any trade or craft, and unemployed inside the pen. Those who could not attain employment with more conventional jobs created their own niches. When the prison first opened, men fished in Foster's Pond and caught plenty of perch, pickerel, bass, and sunfish that swam in from the Chemung River. Foster's Pond soon became polluted with excrement and cookhouse runoff, and when disinfectants were thrown in to reverse these conditions the fishing hole became further contaminated.[70] The chemicals not only gave the pond a distinct green tint, but for days afterward it was also, as inmate Berry Benson noticed, "lined with the white bellies of dead fish" on its banks.[71] Until officials solved the drainage problem, fisherman had to set aside their lines and wait for the following spring season. Temporarily unable to dine on fish, some inmates ventured elsewhere near Foster's Pond for healthy nourishment. Near the pond, on the sandy flat, edible plants were bountiful, including "lambs quarter," the favored herb among gatherers.[72] Yet vegetables alone did not constitute enough sustenance for most, or as Marcus Toney stated, "A prisoner eating this diet will crave any kind of fresh meat."[73]

Late one evening a prisoner was taken into custody for suspicious movements around the prison grounds. The next day he was brought before Major Colt, who inquired "What were you doing?" The prisoner answered "Huntin' sir." Colt wondered what type of game his prison camp offered and asked the man, only to be given the terse reply—"Rats."[74] The rodents migrated into the pen at alarming rates and sizes, hiding under buildings and burrowing in deep holes alongside the pond. Toward dusk, tempted by cookhouse refuse, rats became very active, as did the hunters, who waited patiently with weapons in hand.[75] When a rat emerged, according to one prisoner, "Such a hurrah and such a chase and such a volley of stones! You would have thought it was our Battalion of Sharpshooters in charge."[76] Those less skilled in stone throwing or lacking in a sporting spirit, simply clubbed the creatures with large sticks.[77]

After the prisoners killed and gutted the rats, the quarry was prepared in two different manners: frying or grilling. Prisoners savored either style. "They smelt very good while frying" said one, whereas another preferred the open flame, claiming "a broiled rat was superb."[78] Their taste was likened to squirrels. A cavalryman stated that "I ate rats, myself, several times, and found them really palatable food."[79] Conversely, the refined Anthony Keiley believed the "expedients resorted to by the men to supply this want of animal food were disgusting," in spite of being "assured by those who indulged in them that worse things have been eaten—an estimate of their value that I took on their trust."[80] These "Chinese delicacies" were also an important commodity in the prison camp market, their stock worth anywhere from four to twenty-five cents, "killed and dressed."[81] In trade value, a rat was worth its weight in chewing tobacco, the uniform currency of the pen. One rat could be bartered for five quids of tobacco or exchanged for a loaf of bread. In addition to pacifying urges for food, the hunt might afford prisoners who possessed talents other valuables at the prison marketplace. Other meats were also available for the taking by captives, although the alternatives were never held in the same esteem as the Chemung Valley rat.[82]

Short rations at Elmira once inspired a sentry to say that even if captives were like cats and had nine lives, they still "wouldn't last five minutes in the Rebel prison."[83] Evidently, neither would other domesticated animals. Pets accompanied their masters and strays frequently followed wood haulers or other government contractors and employees into the prison, and many pets never left. In due time they were hunted down and eaten. The inmates regularly preyed upon dogs.[84] One canine connoisseur believed that the "ribs of a stewed dog were delicious," and some compared its flavor to mutton.[85] In one instance, a big terrier, usually bred to hunt, had the tables turned on it when cornered by a couple of inmates. Soon the dog's owner, none other than Captain Whiton, made an investigation into its whereabouts. By that time, the two Rebels had overindulged in the terrier and decided to hide what was left from their feast in their bunks. Captain Whiton, being informed that his dog, or at least part of it, had been discovered, demanded that the culprits be punished. No one had the courage to ask the captain if he were more upset over the loss of the family pet or the implicit insult of what prisoners really thought of his cooking.[86]

A subclass of hunters and gatherers comprised the bottom of the inmate social order. These men could be categorized as "scavengers" and brought shame even to their own kind. They were known, as one Southerner described, "by their pallid color and lifeless movements."[87] What pushed men over the edge depended on the individual and how he responded to his confinement. John Opie wrote, "If any condition in life shows a man in his true character and develops the hog in his nature, it is when he is a prisoner." The captive loses "all feeling and humanity," he philosophized, "and become[s] like so many wolves or hyaenas."[88] James Huffman concurred: "Yet there was a lot of drones or lifeless, do-less persons who moped about, pining away for want of sufficient food to eat, losing their humanity, eating almost anything a brute would eat."[89] Many considered these weak creatures either indolent or gluttonous, and sometimes both, men who lay idle during their captivity and wasted away until death. Some also felt that the food these scavengers scoured to placate their cravings expedited that process.[90]

Erastus Palmer, captured at Front Royal, remembered one day seeing a comrade in back of the hospital and stopped to chat. While exchanging pleasantries, he noticed that the man picked up a discarded mush poultice and began scraping off the side used for treating lesions. The conversation ended abruptly while this person worked the dirty poultice, nonchalantly mentioning that he was preparing to eat it, to which Palmer wrote, "I did not stay to see him do it."[91] Walter Addison, also walking by the hospital, saw men "fish scraps from barrels containing hospital refuse and [devour] it ravenously, although by so doing were poisoning themselves with the putrid filth they were swallowing."[92] Anthony Keiley witnessed scavengers picking out bones in barrels filled with fatty offal, "thrown out in a dirty heap back of the kitchen, to be removed once a week." He added, "I have seen a mob of hungry 'rebs' besiege the bone-cart, and beg from the driver fragments on which an August sun had been burning for several days."[93] Inmates were known to crawl underneath the cookhouse to get at the drainage from the hopper or scour dishwater thrown out by Union officers, so they could pluck out tiny morsels of food.[94]

Dirty fruit and vegetable peelings were collected off the prison grounds and eaten. An Alabama sergeant "once threw down an apple core near where some prisoners were standing, and it was immediately picked up by one of them and devoured."[95] John King wrote from experience: "Hunger often caused people to do desperate things. I myself often watched for the bones, after the meat had been eaten off." The Old Dominion private admitted, "I got up many times in my bunk with a bone and after knawing the soft ends, sucked at the bone for hours at a time. I wasn't the only one."[96] King was fortunate that he survived his stay. Others were too predisposed in searching for more food, some sickening themselves from the pathetic lifestyle they led and held in contempt by their healthier comrades. There was still hope for them. In early October 1864, news circulated inside the pen that an exchange of ill and injured prisoners would soon take place.[97]

5

The October Exchange

At the end of September 1864, Commissary General Hoffman wired Colonel Tracy: "By authority of the Secretary of War all invalid prisoners in your charge who will not be fit for service within sixty days will in a few days be sent South for delivery." This order did not encompass men "who are too feeble to endure the journey."[1] Medical officers under the auspices of Chief Surgeon Sanger were to choose those prisoners healthy enough to sustain the trip. A doctor and guard force were to accompany the exchanged men and the detail would be sent with two day's cooked rations. Nurses and attendants selected from among the prisoners would also accompany the detail, their reward being a return to the South. The men were to be taken by rail to Baltimore, then by steamer to Point Lookout, where they and their parole rolls would be delivered to the prison commandant. From Maryland, the Confederates would be shipped to the exchange base at City Point, Virginia.[2]

Hospital patients who fell under the exchange criteria were given priority over other inmates, and by October 3, three hundred candidates had been selected for transfer. On that day, surgeons started to make their rounds in the regular wards. Around 10:00 A.M., men fell in with their companies and Major Colt ordered those who wished to be examined to take three steps forward. Medical officers and parole clerks then filed down the ranks, segregating those apparently unready for field service due to illness, injury, or age. The task of examining the men and processing their parole papers lasted almost a week, and because it was prominent in the prisoners' minds, it afforded the captives no better moment for clever action.[3] On one occasion, as an examiner approached a Rebel, the prisoner tried to guarantee that his injured arm would keep him out of service. Carefully rolling up his cuff for only the doctor to see, the Southerner revealed not a wound, but a five-dollar bill. The temptation won over the Yankee medic, who had the parole clerk record the inmate as having a "gunshot wound in the left arm."[4] In another instance, a prisoner faked an epileptic seizure, a dramatic performance that won him freedom because he was too poor to buy it.[5]

Paroling captives for exchange continued until the late hours of the following Monday, the eve of their departure. That night indications appeared that the prison medical department was not following orders, even though the examining board instructor had told Sanger "not to send those who were unable to travel."[6] As a parole officer went through the wards getting the signatures of persons preparing to leave, one potential parolee was already dead. Another man died twenty minutes after he signed his name. According to the *Elmira Daily Advertiser*, "The excitement proved too much for him." The paper added, "It is hardly probable that some will reach Point Lookout alive."[7] Anthony Keiley, who assisted as a nurse on the passage, never thought "such a spectacle was seen before on earth," in view of hospital patients who came "on their crutches, on their cots, borne in the arms of friends, creeping, some of them, on hands and knees, pale, gaunt, emaciated; some with the seal of death stamped on their wasted cheeks and shrivelled limbs. . . . On they came," Keiley recalled, "a ghastly tide, with skeleton bodies and lustreless, and brains bereft of but one single thought, and hearts purged of all feelings but one—the thought of freedom, the love of home."[8]

On Tuesday, October 11, about fourteen hundred parolees boarded three Northern Central trains each of which consisted of sixty boxcars. Men who could not walk to the station were taken by wagon then carried on cots to boxcar floors covered with hay. Those in better health walked to the trains, while water and food were packed away for the trip. Major Edgar Roberts, 102d New York National Guard, supervised the entourage and six Union officers and thirteen guards aided him. By the time the men and supplies were on board, darkness was gathering. Around 9:00 P.M., the trains left for Baltimore on a 260-mile course that should have taken the party fifteen hours. The busy roads of the Northern Central made for slow locomotion—a pace under seven miles per hour—and although various stops gave sentries a chance to strip the closest orchards, the slowness did not bode well for debilitated prisoners. At 10:00 A.M. Thursday, the train finally arrived in Baltimore, but five passengers had already died.[9] Josiah Simpson, medical director of the city, was informed by Major Roberts that many others were sick, which prompted Simpson to personally take charge of the patients. His diagnosis was rapid and he discovered

Postwar bust of Col. Benjamin Tracy, who took command of the Elmira Depot when Eastman retired. After the war Tracy went into a successful career in politics and served as secretary of the navy under Benjamin Harrison. Courtesy of the USAMHI.

"a number unable to bear the journey."[10] Simpson swiftly made preparations for their removal to the city's West Hospital, while sending the hospital's chief, Surgeon Artemus Chapel, to inspect the steamer that some prisoners had already boarded for Point Lookout. Medical Inspector C. F. H. Campbell was ordered to examine the rest of the men at the railroad depot in place of Simpson, who wired Hoffman: "The physical condition of many of these men was distressing in the extreme, and they should never have been permitted to leave Elmira."[11]

Meanwhile, Campbell had found sixty invalids "totally unfit to travel" and sent some to the hospital.[12] Attendants lifted the men from the train to ambulances, yet one individual was so despondent that he died while embraced by his carrier, which added a sixth name to the list of the deceased. Campbell documented these specifics in a report that passed through Hoffman's hands and wrote that if the Elmira captives "were inspected before leaving that place in accordance with orders it was most carelessly done, reflecting severely on the medical officers engaged in that duty and is alike disgraceful to all concerned." An embarrassed Campbell deduced that "The effect produced on the public by such marked displays of inefficiency or neglect of duty cannot fail to be most injurious to our cause both at home and abroad."[13] A number of local women tended the "wretched inmates."[14] To be sure, many Baltimoreans sympathized with the Confederacy even before they saw the ambulances conveying prostrated men from Elmira Prison.

By evening, three steamboats awaited departure for Point Lookout. Artemus Chapel made a futile inspection of the cargo before they left and discovered "at least 40 cases that should not have been sent on such a journey, most of whom were in a very feeble and emaciated condition."[15] No room existed for them at the already crowded West Hospital, and the sick passengers onboard were eager to continue rather than stay. Reluctantly, Chapel decided to let them go. At the same time, he charged, "Some one, in my opinion, is greatly censurable for sending such cases away from camp even for exchange."[16] The steamer's departure bell was beginning to sound more like a funeral toll as the steamboats set out into the Chesapeake Bay. The next morning, the vessels arrived at Point Lookout. For many survivors, the journey had come full circle back to the beginning point of their captivity in the North.[17] Only a trip to City Point, Virginia, remained, and they would soon be under the care of their own government.[18]

When Hoffman learned of the exchange debacle, he was livid. On October 14, Medical Director Simpson reported: "The condition of these men was pitiable in the extreme and evinces criminal neglect and inhumanity on the part of the medical officers in making the selection of men to be transferred."[19] Ten days later, Hoffman briefed Edwin M. Stanton and included the accounts given by Simpson, Campbell, and Chapel. Hoffman blamed others in ad-

dition to the Elmira doctors: "From the within reports it appears that both
the commanding officer and medical officers not only failed to be governed
by these orders, but neglected the ordinary promptings of humanity in the
performance of their duties toward sick men, thus showing themselves to be
wholly unfit for the positions they occupy, and it is respectfully recommended
that they be ordered to some other service."[20] Tracy faulted medical examiners
who did not properly diagnose men "too feeble to endure the journey," along
with the inadequate service of the Northern Central Railroad.[21] As for Chief
Surgeon Sanger, he offered the excuse of not being officially advised on the
specifics of the exchange, and was supposedly only "informed by a captain of
the examining board."[22] Each man was at least partly responsible, but neither
was relieved. The ordeal further strained their relationship, which continued
to grow sour.[23]

Colonel Tracy hoped that by relieving the prison of fourteen hundred invalids, the hospital department would be improved. Two new buildings were
added to the six hospitals located by the western wall, and other barracks that
contained seventy beds each were converted into convalescent wards.[24] Ward
doctors had been appointed for the rank and file to examine "the tongues of
the invalids, very much like an inspector would the arms of a regiment. . . .
Blue-mass was the universal remedy for all complaints," John Opie recalled,
"from the tooth-ache to the stomach-ache."[25] More serious cases were sent
to the hospital. One man flagged with chronic diarrhea, with good reason to
walk briskly, regretted seeing how a weaker companion "staggered along until
his shaky legs failed to support him, then he staggered until he was on his
feet again with a ghastly smile trying to bear it bravely."[26] After being admitted to the hospital patients were treated by about a dozen assistant surgeons,
supervised by Sanger, whose office and dispensary were nearby. Inmates also
worked as wardmasters and nurses. Their duties included reading, talking,
singing, and praying with patients, and they tried to lift spirits, even when
there was no hope.[27]

The week after the exchange took place, Colonel Tracy sent Hoffman
an urgent message regarding substantial amounts of sickness at Barracks
Number 3. He admitted that "mortality in this camp is so great as to justify,
as it seems to me, the most rigid investigation as to its cause." If the dying
continued at the current rate, "you can easily calculate the number of prisoners there would be left here for exchange."[28] As October drew to an end,
at least Captain Munger was somewhat optimistic, his final report for the
month stating that the "number of deaths this week is but 40." Two weeks

earlier he had counted 44 dead, and with 588 in the hospital, plus 1,021 others needing medical attention the prospects had been gloomy.[29] Tracy believed that an outside inspection was required to find reasons for the widespread illness, which might include lack of food or clothing, the virulence of Foster's Pond, or surprisingly, "the competency and efficiency of the medical officers on duty here."[30]

On November 1, Sanger drafted a detailed report, which nine of his assistants endorsed, and delivered it to Surgeon General Joseph K. Barnes. Sanger's intent was to "free" his department "from censure" due to the overwhelming sickness and mortality among prisoners. The report also offered him an opportunity to reply to Tracy. Sanger said that he averaged 1,052 sick men at the pen, more than half of whom were not even admitted into the hospital wards. "At this rate," he computed, "the entire command will be admitted to the hospital in less than a year and 36 percent will die." He reiterated various ailments that afflicted prisoners in the pen, as outlined in earlier reports, and meticulously documented the exact day on which they had been reported. To Sanger, his work seemed unappreciated by prison administrators, especially since vegetable supplies were limited and hospital facilities too small. Foster's Pond, he wrote, "remains green with putrescence, filling the air with its messengers of disease and death, the vaults give out their sickly odors, and the hospitals are crowded with victims for the grave." In addition to these shortcomings, something else more recent also bothered the doctor.[31]

Under Commandant Eastman, the prison's medical business was conducted efficiently. The chief physician reported directly to the depot commander to describe prisoners' needs. When Colonel Tracy had taken charge of the depot, close communication between the offices of Tracy and Sanger had ceased, and Sanger had to report to a liaison, a junior officer "who merely has forwarding power." All requisitions had to go through him, "subject to his approval or disapproval," without any guidance except "common sense." "Common sense is a very good thing," Sanger sarcastically added, "but does not work in the physic." The results were more delays, not only in procuring medical supplies but also in building better hospital facilities. Sanger preferred his previous role because "as senior medical officer of this post the whole administrative duties should be intrusted to my care."[32]

Barnes quickly ordered an official to investigate these matters. On November 14, Dr. William Sloan agreed that Sanger's requests and suggestions were being hampered or ignored, "although an undue warmth of language may have been exhibited." When Sloan confronted Tracy, the punctilious

Maj. Eugene F. Sanger, the controversial head surgeon in charge of Elmira Prison's medical department. Courtesy of the Massachusetts Commandery, Military Order of the Loyal Legion, USAMHI.

colonel responded that all applications connected with prisoners of war had to be approved by the Commissary General's Office.[33] This response may have been taken as a tacit indication that the colonel, too, could be restrained by governmental red tape. Even as post commander, Tracy was subject to the influence of superiors in Washington, as were other Elmira Prison officials. By the third weekend in November, Tracy had learned this lesson and was measuring up to the task. On November 18, the Sanitary Commission's leading lady, Dorothea Dix, arrived in Elmira for a special examination of the prison and its hospital.[34] With Tracy as her personal escort, Dix toured the prison and then left the city "highly gratified since prisoners were receiving all necessary care."[35] Evidently, Tracy's social skills had more of an impact than any disagreeable sights inside the enclosure. Tracy nurtured public relations throughout his career, and it was no accident that the country lawyer turned into a seasoned politician, eventually becoming secretary of the navy. Sanger, conversely, had limited public relations skills. His New England accent might readily bite with a caustic tone. This tendency was apparent in the way he handled some associates, and worse yet, it did not matter if they outranked him. Sanger's bickering also went beyond the depot commander, going so far as to voice displeasure with other individuals in Elmira.[36] He did not work happily with Elwell or Sappington, and complained that some unnamed local inspector "takes liberty of entering my wards at all times, instructs my ward-masters and nurses, finds fault of them to my management, and quizzes them. . . . I cannot be held responsible for a large medical department with over 1,000 patients without power, authority, or influence."[37]

Yet Sanger and his department were held accountable. As with the medical offers he supervised, Sanger's ability was scrutinized throughout his tenure in Elmira by colleagues in Baltimore, the military commander in the city where he worked, and finally, the patients he treated. Southerners were not restrained in their estimates of his staff's medical acumen or indifference toward them. After a Confederate ward doctor admitted one of his men to the hospital "for a clear case of inflammation of the bowels," but then saw the prisoner return with "a styptic so powerful it is used to stop hemorrhage!"he refused to send any more of his patients to the hospital.[38] Walter Addison, who worked in the hospital, expounded on the "deplorable ignorance of the medical men in charge."[39] One day, Sanger was summoned to diagnose three men whose strength was declining. He recommended that the patients be given "four or five drops of Fowlers solution of arsenic," but the ward surgeon, Dr. Ira Van Ness, failed to include the word "or" in the prescription. Apparently, forty-five drops of the solution were distributed according to directions, ingested, and, consequently, each patient died. Sanger imposed no penalty and Van Ness remained on call until he requested his own dismissal from service.[40] These and other incidents caused prisoners to worry not only about the competence of subordinate surgeons, whom they believed were learning on the job, but also the integrity of the entire staff, particularly its head. A few visitors to the hospital even suggested that Sanger was not inept at all, but instead very deliberate in aiding the Union cause.[41]

Anthony Keiley was one of the most severe critics of the medical department. His strong sentiments took shape while he worked as a clerk in headquarters, an experience that gave him an opportunity to earn credit from the sutler, extra cups of coffee from the commissary, and cigars from Major Colt. Keiley's duties included tabulating the number of deaths each morning, which brought him routinely through the hospital wards.[42] After one such visit he wrote about the shocking mortality in the pen: "As I went over to the first hospital this morning early, there were eighteen dead bodies lying naked on the bare earth. Eleven more were added to the list by half-past eight o' clock!" A few weeks before the October exchange, Keiley elaborated on such matters: "The deaths yesterday were twenty-nine. Air pure, location healthy, no epidemic. The men are being deliberately murdered by the surgeon, especially by either the ignorance or malice of the chief."[43] James Huffman, a hospital attendant, allegedly heard a doctor say "he killed more Rebs than any soldier on the front," and another Southerner reported similar conversations.[44] Some also suggested that drugs in the dispensary, which was stocked with quinine, opium pills, and whiskey, were used at times by people who did not qualify as patients.[45]

Anthony Keiley did not hide his feelings toward the chief surgeon. "Sanger is simply a brute, as we learned the whole truth about him from his own people. If he had not avoided court martial by resigning his position, it is likely that even a military commission would have found it impossible to screen his brutality to the sick."[46] Local opinion held that "something [was] wrong with Dr. Sanger." Many believed that he "took a very considerable amount of the 'medicine' which the Government furnished for the sick prisoners."[47] Further indictments came from within the hospital. Medical steward W. P. Whitesides commented that there were "plenty of stimulants, but a good deal of it drank by the doctor."[48] Sanger was never brought up on any charges and it seems unlikely that he or his staff intentionally harmed the prisoners, let alone killed any. Then again, personal addictions can affect an individual's performance, as already demonstrated in the Shohola mishap; and escapism through an addiction could not be ruled out. Sanger's acerbic personality did not help, and what the major lacked in tact and ability to follow orders he made up through an enlarged ego. Perhaps pride in his professional standing as a doctor made him feel that he outranked anyone, even in the army. Sanger wanted to escape his duty at Elmira, admitting that from the moment he entered the Chemung Valley he wanted out—and when Sanger left, controversy followed him.[49]

Sanger's personal records and events after he left Elmira aid in understanding this enigmatic figure. As early as September 16, a little more than a month after he reported for duty at Elmira, Sanger requested that Surgeon General Barnes relieve him. Before the exchange fiasco and the hostilities with Tracy, Sanger claimed to be "predisposed to asthma[;] it had returned with unusual violence, rendering me almost unfit to perform my duty. . . . If retained here much longer," he warned, "I must give it up." Sanger insisted that he had "reason to believe the atmosphere of Elmira peculiarly obnoxious, as I have suffered more at this place than all my experience on the Potomoc and in the Dept. of the Gulf."[50] The major hoped he could either resume his old job as medical director of the 19th Corps in the Shenandoah Valley or at least be given a supervisory role at a general hospital in another city.[51] Unfortunately for the New Englander, he jotted down a note on the last day of November reminding Barnes that "I continue on duty at Elmira, N.Y. with prisoners of war."[52]

On December 23, Barnes finally consented to Sanger's appeal and replaced Sanger with Maj. Anthony E. Stocker of the U.S. Volunteers.[53] At the end of the following week, with Sanger out of the way, Stocker wrote Tracy, "I hope soon to establish more order and system in the general management of the hospital both as regards officers and employees." It would not be easy, because Stocker's wards required "an increase of at least one-half their present capacity, there is a steady demand of seventy-five persons daily who should be placed in the Hospital at once."[54] Meanwhile, Sanger had his own problems as he awaited orders and wrote Barnes that he preferred field service with Generals William T. Sherman or George H. Thomas.[55] Commissary General of Subsistence Eaton hounded the major, threatening to stop his pay unless he rendered accounts for stores requisitioned four months prior to his arrival in Elmira. Sanger replied that his commissary officer, Capt. Henry Sibley, had told him he did not need to account for the provisions. Sibley, however, had "no recollection" of giving Sanger such advice.[56] Evidently, these finances were eventually settled, but by that time Sanger was in Detroit, his next assignment after leaving Elmira.

In the Northern Department, Sanger was appointed chief surgeon at St. Mary's and Harper General Hospitals in Detroit. On January 19, 1865, he requested that orders be "modified" to make him superintendent, but really hoped that they would be altered altogether. "I prefer to be sent to the field, to any post duty in the rear, unless I can board my family in becoming style, on my army pay."[57] He stayed in Detroit until early 1865 and was promoted to medical director of the Michigan District, although he quickly put this job in jeopardy by directly disobeying orders from a superior.[58] A message from the Northern Department's headquarters in Cincinnati sanctioned by the Surgeon General's Office in Washington required that Sanger send one of his assistants, D. O. Farrand, to help transfer a contingent of ill soldiers. On April 5, Sanger wrote his department head, Col. Charles S. Tripler, that it was "absolutely impossible to spare him [Farrand] at present without serious detriment to Harper Hospital." Sanger's arrogance incensed Tripler, and on April 7, he called for Sanger's dismissal from his department. This incident was not the only time Sanger refused orders, nor was it the first time that this particular superior was struck by Sanger's insubordination. "This officer has," wrote a perturbed Tripler, "in several instances failed to carry out instructions from this office, but they were of too unimportant a nature to require any severity of rebuke."[59]

Tripler demanded that Sanger have his assistant delivered "immediately," but instead of receiving Farrand in Cincinnati, Tripler was greeted with another one of Sanger's telegrams, "taking altogether different grounds from his report, inconsistent with itself, and threatening me with an appeal to the Surgeon General, if I attempt to enforce my order." A furious Tripler concluded that he could not "rely upon such an officer to carry out an order," and he brought the matter to Maj. Gen. Joseph Hooker, commander of the Northern Department.[60] Sanger would be swept off to yet another department, but not before appealing to the surgeon general.

On April 8, Sanger wrote Barnes a "private and unofficial letter." He reflected on a meeting that the two had had in Washington the year before, after he had returned with the 19th Corps from the Red River campaign. Sanger believed that Barnes inadvertently supposed he "desired an easy duty in the rear." The frustrated doctor revealed much about himself and his true ambitions: "I have lived in constant hope from the time that I was ordered to Elmira that you would send me to active field duty—either with Gen'l Sherman or Grant's Armies." Now that the end of the war was near, Sanger continued, "I don't feel a bit satisfied to terminate my career at a rear station," and "always desired to participate in some of the eventful conflicts of the war."[61] He was convinced that he "came into the service for different purposes and deserve[d] to terminate my relations with the army in a little more immediate proclivity to the scenes of active strife. . . . Events are stirring and foreshadow the speedy surrender of Gen'l Lees Army," but Sanger wanted to "be there to participate in the last death struggles of this eventful rebellion."[62] Sanger's dreams never materialized. Rather than being sent to Virginia he was ordered to the District of East Tennessee, under the Department of the Cumberland. He worked as the district's medical inspector, then its chief surgeon. Sanger was mustered out of the army in September 1865.[63]

After the war, Sanger returned to Bangor to reestablish a practice that had gained much respectability in the public eye, but he was also plagued by personal setbacks. His profitable surgical practice was one of the largest in eastern Maine, and in his spare time he served as an examining physician for the Pension Bureau. He was appointed surgeon general of his state by fellow Civil War veteran Governor Joshua Lawrence Chamberlain, and five years later, in 1876, was named president of Maine's medical association. Ironically, he was also given honorary memberships to medical societies in Baltimore and Detroit, two places at which he had left behind less than favorable impressions during the war. His postwar scholarly pursuits included published articles on "Resection of Joints," "Abscesses of the Lungs," and "Malpractice," a subject that some contended he knew far too well.[64]

In 1887, Sanger's family life fell under scrutiny because of his spouse, who opted for a more secure life than the prominent and well-to-do doctor could provide. By the middle of December, wife Emily had decided she could no longer bear her husband's conduct, or the marriage, and she divorced him on grounds of "cruel and abusive treatment."[65] Three years later, Sanger remarried, but this relationship lasted only seven years. On July 24, 1897, at the age of sixty-seven, former chief surgeon of Elmira Prison, Eugene Francis Sanger, died.[66] A post mortem discovered that Sanger had succumbed to heart disease, although a few Southerners felt he had a tainted heart long before his old body was stretched out on an examining table in Bangor, Maine.[67]

6

Winter's Torment

The brilliant fall foliage of the Chemung Valley gave way to a harsh and barren winter. In October, there were 1,038 "A" tents pitched inside the enclosure, each of which could house up to five prisoners. A total of 5,190 men camped outdoors, while 3,873 were housed in thirty barracks.[1] Inquiries about better housing had been addressed to Commissary General Hoffman long before the approach of winter, and as the cold season drew nearer Colonel Tracy echoed his predecessor's sentiments: "Many men are in tents without floors or blankets. Barracks should be erected instead of tents." Captain Munger affirmed that the "weather is cold for the season, and those in tents especially suffer." Hoffman, who had denied permission to construct additional buildings for inmates and guards earlier in the year, granted approval in the middle of October.[2]

Quartermaster John J. Elwell received the ground plans for the immense project and supervised the construction of the winter quarters. The barracks were to be 100 feet in length and 22 feet in width, and were designed to accommodate 120 men each, although each would be filled with more. Floors were to be raised to discourage tunneling and roofs fabricated with felt for insulation. Three rows of bunks were to be built down the long walls of each barrack. Hoffman ordered the design of the barracks to be the same as those built at Camp Chemung, and "in every way the closest economy will be studied." He added that the "lumber and other materials and the hire of the workmen will, as far as practicable, be paid out of the prison fund."[3] If the purchases exceeded that amount, the Quartermaster Department would pay the difference. A qualified carpenter would be selected to direct the workers, who were needed now more than ever. Civilian laborers comprised a combined

A picture of Elmira Prison before the winter barracks were constructed. Notice the men lined up for roll call. Courtesy of the Library of Virginia.

workforce of about eighty men, with carpenters earning up to $2.75 daily and teamsters the usual $40 a month. Prisoner laborers came much cheaper, 5 cents daily, whereas prisoner carpenters commanded twice that amount. Prisoners were also compensated with bonus rations. Workdays were long and tedious, beginning in the early morning and ending in late afternoon.[4]

In mid-October, Colonel Tracy also reintroduced plans to drain Foster's Pond, which was producing a "continued prevalence of disease and death in this camp."[5] This matter was one of the few concerns over which he and Sanger never differed, as the doctor demonstrated in an observation recorded before he left that described the pond as "a festering mass of corruption, impregnating the entire atmosphere of the camp with its pestilential odors, night and day." Tracy felt that "a due regard for the lives of prisoners confined here requires that some method of introducing a running stream of water through this camp should be adopted."[6] His approach was to build an underground drainage sluice. Unlike his predecessors' open-trench plan, a scheme that property owners had blocked, the tactful Tracy persuaded the property owners that a pipe laid underneath the soil would not interfere with their land or lower its value. He hired a surveyor, who determined that around six thousand feet of six-inch wooden pipe was required, priced at almost six thousand dollars, but well worth the expense. To convince his cost-conscious commissary, Tracy insisted that the War Department would actually save money because inmates could perform most of the work. The Quartermaster Department could also provide most of the tools.[7]

Hoffman supported almost everything that Tracy proposed to remove "the material exhalations from the stagnant water," but he balked at the price. To him, it was obvious that inmates could do all the work and that the prison fund could afford them, along with the cost of lumber. The only conduit Hoffman would approve had to be built with less expensive two-inch pipe, its ends beveled into six-inch sections. "Constructed this way," Hoffman wrote, "the whole work should not cost over $120." He reminded Tracy that "fall rains may be expected to come on very soon, which for this winter will do away with the necessity for the work."[8] Cooperation from Mother Nature could be forgotten, and if Elmira officials wanted Foster's Pond drained, they had to do it themselves. So at the end of October, 150 prisoners started digging a ditch to connect the river and pond. Darius P. Smith, a civil engineer, supervised the prisoners for six dollars a day. Shovels were the primary implements for the task, but the purchase of other equipment helped expedite the job. Eventually, a prison camp carpenter shop sixteen-by-thirty-by-twelve feet was built that stored not only shovels, but also a large number of spades, saws, axes, wheelbarrows, hammers, hatchets, and wooden pails. With so many tools at the prisoners' disposal, one might have believed Colonel Tracy when he said that the project should take only a couple weeks.[9]

While plans for the barracks and drainage sluice were being finalized, Elmira's Quartermaster Department faced another problem. Captain Elwell and Assistant Quartermaster S. P. Suydam were driving their buggy toward downtown, their horses riding in full stride, when the bolt that joined carriage and team loosened. The buggy disconnected and flipped, hurling both men to the ground as the startled horses raced down Water Street.[10] Eyewitnesses "pronounced it a most thrilling sight as none supposed it possible for the occupants to escape alive."[11] Captain Suydam received only superficial wounds to his side and head, but Quartermaster Elwell fractured his leg again—in the same place as he had in South Carolina. While they recuperated, construction slowed, not so much because of the accident as from the shortage of building materials.[12]

Despite shortages in timber, progress had been made by the middle of November. Carpenters and shovelers toiled in earnest. Six new barracks provided lodging for captives and four others barracks were almost finished. An extensive labor force of civilian and prison labor working together enabled one building to be constructed each day, each at at an estimated price of one thousand dollars. Older barracks that had deteriorated were patched with clay to keep out winter winds. Major Colt petitioned for a guardhouse to be built at the cost of $365 inside the pen to protect sentinels on duty. Near the river, about 125 inmates spent eight hours each day breaking the frosted ground, which became harder and harder as they moved along. On November 20, the project reached halfway point, with three thousand feet of trench opened and one thousand feet of wooden pipe fit together and covered. The immense amount of lumber required for these and other improvements brought enormous profits to suppliers. Spaulding and Haskell sold more than $13,500 worth of lumber, whereas the mill of Hatch and Partridge sold $12,221 in supplies. However, neither firm could prepare the wood as fast as needed. Cook and Covell provided the necessary hardware.[13]

Preparations for cold weather were also made at the prison hospital. As one doctor explained, "Winters are exceedingly cold and bleak at Elmira."[14] Patients' clothes, some six hundred items per day, were washed in a kettle, outdoors, leaving the nine laundry men unhappy. A larger facility with increased loading capacity was built so that the detail could work faster and be better sheltered. Colonel Tracy also urged that the hospital patients be protected better and hoped that the wards could be better insulated. Upgrading the hospital would be costly, but Hoffman proposed that it be treated like the regular wards and sealed with clay. When drafts still slipped through their wards, additional stoves had to be ordered.[15]

In early December, as buildings were under construction, lumber supplies dwindled.[16] Captain Elwell apologized to Quartermaster General Meigs for the shortage, noting that in addition to providing for the improvements at the prison, lumber was also being used to develop Camp Chemung. "These jobs and smaller ones have required immense amounts of lumber," Elwell wrote to Meigs, "more than the market afforded." As more trees were cleared and processed, Elwell reassured his superior that "as many carpenters have been worked as much as possible." God fearing or not, the men also hammered their nails on Sundays, "early and late." Indeed, from September through December, the prison fund paid $2,652 for carpenter labor.[17]

Ever since the buggy accident, Elwell had recuperated in his second-floor office rather than resting at his regular quarters. For the next seven weeks, he conducted business for his department, but on December 6 bad luck struck once again. Hobbling on crutches outside his office, Elwell slipped and tumbled down a staircase. Elwell fractured his right leg, this time near the thigh. This incident represented the third time Elwell had broken the leg in less than two years, yet he took up his overused crutches and went back to work.[18] The local press could not help poking fun at the captain's latest misfortune, hoping not only for a more successful recovery, but also for a final one, so that Elwell "may not experience more danger or rougher service in Elmira than in the field."[19]

A week before Christmas, Elwell's work crew took a short break from working on the unfinished barracks, not on account of the holiday but again because of the scarcity of lumber.[20] H. H. Rockwell, a citizen who lived in the Chemung Valley during the Civil War, later recalled how the "hills around Elmira were denuded by their owners to furnish the barracks of the Union soldiers and also the prison camp with wood." Rockwell knew firsthand that timber "brought a very high price and was purchased in unlimited quantities."[21] In addition to buying manufactured lumber, the Quartermaster's Department also hired locals, particularly farmers, to gather and haul wood to the stockade because captives had to be allotted four sticks each day for fuel.[22] Elmira resident J. Marvin, for example, had been supplying the depot with wood since late summer, receiving five thousand cords of wood at $7.25 apiece. His contract

A view of Elmira Prison after the winter barracks were constructed. Courtesy of the Massachusetts Commandery, Military Order of the Loyal Legion, USAMHI.

was renegotiated in early fall to continue through the winter and included dry hardwood, green hardwood, and softwood.[23]

On Christmas Day, temperatures rose, slightly warming the nine hundred men who still lived in tents. An even better gift came when Tracy was given permission to replace the wood burners with coal stoves. Because coal burning was more efficient and less hazardous, it was adopted as the primary heating source at the prison camp. The decision to purchase two coal stoves for every barrack was appreciated by Cook and Covell, which had already sold the camp its wood burners. The hardware merchants immediately sold 150 coal stoves at Barracks Number 3, along with 90 feet of stovepipe for every unit. Each stove cost about $28 and burned 3 kegs of coal daily. Moreover, utilizing coal for heating Barracks Number 3 was not inexpensive. The prison camp could burn almost 375 tons a month at a cost more than $4,000 per month.[24]

On New Year's Day 1865, all of the prisoners were sheltered in barracks, but overcrowding was common since almost two hundred men occupied each ward. The twenty original barracks were supposed to house one hundred men each, whereas the more recent structures fit 120 to 150 prisoners. Two coal stoves warmed each building.[25] Supported by a visiting medical inspector, Tracy had convinced the prison commissary's office to line the hospital wards, which helped keep sick patients warm, although at a total cost of $3,500.[26] Tracy also had "the honor to . . . report that the conduit for conducting a stream of water from the Chemung River through the prison camp is fully completed and works like a charm." The mile-long pipe took about two months to complete—longer than expected—because it became "a more serious job than anticipated, owing to waste and quicksand in the bottom of the cutting." Its price, not including labor charges, was $2,000, but Tracy contended that it was "worth twice its cost."[27] He did not have to be overly apprehensive regarding the price because he now reported to a new superior, Brig. Gen. Henry Wessells. An increase in Southern prisoners had led to expansion and division of command in the prison commissary's office. Wessells had charge of the territory east of the Mississippi, and Hoffman presided over the west. The arrangement did not last long because, as more prisoners were exchanged, Hoffman assumed overall command in February 1865.[28]

Even with improved shelter and heat, many Southerners lost the fight against Elmira's winter. One North Carolinian had noticed in September: "It is very cold, worse than I have seen it in the South in the dead of winter."[29] Ever since these captives had been condemned to this forty-acre plot, Mother Nature had multiplied their difficulties. During the summer, a drought had

stagnated the drainage system and wilted the food. At the beginning of au-
tumn, a cold rain had turned to snow.[30] One Texan remembered the winter:
"If there ever was a hell on earth, Elmira prison was that hell, but it was not a
hot one."[31] Twice during the winter, the temperature plummeted to eighteen
degrees below zero, although wind chills made it feel even colder. Blizzards left
several feet of snow and incapacitated those who lived within and outside of
the city.[32] If anyone needed reminding, the well-traveled Keiley warned that
Elmira was "in the hyperborean regions of New York, where for at least four
months of every year, anything short of a polar-bear would find locomotion
impracticable."[33]

Winds whistled through unsealed cracks in the barracks; stronger gusts
rattled planks and tore away shingles. Prisoners huddled around stoves, and
sometimes each other.[34] Hundreds of men crowded in their quarters trying to
stay warm, but the space indoors might still be as cold as the outside environment. "Imagine if you can," wrote John Opie, "with the weather ten or fifteen
degrees below zero, one hundred men trying to keep warm by one stove. Each
morning the men crawled out of their bunks shivering and half frozen, when
a scuffle, and frequently a fight, for a place by the fire occurred. God help the
sick and weak as they were literally left out in the cold."[35] Stoves were installed
in the open aisle thirty feet apart at each end of the barrack. They were fired
up twice a day, at 8:00 morning and night. A three- to five-foot "deadline"
etched in chalk encircled each stove to prevent men from getting too close.
Each barracks took about four hours to heat, and the hours between were less
than hospitable.[36]

If they could be acquired, blankets served as both bedding and linens
for the three-tiered bunks. W. S. Riddle complained to his ward sergeant
about sleeping arrangements because "that board nearly breaks my back."[37]
However, the men were not allowed to cushion their bunks with straw or
shavings, because authorities feared the material as breeding grounds for
lice, to which John King replied, "we were already well supplied."[38] Bunks
extended four feet off the wall, and a six-inch rail surrounded them to keep
men from falling out. The bunks were built to hold two men, but during the
colder months as many as four slept close together to provide extra warmth.
In the evening, not long after the coal stoves were turned on, the lamps that
kept the wards lighted were extinguished for the night. Wilbur Grambling
recalled about one night that he did not "expect to sleep, . . . as I only [had]
one blanket to cover with and it [was] quite thin."[39] Others managed to doze
off and let dreams carry them far away from their dreary abodes. In the dead

of Elmira's winter, Willie Campbell, an "affectionate" but uncertain brother, needed reassurance from his "Beloved sister Zoe," home in Louisiana. "In the stillness of the night, my imagination takes its flight to happier scenes, and the contemplation of future happiness causes a temporary forgetfulness of my present condition. I am a patient under trial—resigned in suffering—for hope dwells in my heart? . . . Other days will come?"[40]

As the morning sun rose to bleak dawn skies, prisoners awakened, folded up what blankets they had, and lined up outside for roll call. They stood at attention longer than they wanted, their breath made visible in the frosted air. The prisoners, some with holes in their shoes, other with no shoes at all, grew even more agitated when they looked down at the snow heaped to their ankles.[41] "This was very rough on our boys from the extreme South," a border state comrade noted, "and they shivered with the chills."[42] After morning roll, captives might stay behind their quarters, shielding themselves from winds, until they returned inside, where they wrapped rags around perhaps throbbing, frostbitten feet. The more venturesome and better clad prisoners stayed outside longer and even tried to ice skate on Foster's Pond.[43] But these individuals were in the minority. The more typical Elmira inmate wondered how he was going "to live this winter without more cover."[44]

Although shelter had been crucial at the beginning of winter, clothing became even more imperative as the season progressed. Earlier warnings were not heeded. A week after the prison opened, a visiting medical inspector mentioned that inmates lacked proper shirts, pants, blankets, and shoes.[45] A month later, a *New York Post* correspondent watched a number of Southerners enter the stockade "barefooted, and others bareheaded; many have not, apparently the slightest regard for their personal appearance."[46] Nor did they care. Men captured in summer campaigns never imagined themselves in New York during the winter. Confederate soldiers seldom dressed uniformly to begin, and clothing was never a top priority in their warmer environs. Yet those transferred to Elmira during the summer and early fall could at least attempt to acclimate themselves by collecting any apparel they could find, in contrast to men thrown into the mix when the bitter cold season was already upon them. This problem held true particularly for the 2,129 prisoners received after the October exchange. Two-thirds of them came straight from Fort Fisher, North Carolina, and Ship Island, Mississippi, and proved susceptible to pneumonia.[47] John King could caution them that Elmira "was a pleasant summer prison for the southern soldiers, but an excellent place for them to find their graves in the winter."[48]

At the end of October, Inspector Munger warned, "Another supply of clothing is needed, as weather is becoming cold and many are still poorly clad."[49] One month later, another inspection confirmed that clothing was "insufficient," and a troubled Colonel Tracy notified his superiors that "pneumonia is prevailing and is alarmingly fatal."[50] As the disorder circulated through the pen, Union authorities provided prisoners with limited clothing, mostly old army overcoats with one of their tails removed so that inmates would not be confused for guards and sneak out. When this defect was explained to a captive, he answered, "I would have attempted it."[51] A more fashion-conscious comrade was less grateful for being made more distinguishable: "They helped keep us warm, but should we have been out in the world in such a costume, one might have mistaken us for scarecrows eloping from the neighboring cornfield."[52]

On December 4, a busy Captain Munger reiterated that clothing was "insufficient for this climate" and counted 1,666 prisoners "entirely destitute of blankets."[53] That week the Quartermaster's Department filled a requisition for four thousand blankets, which inmates cherished for their extra insulation during chilly nights in tents and barracks. In addition, Captain Elwell brought additional relief with 2,500 jackets, 162 coats, 2,000 pants, 3,011 shirts, 1,216 underpants, and 6,065 pairs of socks. However, as this supply arrived, so did more prisoners. Of the 110 men that came from Old Capitol Prison in Washington, only nine had blankets and a number were clothed poorly. Not only did these arrivals need provisions, but others already in camp were shown to need shoes and pants during the year's last inspection.[54]

In the meantime, prisoners privately solicited garments through the postal system. They wrote countless letters to friends, relatives, and anyone else willing to mail them clothing. By Union military regulations, the clothing had to be gray or have a dark color stitched into the fabric so that inmates could not be mistaken for Union soldiers or civilians.[55] Prisoner D. Bruin emphasized that his family must not "have me any fine or costly clothes made, but something *heavy* & comfortable, suitable for this climate." He asked for the clothing "as soon as possible," gave his measurements, and reminded his family that they be "Gray or mixed coulor."[56] Another Rebel's "joy was unabounded" when a fellow inmate shared a package of clothes with him.[57] James H. Hardaway, who lived in "Barracks 3 ward 35 Elmira New York" was "very thankful" after Edwin G. Booth, who resided in Philadelphia, sent clothes to him.[58] A shy Wilbur Grambling, the recipient of a box from one "Mrs. Sawyer," appreciated her kindness, as well, until he opened it and discovered "a pair of girls drawers."[59]

Larger donations were attempted with less success. Toward the end of the year, a group of Baltimoreans raised clothing for Elmira prisoners. Their representative, John Van Allen, arrived in Elmira "when the bitter sleets and biting frosts of winter had commenced." As he stood outside the stockade, a sympathetic Major Colt approached. Van Allen told the major about his mission and his desire to enter the enclosure to meet the captive's needs personally. The commandant "treated me with consideration and kindness, and informed me that they were very destitute of clothing and blankets. Yet he stated he could not allow me to enter the prison gate or administer relief, as an order from the War Department rendered him powerless." Although army regulations did not allow most civilians inside, Colt wired Washington on the group's behalf anyway, yet his efforts were to no avail. The closest Van Allen ever got to the inmates was a visit up the observatory after "a money consideration was exacted and paid." He looked down into the prison, at the captives "bare feet . . . clothes in tatters . . . without blankets. I say these men suffered bitterly from the want of clothing," wrote Van Allen, "but [were] denied the privilege of covering their nakedness."[60]

Not long after this visit, Colt's tenure as prison commandant ended. He had recovered from his accidental fall on the Peninsula and was ordered back to his regiment. Before he left, friends he had made while on duty at Elmira gave him a gift, an expensive overcoat, tails intact.[61] The Southerners he commanded appreciated his fair treatment no less, but being short on clothing they awarded him instead with an ornately designed chalice. It was whittled from a coconut shell, set on a silver stand, and engraved—"To Maj. Henry V. Colt 104th N.Y. Vols. Commandant U.S. Military Prison Barrack No. 3 Elmira, N.Y."[62] Colt's replacement was Lt. Col. Stephen Moore, previously in charge of Camp Chemung. An officer in the 11th New Jersey Volunteers, Moore had suffered a severe case of sunstroke during the Battle of Chancellorsville that had impaired his sight, memory, and general health. The New Jerseyite, in his early forties, about 5 feet 10 inches tall, and weighing 140 pounds, needed to fill large shoes after the departure of the personable Colt. However, Stephen Moore was equal to the challenge and continued the tradition of his predecessor, becoming well liked by those within and outside the stockade as he guided the prison through the new year.[63]

By the beginning of 1865, the Confederacy had taken upon itself the responsibility to clothe its own captured men. Each side had occasionally supplied its own soldiers in prison, and in the fall of 1864 the Confederacy considered shipping a cargo of cotton to the North for similar purposes. The

Lt. Col. Stephen Moore, who replaced Colt as Elmira prison commandant at the end of November 1864. Courtesy of the Bureau of Archives and History, New Jersey State Library.

opposing sides decided that one thousand bales would be sent from Mobile, Alabama, to New York City, where it would be sold and the proceeds used to buy clothing for Southerners in Union prisons. In return, the Yankees would send provisions for their soldiers held in Southern captivity. Confederate brigadier general William N. R. Beall, a former prisoner himself, was placed on parole and appointed the chief officer in charge of disbursing Southern clothing from his headquarters in New York City. Three other Confederate officers, also paroled and under Union guard, were to distribute the requisitions. Elmira Prison was high on their list, but it had no commissioned officers among the prison population, and since only officers could supervise the distribution of clothing, Elmira inmates had to wait until three higher ranking men were transferred from another compound.[64]

Final terms of the deal, delays from ocean travel, and the wait for Confederate emissaries, impeded progress. On January 5, Tracy wrote to Wessells that for a month his prisoners had awaited 3,000 pants, 8,000 drawers, 1,000 jackets, 2,500 shirts, 4,000 boots, 7,000 socks, and 1,500 hats.[65] Tracy's solution was to have Quartermaster Elwell furnish them garments, but the commissary general's office denied the request due to "the necessity of strict economy in the issue of clothing."[66] The only consolation came when Elmira Depot received a small shipment of clothing. The delivery was in error, but Tracy, perhaps thinking it was clothing from the Rebel authorities, let the prisoners don them before realizing the mistake. On January 27, the Rebel cotton shipment finally reached New York Harbor, yet clothing was still desperately needed upstate.[67]

On Tuesday night February 7, three Confederate emissaries finally arrived in Elmira, coming from a prison exclusively for officers on Johnson's Island, off Sandusky, Ohio. Majors Daniel S. Printup and John Thompson, and Lt. Col. Henry J. Price comprised the committee. However, they arrived before any shipments of clothing, and because two and one-half feet of snow had postponed rail service they decided to go to the prison on Thursday without supplies to at least make an initial assessment. After returning to their rooms at the Brainard House, where other military officials boarded, they faced another problem. Colonel Tracy was ordered not to allow the three officers quarters inside the stockade, so they temporarily stayed at the more expensive city hotel under the watchful eyes of guards. While there, they incurred an unexpected hotel bill, and, short on cash, they asked their quartermaster general to pick up the charges. At the end of the week they solved this problem by moving to less expensive quarters, closer to the prison.[68]

By that time, the Confederate officers were receiving packages from the express company and distributing them among Elmira inmates. A large number of the blankets and socks were secured, while other boxes containing a greater variety of apparel were still on their way. As the emissaries waited, they negotiated on their own. Providing clothing for prisoners was one market that locals had trouble cornering because the Confederate government had main responsibility for that business. [69] However, Elmira Prison authorities had given J. Gladke the impression that he could design clothes specifically for the Rebels and had led him to believe "that he would be permitted to sell them." When a dismayed Gladke "was prohibited from doing so," he found himself left with a large supply of garments "expressly for the prisoners." The Confederate's chief spokesman, Major Printup, wrote excitedly to Beall that the Elmira clothier wanted to make a deal with the Rebels to sell this lot, plus more: "We understand him to have only about $5,000 worth but see from his proposition that the amount has wonderfully been enlarged." Printup remarked that Gladke's merchandise was "of good quality & seems to us fully worth the price asked." Nothing else in the correspondence between Beall and Printup mentioned the matter, and it can only be concluded that Gladke had offered a sensible proposition, particularly considering the savings in shipping and handling. [70]

On the last day of February, thirty-six cases of apparel arrived in Elmira from Brigadier General Beall. Prisoners who needed clothing most were given preference. The boxes contained 995 jackets, 1,530 pants, 550 shirts, 780 drawers, 1,000 pairs of socks, and 1,040 pairs of shoes. [71] However, an inspection after distribution of the garments reported the following: "The clothing sent here by the Confederates . . . [is] not in quantities sufficient to supply all that are in need." [72] On March 6, an additional 454 blankets, 980 jackets, 900 pants, 950 shirts 1,200 drawers, 500 pairs of socks, 1,020 pairs of shoes, and a bonus of 196 packages of tobacco came from Beall in New York City. It was still not enough. Seeing no end to the work that lay ahead, Printup asked the next day that Beall have their paroles extended. [73]

Clothing concerns continued late into winter. On March 12, Printup informed Beall that the supplies recently issued did not fill the quota of shirts, underclothing, or shoes. [74] That day, Prison Inspector James R. Reid verified, "A small amount of clothing had been distributed but not enough to supply all that is needed," and furthermore stressed that what inmates currently wore was "Ragged and Inadequate." [75] The prisoners received more shipments throughout the month, including 500 blankets, 450 jackets, 110 pants, 600 shirts, 300 drawers, 100 pairs of socks, and 200 pairs of shoes. But, again, Printup wrote Beall, bothered that the "demand has been and still is much greater than the supply." Printup emphasized that "we need *underclothing pants & shoes* more than anything else."[76] The Confederate emissaries would still be disbursing clothes at Elmira after the Army of Northern Virginia surrendered in April 1865.[77]

Even when the weather became warmer, nothing indicated that General Beall would be able to clothe the Elmira inmates. Camp Inspector William Stanhope verified that point in a letter in which he had "the honor to call the attention of the commanding officer to the neglected condition of clothing for Prisoners of War. . . . After careful investigation," Stanhope concluded, "I find the wants of the prisoners in this respect have been greatly overlooked." Evidently so, for his report was dated May 20, 1865.[78] Clothing woes were exacerbated when the Union and Confederate governments became less interested in clothing for prisoners after they revitalized the exchange system in late winter. In February 1865, many at Elmira hoped for such a possibility.

On February 4, Hoffman telegraphed Tracy that he could begin making out rolls for exchanging three thousand inmates. As with the previous exchange, prisoners in poor health would be given preference as long as officials deemed them fit to travel. The next day, Tracy informed Hoffman that the past performance of the Northern Central railway concerned him, as did its inferior cars and the slowness of service caused by recruits heading south. Tracy reminded Hoffman: "The detachment of prisoners that was sent from here last fall were forty hours in reaching Baltimore, a run which should have been made in fifteen hours."[79] He pleaded for permission to send the men on the Erie Railroad to New York City: "To keep sick men upon the road at this season of the year in cars without seats and without water-closets or any of the conveniences usually provided for the transportation of passengers will result in much suffering." Tracy wrote with words to which Hoffman could relate: "It will cost no more to transport these men to New York than to Baltimore, while the Erie Railroad has a large number of second-class passenger cars and can move a detachment of 500 men on a few hours' notice and land them in New York within twelve to fifteen hours from starting. . . . Unless facilities for water transportation from Baltimore are greatly superior to those from New York," Tracy contended, "it is greatly desirable that they be forwarded via New York City."[80] For one reason or another, Hoffman demurred. At least for Tracy, this time his conscience would be clear.

At 5:00 P.M., February 13, guards put the first five hundred prisoners on a train of the Northern Central railway under the charge of Lt. Col. Frederick E. Trotter, 1st Veterans Reserve Corps. Two days later, at 10:00 A.M., the prisoners arrived at Baltimore's Bolton Station.[81] Three men had died on the way and nineteen others counted incapable of traveling further were sent to local hospitals. Although casualties were not as high as in October, the scenario was all too familiar for the city's medical director, Josiah Simpson. Simpson wrote Hoffman on February 18: "Proper care does not appear to have been exercised by the medical officer at Elmira in the examination of the prisoners for transfer, for it is not possible that so short a journey could have brought about the condition in which these sick men were found on their arrival at this point." Hoffman sent Tracy a terse message that "instructions from this office directing invalids who were well enough to bear the journey should be forwarded does not appear to have been obeyed."[82]

Tracy replied to Hoffman with his own account of the trip, as given by Lieutenant Colonel Trotter: "During the night of February 14 neither water nor lights were provided for any car upon the train, as required by terms of the contract, and three of the prisoners died from the continued exposure. The train consisted of seventeen cars, with only one brakemen for the entire number, to which ten or more cattle cars were added when the train left Williamsport. I would beg leave to call attention to the indifference of the officials of the Northern Central Railroad, who paid not the least attention to the repeated applications for lights for the cars, which I was finally compelled to purchase myself. Neither did they supply any water or fuel after the train left Elmira."[83] Tracy added his personal evaluation: "The surgeon was strictly charged to send no one unable to endure the journey. It requires a pretty strong man, however, to endure a railroad journey of forty-one hours during such weather as prevailed at the time this party of prisoners was forwarded."[84] Hoffman did not respond. Fortunately for the Elmira prison officials and the Confederates, future exchanges ran much smoother.

In fairness to Dr. Stocker, other matters preoccupied him during this period. Smallpox had proven more deadly than pneumonia most of the winter. Smallpox, a highly contagious disease introduced by newly relocated prisoners, had begun to break out with the arrival of cold weather.[85] The earliest reported case, at the end of October, was carried by a Fort Morgan captive, who recovered before passing it on to others. However, in the middle of December, a number of prisoners suddenly came down with the disease. One man died and was buried inside the prison, apparently to prevent panic outside. On

Christmas morning, it was reported that the virus had been transmitted to sixty-three men, not including the two it had already struck fatally earlier in the week. By New Year's Day, the disease had surged to ninety-five cases, nine men succumbing that week, which caused genuine fear of an epidemic.[86] On January 5, Asst. Adj. Gen. Wilson T. Hartz notified Tracy that if the disease spread further he should isolate the carriers by building a hospital some distance away from the regular population. Three days later, 126 cases and 10 deaths were reported, even while prison officials had been putting into action plans to check its progression. "A" tents were quickly erected beyond Foster's Pond to serve as a temporary hospital and Chief Surgeon Stocker prepared the antidotes for vaccinating the camp.[87] With these measures, Tracy wrote his superiors, "We hope we have got control of this disease and will be able to keep it within bounds."[88] By the end of the month, so many smallpox victims had crowded the tents that officials decided to construct a more permanent smallpox hospital.[89]

Stocker and his staff busily administered vaccinations; men lined up with bare arms in ready position and a doctor immersed a lancet in the vaccine matter then pushed it through the flesh.[90] One Floridian's "vaxnation" took "finely," but others were not so lucky.[91] An Alabaman did "not charge there was any intention of doing harm," but the vaccine prescribed by the government was not of the best quality, sometimes causing "loathsome sores completely covering the arm."[92] Some prisoners hinted that amputation resulted when the antidote did not take. John Opie was not alone when he admitted that he feared "the vaccination more than the small-pox." The former cavalryman, already disabled, preferred not to put another limb in jeopardy and managed to elude both the disease and its intended cure.[93] His trepidation seemed well founded when an anonymous assistant surgeon criticized the government after the war for not providing better medicine when the smallpox "raged through the camp." Vaccinations often produced "horrible ulcers and eruptions" and were "too frequent and obvious to be mistaken."[94]

In January alone, 5,600 vaccinations were given, a result of the 397 smallpox cases reported up to that time. The communicable disease might first appear in the form of chills, fever, and pains to the back and head. Pimples then broke out, developing into puss-filled blisters. Within a two-week period, scratching the irritating sores might cause them to open. Scabs closed the wounds, but the scabs would fall off and sometimes leave permanent scars. Individuals who survived the scourge generally became immune—a welcome lifetime exemption.[95] Confederate ward sergeant Marcus Toney thought he was one such person because he had contracted a milder strain of the virus earlier in life. When he again came down with a few symptoms, he did not fret, but his condition worsened and he slipped into a delirious state during which he climbed in and out of his bunk. The Tennessean regained some of his faculties two days later and in the middle of mumbling out his name for roll call was immediately ordered to the smallpox hospital.[96]

Prisoners admitted to the smallpox hospital might be taken by stretcher or go under their own power. Each "A" tent sheltered three patients on cots, which were squeezed closely together.[97] However, smallpox patient Miles Sherrill, although "sandwiched in this way," soon discovered he had more room after awakening one morning to find one bunkmate dead.[98] A similar experience occurred with Marcus Toney, who understandably felt very uneasy: "The second night one of our bedfellows died, and all the vermin came to us, and we had plenty of company."[99] Men turned into corpses overnight, their cold bodies frozen in the position they slept, unyielding and unbending until wedged into coffins. Toney wrote, "It was horrible to see attendants breaking their arms and legs in order to force them into their coffins." Their living roommates could only watch in despair, wondering if they would live to see the morrow, or be dragged out and prepared for burial in the same manner.[100]

Doctors, nurses, waiters, and wardmasters resistant to the disease did what little they could as smallpox ran its course. Wardmasters assigned patients to bunks and kept order over the accommodations.[101] Waiters delivered special food such as tea to the sick, although one patient regretted that, with "the weather below zero, the tea was cold when it reached us."[102] Georgian Tapley Stewart remembered how nurses tended to men who became "insane" by the nagging sores, until the nurses were forced "to tie their hands to keep the patients from tearing their flesh."[103] The few doctors assigned to the crowded wards were unable to treat everyone. One frustrated doctor recalled how "the simple movement of one of them would cause his neighbor to cry out in agony of pain." The reason, the doctor continued, was because the "confluent and malignant type prevailed to such an extent, and of such a nature, that the body would frequently be found one continuous scab."[104]

When doctors were confident that a patient had fully recovered, he was discharged from the smallpox hospital. However, before returning to the regular wards, a recovered prisoner had to undergo another treatment at the bathhouse to remove any traces of the disease. Not everyone wanted to take this plunge because it occurred during the cold season, but the released prisoners had no choice. After removing contaminated clothes, which were promptly burned, they climbed into the tub's effervescent waters.[105] One inmate at first found the ablution "almost too hot to bear," but changed his mind after an attendant experienced a delay bringing him his clothes. "The atmosphere of the room," believed the water-logged Southerner, brought the bath down "to nearly the freezing point."[106] When men finished the cleansing, they were issued new apparel. This gift had implications for the entire camp, especially for men not directly affected by the disease.[107]

A good portion of clothing doled out by the Confederate emissaries went to reclothe smallpox victims. Because part of their treatment included getting rid of clothing they wore when infected, prisoners who recovered from small-pox had priority over the regular population. When Major Printup received a shipment of clothing, he needed to set aside a portion for that purpose. Printup documented this practice thoroughly in his fastidious records, which includes individual checks beside each garment given to those discharged from the smallpox hospital.[108]

More than four hundred men perished from smallpox during February and March. At the beginning of March, additional steps were being taken for its containment. A permanent, 30-by-100-foot smallpox hospital building was completed. On March 7, Printup received 150 suits specifically for smallpox patients. Quartermaster Elwell was able to pitch in, and furnished 120 pairs of shoes so that prisoners did not need to walk barefoot after their release. Most encouraging for smallpox patients—and the rest of Elmira prison-ers—was the break in the weather. Warm weather was a welcome indication that the cold season was departing and that the chances for exchange might improve. If not, at least the vexing winter of 1864–65 had passed, making it easier to forget as the temperatures rose. The only precipitation that fell in March was rain, and the snow in the Chemung Valley melted. Commissary General Hoffman's long-anticipated rains had finally arrived, but he should have been more careful about his wishes. Mother Nature had always been excessive in her treatment of Southerners, and a downpour in the middle of March proved to be another example of her unbridled power, which washed away more than the remnants of her bitter winter.[109]

7

Economics on the Inside

The Prison Market, Employment, & the Inmate Social Order

In September 1864, the *Elmira Daily Advertiser* observed that "New buildings are going up at the rebel prison camp for their [prisoners'] better accommodation. It is quite a small city, busy and active, within the enclosure, where they are confined."[1] Berry Benson, a temporary resident living behind the fence, expressed similar sentiments: "The prison kept growing in population till there was said to be 10,000—quite a little city in itself."[2] Indeed, contemporaries inside and outside the enclosure viewed the prison as a sort of a city, crowded with inhabitants and dictated by a distinct economy, which centered on its market.

The Elmira Prison market had its genesis on the Maryland shore. Most of the early prisoners sent to the Chemung Valley came from Point Lookout, where they had frequently traded for apples, onions, crackers, and shellfish. They also made items, including rings, buttons, and chains, which were exchanged with a sutler for food. Inmates who found other employment, mostly digging fortifications around the vulnerable coastal confines, were compensated five cents credit per day and given a whiskey ration. Because they were allowed to take the whiskey back into the enclosure, a black market flourished. Union officers attempted to dry out the prison by requiring prisoners to consume the beverage before reentering the stockade. However, to their dismay it continued, laborers being capable of holding the alcohol in their mouths until returning inside, then spitting it into cups. Hence, "spit whiskey" was available until employers made swallowing a part of the job requirement. Prisoners from Point Lookout brought such resourcefulness to Elmira: rats were caught instead of crabs and tobacco regarded more highly than whiskey, and, with no ocean waves to wash in material for their handi-work, the prisoners had to rely on other sources.[3]

It did not take long after passing through the gates of Elmira Prison for one to be drawn to music playing in the distance. As one approached the center of camp along the main boulevard voices grew louder between the twenty original barracks and the mess hall. At that spot was one of the most interest-ing sights of any Civil War prison, which inmates appropriately termed "The Market." Men crowded together, yelling, selling, buying, and bargaining, at different rates of exchange primarily based on chewing tobacco.[4] Maryland transfer Berry Benson wrote that "at Elmira there was a regular market place where all the trading was done."[5] James Huffman, also a Maryland transfer, wrote, "I tell you we did as much business in a small way as a town or city."[6] Another former Point Lookout captive, John King, said that Elmira's market offered "a strange medley of things in progress that could never have been seen elsewhere."[7]

A fiddler carried his tune far across the crowded marketplace trying to persuade someone to buy an instrument designed from a cracker box and string. As men listened intently, his homespun chords would be drowned out by a chorus attempting to divide the audience's attention. "Here's your nice hot coffee, a cup full for a 'chaw' of tobacco," bellowed a man lugging a cumbersome boiling pot. Another peddler offered a slice of bread for "five chews." "Here's your two rations of meat and ten chews of tobacco on it," chimed a meat vendor. Some dealers specialized in fruits and vegetables. Many built makeshift stands from old pine boxes so they could sit while displaying their foodstuffs. Behind one of these men another could be seen dangling a rat by the tail for prospective buyers, his free hand casually waiting to accept the five quids of tobacco the large specimen brought. No part of the animal was wasted either, particularly in the colder months when the skins of such creatures were sewn together and sold as winter gloves. There was constant motion as men came and went, bringing their prepared food from the numer-ous fire pits dug beside Foster's Pond so that deliveries could be readied for market.[8]

Throughout the marketplace, prisoners improvised shops with signs that advertised specific services. Tailors stitched frayed clothes, their placards declaring, "A small patch for four chews, and a large one six." A cobbler advertised "Shoes mended for tobacco." Barber poles were sunk into the ground, and signs offered a haircut for ten chews or a shave for five.[9] Other barbers took up a traveling kit, a wood box with scissors, a comb, and a razor, and sought out their clients. After seeing them with razors in action, Marcus Toney expressed preferrence for a scruffy face rather than risking his neck to their shaky hands: "They never used a hone or strap except their boots and shoes, and it was hard to tell which was the worst sufferer, the barber or his customer."[10] Some pursued altogether different types of hands. Faro boxes were constructed out of old sardine cases with a spring inside, which dealt cards "for chews of the weed."[11] In addition to tobacco, food was gambled away. High rollers tried their luck at keno, money bets being substituted for bread crusts given with daily meals. As with the game's longer version, bingo, tension mounted with an accumulating pot, literally bread, until the air was broken with a shout of "keno." Oftentimes winnings were turned in for the regular currency of the prison: "Here is your Keno ration with five chews of tobacco on it."[12]

Inside Elmira Prison, tobacco was an ideal substitute for money, which military edict prohibited. Tobacco could be easily divided, did not spoil, and was readily available. Black navy tobacco was a common variety used at the pen, and was worth about one dollar a pound. One pound could be divided into twenty small squares, and each unit—called a quid or chew—was worth five cents in hard money. The nonperishable segments could be distributed easily throughout the stockade, especially by the camp sutler, because it was one of the few plentiful crops in the area. The abundance of tobacco showed in the sutler's tobacco sales to inmates, which sometimes earned him over $100 a day. Adding to the Chemung Valley's high yield was a share that the Confederacy sent to captured soldiers in Elmira, as well as their own unrelenting requests to outsiders.[13] "But if you are like myself, a slave to the 'Indian Weed' you can appreciate my situation being without Tobacco," was an appeal to a Philadelphian from a letter writer in Ward 49.[14] James Montgomery, tobaccoless and friendless, begged Mr. F. J. Fergeson for "10 or 12 plugs," since he "would soon as do without half my rations, as to be without tobacco."[15]

Marcus Toney watched men "go hungry a day and save their rations and trade them for tobacco."[16] Prisoner L. B. Jones "saw a man coming from breakfast exchange his slice of bread for a chew of tobacco, saying the tobacco would pacify his stomach for two hours, while the bread would only aggravate it."[17] Clumps of discharged wads were collected off the prison grounds and used again.[18] A fisherman from Florida nicknamed "Old Picket" was notorious for this practice, one of his comrades saying that he "watched from morning till night for the chews of tobacco others had thrown away. He threw them into his mouth as though his life depended on it."[19] Inmates also took to smoking discarded tobacco, drying out the juiced leaves and packing them in pipe bowls.[20] One Southerner was dumbfounded after witnessing a white man solicit "a negro to give him the quid of tobacco he was chewing" to use for that purpose.[21] The individual who benefited the most from the prisoners' proclivity for tobacco also monopolized other necessities of prison life.

Woodman Demorest was awarded the prison sutlership. The long-time Elmira citizen set up shop at the intersection of the camp's main boulevard and the macadamized street that ran by the market. Demorest hired an assistant, George Mosher, who helped him with the store that Demorest operated inside the stockade, while he tended to his sutlery for guards and officers at Camp Chemung.[22] Contrary to the more competitive outside economy, the prison camp market depended exclusively on his business, which Demorest based on the credit system. If captives had money when they arrived in Elmira, or if they received any in the mail, the prison treasurer, Lt. Joseph Groves, took it. Groves placed the money in the prison fund, then took the exact amount and registered it in the ledger books at headquarters. Afterward, prisoners received credit that they could combine with earnings from employment and open an account with Sutler Demorest. Thousands of sutler order forms were provided so transactions could be documented, each slip labeling purchases such as tobacco, fruits, vegetables, postage stamps, and stationery.[23]

An order by the commissary general of prisons specified that sutlers sell goods at fair rates relative to local markets, but prices were actually higher in the prison than in Elmira. For example, the same plug of tobacco that could be purchased on the free market for ten cents sold inside the prison for about fifteen cents, and the same ratio generally held true for other articles. This modestly high exchange rate made Southerners feel as though Demorest was getting the best of them. James Marion Howard wrote that Demorest's "things were sold at enormous profit."[24] A fellow Alabaman felt that the entire system's object was to "force the money into the hands of the sutler."[25] A Virginian complained, "We had but little money and prices were high."[26] More specifically, flour and cornmeal sold at five cents a pound, cabbage at ten cents, and onions at fifteen cents a pound. One cup of milk cost fifteen cents and an apple five cents; beeswax, coffee, and sugar each sold for ten cents. Jackets were priced at a dollar, a pair of pants or shirt cost twenty-five cents, socks twenty cents, and shoes twenty-five cents. One postage stamp cost thirty cents, as did a piece of paper or an envelope. Soap commanded five cents, a pipe ten cents, and a pocket knife twenty-five cents.[27] A newspaper correspondent with the *New York Post* understated the case when he reported that Demorest's "store does considerable business."[28]

Military authorities monitored the prison camp economy closely. They made sure that Demorest did not stray far from the city's prices and watched to see if he sold items like fruits and vegetables or alcohol that the War Department had not approved. Treasurer Groves was a principal player in the pen's fiduciary operations. His assignments included withdrawing money from the prison fund for discharged prisoners and adding to it by collecting a three and one-half–cent sales tax imposed on the sutler for every dollar he earned from customers. That amount was significant, as documented by the First National Bank of Elmira, which cut weekly checks to Demorest that typically totaled thousands of dollars each payment. From the period when the prison was organized until January 31, 1865, Demorest sold $30,668 worth of goods and had to pay Lieutenant Groves a $1,073 tax for the prison fund. From February 1, 1865, to the time that the prison camp was disbanded, the sutler took in $19,368, remitting $678 to the Treasury Department. All told, Demorest grossed $50,036 from Elmira prisoners, and paid $1,751 for the right to do so.[29]

Woodman Demorest could thank many of his Southern patrons for his profits. However, many individuals found it difficult to get credit at his store. Prisoners who received no money to open an account or were not employed by prison authorities had to become more self-reliant. Such was the case with twenty-four-year-old James Huffman. A native of Naked Creek, Virginia, Huffman had lived simply before the war, his life experiences restricted to working farms and sawmills. As he contemplated captivity, he recognized that some of his associates "went to work making very pretty things and selling them for big money. We looked on with stomachs pinching, until the thought came, 'I wonder if I could make anything.'"[30] Like others at Elmira, he "had no tools, no material and was shut up in prison. . . . Here is one of the most important lessons of life," he thought. "Believe you can do a thing and have patience and try it thoroughly."[31] Huffman made a hammer by pushing a six-inch nail into a stick, and with what little credit he had, he purchased a file. He then explored the prison yard for anything he could use in his new "outfit," which fortunately for him, turned out "nice rings that sold well and at good prices." The young man was part of an industry that not only kept him busy, but also improved his chances at survival.[32]

Barracks Number 3 could have been considered the city's jewelry district. Unlike other items sold in the controlled economy, personal adornments that prisoners created were in demand throughout the Chemung Valley. At

Elmira Prison, producers of jewelry and trinkets dominated all other inmate occupations.[33] Making jewelry was an attractive path to pursue because no prior education or experience was required, so nearly anyone could learn and participate if he simply took the time. And if these confined men had anything they could spare, it was their time.

Men spent hours searching throughout the prison yard for bone, wood, lumber, animal hair, fabric, and gutta percha buttons. After they purchased, borrowed, or made tools, men sat behind tables around the marketplace meticulously carving, whittling, and crafting day after day. Some prisoners used only pocket knives or files to shape pendants and charms. Others used crochet needles pared from pine sticks to braid hair from the manes and tails of horses into finely designed necklaces, bracelets, and watch chains.[34] Rings were the easiest item to mass-produce. Prisoners constructed rudimentary drills out of old boxes, strings, and needles, some attaching a rotating fly wheel. Rings were shipped out, which attracted mail orders from friends north and south.[35] Throughout their imprisonment basic filers could advance into larger enterprises, and one onlooker marveled at how "men would secure a few cents, and on that little capital would build up quite a business."[36] "Some of us were manufacturing, some selling at wholesale, some retailing," wrote a successful ringmaker, "altogether making a perfect network of business."[37]

Such networking required partnerships. Union guards brought bits of silver, gold, pearl, and mussel shell to be inserted into their jewelry. The officers did not discourage such fraternizing, since they, too, participated. Government contractors also dealt in Confederate products during routine trips. These active "partners" were more essential for supplies rather than distribution. Some middlemen bought rings directly from the prisoners and then sold them elsewhere, but doing so required money up front, so more often the seller required a commission of half the price. After selling items, the partner would apply the agreed-upon earnings to the credit books at headquarters. Entrusting others to distribute trinkets outside and receive a fair return inside could prove to risky, especially since products were such time-consuming endeavors. However, prisoners were in no position to find how much profit the other party actually made.[38] One Elmira guard noticed his peers were more than obliged to help, stating, "Very kindly they did it."[39] One Southerner believed "in nearly every instance the guards were honest in returning a part of the proceeds of the sale."[40] "Capt. Munger and Capt. Peck, secured the material and after the articles were completed sold them in the city for the best price possible, always remitting the money" wrote John King.[41] On the very day that King was taken prisoner, a Union captain led his men into hand-to-hand combat on the same field. He ended up at Elmira Prison for a different reason, but could have enlightened many Southerners about money made in the ring trade.[42]

On May 12, 1864, Union forces fought an entrenched enemy on the rain-soaked fields of Spottsylvania, Virginia. Much blood saturated the soil that day, including that of Capt. John S. Kidder of the 121st New York Volunteers. Around noon, Kidder was struck by a ball that drilled through the left side of his head, went into the cheekbone, and left through his ear. What had been filled with the sounds of booming cannon and piercing fire abruptly became silent and clogged with blood. Kidder staggered back in retreat, his face swelling terribly, and a field doctor attended him. Odorous pus began draining from his ear. Fearing partial loss of the organ and full loss of its function, the thirty-four year old was transferred to an officers' hospital in Annapolis, Maryland. While there, he discovered that his condition paled in comparison to that of other patients, especially some released from the infamous Libby Prison in Richmond.[43] "It is terrible to think what those poor fellows have suffered," Kidder wrote in June.[44] A month later, Kidder's ear healing but his hearing still gone, army officials were determined that the captain was incapable of field service but ready for light duty. Kidder might have trouble hearing, but he could soon see for himself whether his government cared for its captives any better than did the Confederacy.[45]

After a prolonged leave in Laurens, New York, Kidder reported for guard duty at Elmira in early September. Perhaps he would have reported sooner had he known what perquisites his service at Elmira Prison had to offer. Two days after arriving, Kidder began dealing in Confederate rings, which promised to be very remunerative. On September 10, in a letter to his pregnant wife, Harriet, he sent a number of finger rings, telling her that inmates "make them with Jack knives." In the same correspondence he asked her to notify a friend of theirs about the booming industry: "Send Charley Matteson here . . . immediately, he can make money like fun. I can put him in a way of selling rings as many want them and I can furnish him all that he can sell. He can make a pile of money if he comes."[46]

On September 25, Kidder made another appeal to his wife, hoping that "Charlie will come soon." Yet the captain was already doing fine on his own. On duty at Elmira Prison for less than three weeks, he confided to his wife the following: "This you can keep to yourself. I have made $200 since I came here in the ring trade." He also mentioned that prisoners were extremely susceptible

Capt. John S. Kidder, who profited in the ring trade at Elmira Prison. Courtesy of the

to disease, and proved it by sending her the morning death reports.[47] By the beginning of October, his friend Matteson had finally arrived in the city, and he began selling rings under the captain's auspices. Their enterprise expanded to include hair buns, chains, and pins, and, indeed, they made money "like fun," just as had Kidder predicted. In addition to briefing his wife about his successful business affairs, Kidder commented that "the Rebs are dying quite fast from 8 to 30 per day."[48]

From a financial standpoint, Kidder was probably sorry to hear—which he could evidently do well enough by January 1865—that he had to return to his regiment. He did, however, continue to collect back pay owed to him for the sale of rings and chains even after he left the Chemung Valley. His eventual earnings in jewelry merchandising at Elmira Prison exceeded five hundred dollars, which almost doubled his income for that year.[49] Even after he left the prison, a former inmate still held a supply of rings for the captain. A couple weeks after Lee's surrender, Kidder was at Petersburg, Virginia, having a reunion with old Southern friends once in prison: "Two of them were merchants, one a lawyer and member of the legislature of Va." He dined with the latter gentleman, "a Mr. Keiley." If Kidder still wanted to conceal that he was a successful ring trader at Elmira, it would have been wise for him not to disclose it during his dinner conversation.[50]

Anthony Keiley was most articulate in expressing dissatisfaction over the way that Confederates were treated in prison, particularly at how they were slighted in the Elmira jewelry trade. This dissatisfaction was due in large part to a Union captain the Petersburger singled out in his diary, who was "ostensibly engaged in taking charge of certain companies of 'Rebs,' but really employed in turning a penny by huckstering the various products of the prisoners skill. . . . Many of them have told me," Keiley added, "of the impossibility of getting their just dues from the prying, round shouldered captain."[51] Certainly to the relief of Kidder, although this individual sounded familiar the "purloiner of rings and chains" of whom Keiley spoke was not Kidder, but another officer at Elmira named William Peck.[52] Peck's name, however, could have been synonymous with other persons at Elmira who took advantage of their authority. As Keiley surmised, the jewelry trade was "an occupation very profitable to Peck, but generally unsatisfactory, in a pecuniary way, to the 'rebs.'"[53]

Not all who sold the prisoners' handiwork were unscrupulous. Other guards, officers, and citizens were honest in their exchanges. Will Ellet, hired to drive supplies inside the prison, had to keep a careful eye on his horse, "to keep the 'Johnnies' from stealing all the hair out of his tail." As Ellet became more familiar in camp, inmates came to respect him and his animal, since "they found I could be of service to them." They brought Ellet jewelry, which the Elmira native sold in the city; he brought them back either their proceeds or a popular delicacy of the day: pints of oysters.[54] James Dumars, the son of an officer posted at the pen, frequently ran errands for his father. The youngster did much the same for prisoners, not only bringing material in to them, but also selling their finished products to friends in town.

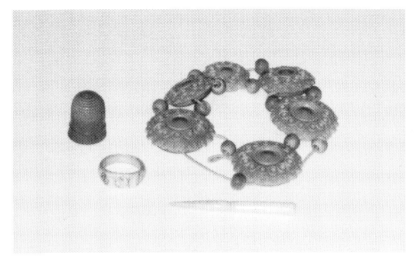

Trinkets made by Elmira prisoners; from left to right, a thimble, a ring, a toohtpick, and above, a necklace. Courtesy of the Chemung County Historical Society.

Buyers interested in the Confederates' work could also bypass the middleman altogether, and go directly up Water Street near the front of the stockade.[55] At the officers' quarters, by the prison's main gate, a large display case housed trinkets for anyone to purchase. Lieutenant Groves kept in his treasury files a detailed account book that tabulated each prisoner's work, his name, his ward number, any items that he sold, and the prices of those items so that money could be credited to the proper account.[56] Between sales at headquarters and those of partners who worked the valley, Southerners touched the multitudes, and it was not exclusively because of the fine quality of their keepsakes. If large numbers of people paid admission just to observe the enemy in prison, imagine the excitement and fascination of owning an item made in captivity. Indeed, one Elmiran marveled at how the "country was flooded with canes, finger rings, watch chains and charms, products of genius of these prisoners." He continued: "It is a fact that during that period old men and women, young men and maids, throughout Elmira and vicinity, were decorated largely with these thousand and one devices made by these Confederate prisoners."[57]

Nor should the monetary value of trinkets made by prisoners be underestimated. By selling rings, prisoners could earn credit for better food, which could help fight many ailments. Miles Sherrill, who described the "fare" at

Elmira as "not enough to sustain life," and if prisoners "could not make something—make rings, etc.,—and thus secure something from the sutlers, many, yea hundreds of poor fellows would be attacked with dysentery."[58] Another Georgian, J. A. Hooper, stated "I did not live on the rations I drew entirely. I made watch chains out of horsehair, and finger rings out of gutta percha buttons, and sold them. I could buy anything from the camp sutler."[59] Rings and chains might earn an inmate anywhere from thirty cents to over a dollar, depending on design and quality, which increased if inset with a stone or mineral. Some jewelry could be fitted on the spot, and engravers could add a personal touch for an additional twenty cents.[60]

Other items manufactured in Elmira Prison varied in form and price. Fancy toothpicks sold for seventy-five cents; fans made out of pine and colorful ribbon might fetch as much as two dollars. Larger products, such as canes and parasols, were designed in a similar manner but made on a grander scale, which led to higher prices.[61] Some craftsmen built a reputation for their handiwork. G. N. Saussy, "a guest of the Nation at Elmira," carved goblets from coconut shell.[62] Also well known was an inventor who made a clock from bone and a stationary steam engine out of old camp pots.[63] Skilled woodworkers made furniture for the Union officers.[64] In November 1864, John S. Kidder, a new and fairly proud father, wrote to his wife that he "had expected a boy but . . . there is plenty of time for that." A month later, perhaps because the birth still weighed on his mind or he was just lonely because "several officers have their wives with them," Kidder invited his family to winter with him in Elmira. He said he had ample room, and abundant fuel in his residence made Elmira warmer than their home in Laurens. As for sleeping arrangements, he had a bedstead and "could have the rebs make me another cradle in half a day."[65]

Employment opportunities were also available directly from the prison itself, which offered work in the four main departments that functioned inside the camp: the adjutant's office, the commissary department, the hospital department, and the detail for manual labor. Clerks, personal assistants, orderlies, bakers, mechanics, and carpenters were paid at a daily rate of ten cents. Common laborers earned five cents. All employees on public works were to report to their department head each morning, and all were given additional rations, including bread, meat, and coffee, along with the credit they tallied up in the sutler books. About four hundred prisoners were thus employed daily.[66] John King did "not want to leave the impression that every prisoner was sick, poor, ragged, and weak like the majority of us, for there were many that escaped sickness and numbers who were kept at detail work."[67] T. S. Terrell was more succinct: "I worked while in prison and therefore fared better than the rank and file."[68]

Prison authorities showed some favoritism when reviewing job applications. Southerners who indicated a desire to take the oath of allegiance to the United States and abandon all ties with the Confederacy might be rewarded with a job. Viewed as traitors by the more loyal longer committed Southerners, these "galvanized prisoners" wore a red badge as an outward sign of their new allegiance as they performed their chores. A less-visible group, which stretched far and wide before and after the war, was also given preference in the pool of applicants. Any prisoners involved with the Freemasons enjoyed privileges, especially during the term of Stephen Moore, who was an active member.[69] However, a more prominent class rose to the top, not because of the secret society to which they belonged or because of whom they had betrayed, but because of what they possessed. If one were educated or skilled, he held a distinct advantage over other captives.

Not long after the prison camp opened, an appeal went through the various wards in an attempt to enlist Southerners who had been accountants, bookkeepers, and others familiar with office and clerical work. A handsomely written application in calligraphy, error free, might be the first step toward an interview. Education, particularly in spelling, handwriting, and mathematics, was paramount for these positions, which in essence were the white-collar jobs of the prison. Accountants kept the camp rolls, sutler orders, and treasury records. Groves alone had seven clerks, which did not include those needed in other departments. Pay for these jobs was twice that of most other jobs, but benefits in personal conveniences and contacts were even more rewarding. Office jobs were prized because many employees were given warm and comfortable rooms away from the regular wards. In addition, their work brought them into close association with officers in charge, which put them in prestigious company.[70] Anthony Keiley quickly ascended the clerical ladder, particularly after he admitted to having a diploma, and was elevated to chief clerk at headquarters. At first, his job seemed to have an adverse effect because he was not selected for the October exchange. "Individually my case is pitiable indeed," the Virginian quipped; his employment allowed him better food and housing than regular inmates, which left him "in an awkward exuberance of health." When he applied to assist the sick on the journey, Union officers said Keiley would "be 'the last secesh that should leave the pen;' an honorable distinction, for which I was indebted to the circumstances that I was considered the worst 'rebel' in camp." However, if it were not for his job, he may never have formed a friendship with Major Colt, who made sure he was included on the trip.[71]

One of Keiley's successors was James Ford, a youthful Georgian who earned himself a cozy room with a bed and developed friendships with Northern men beside whom he worked, particularly his supervisor, Adj. H. H. Mott. Ford's privileged position also afforded him special treatment. On Christmas Eve, Ford celebrated with a Union friend and coworker but overindulged on eggnog. When their party broke up, the Georgian had to walk to his quarters across a slippery and snow-covered prison yard. "In my endeavor to reach my room, due to the uncertain condition of my pedal extremities, I think I must have fallen in the snow say a dozen times or more." Ford ended up in solitary confinement for being drunk. The next morning at the headquarters, when neither Ford nor his consolidated report were present, Captain Mott wanted an explanation. When told that Ford was being punished, Mott immediately ordered his release. Upon Ford's return, Mott confronted the wide-eyed Georgian. The Captain was happy to learn that Ford had partaken of some Christmas cheer, but advised him that "in the future when you feel that a toddy will do you good, just let me know and I will see that you get it. Sit down young man, and make up the morning report."[72]

William Lambert Campbell was another member of the clerical elite. The Louisianan, who at one point questioned his ability to survive in prison, used his fine penmanship to become an assistant to Maj. S. W. Beall, second in command to Stephen Moore. Campbell said that his "office confer[ed] a great many privileges," such as credit, food, and a room. Early in the winter, he reassured his sister Zoe, "I am in very good health and quite comfortable; I have a nice room and do not suffer from the cold. I do not think there is a prisoner who feels more comfortable than I do."[73] On February 1, Campbell even wrote that he was going to send her some rings and "a variety of articles made by the prisoners." In March, the Louisianan's writing got him in trouble, for he was implicated with others for smuggling letters out of prison. Instead of being fired, however, he was transferred out of headquarters to the hospital department, where he assisted Dr. Stocker. Even after this transition, he was still "doing splendidly; all my wants [were] supplied."[74]

Skilled workers or artisans did not have everything supplied, but their prison life seemed less harsh compared to those without work. Among the highest paid tradesmen, equal to those in business occupations, were carpenters. Their work was highly regarded from the outset, being needed for building up Barracks Number 3 and making furniture for military personnel, all of which might result in gainful employment throughout an imprisonment. Men who comprised the lower echelon of manual laborers received half the pay of carpenters. Plumbers who expeditiously laid pipe for the drainage sluice had special incentives. In addition to collecting thirty-five cents at the end of their work week, along with the extra rations during breaks, they received whiskey in the evening. Plumbers dug wells to provide water for the camp, which in part led to one of their less desirable assignments: liming the smelly sinks around Foster's Pond. When the sinks were beyond the point of sanitizing, new ones had to be excavated. Some prisoners worked as painters, whitewashing dull prison buildings. Street graders smoothed prison roads, and street cleaners removed scattered debris. At dawn, a gang of fire extinguishers put out the kerosene lights that hung on the stockade wall. Other men sawed and chopped firewood for the camp, or excavated the ground for various purposes. Among the latter group was a contingent of prisoners who work in the graveyard, burying their brethren in return for food and pay.[75]

Service-oriented jobs kept many busy within the commissary and hospital departments. Southerners employed in the kitchen and mess halls worked at baking, cooking, and cleaning. Wilbur Grambling was a waiter in the mess room and had "much work to do and . . . plenty to eat." He rose early in the morning to set, wait, and clear tables, then repeated the task in the afternoon session. Grambling kept this up, "but [didn't] like it much" because he received no raise after his station expanded to three tables with 135 men each, whose dishes he needed to wash, as well. However, Grambling continued to work and carefully watched his money during the summer. In early October, he complained that he would not make it through the cold weather "without more cover." On November 19, the Floridian purchased a blanket for seventy-five cents with money he had saved. The three daily meals he took allowed him to survive the winter, and he wrote in February that his "health remain[ed] quite good."[76] South Carolinian J. H. Michaels worked in the hospital. He, too, mentioned the importance of his work: "I was never in the hospital as a patient, but for some time was on detail in hospital service. Then I got plenty to eat, as did all those who were employed in any way, but the rank and file did not." Like Grambling, Michaels survived his confinement.[77]

At the end of August, an Old Dominion soldier who had graduated from the University of Virginia founded a school within the stockade. Elmira ladies contributed books, slates, and pencils, while colleagues familiar with the profession assisted him. Teachers evidently did not share their knowledge for free, and camp officials allowed each an additional ration as a stipend. Altogether, a ten-member faculty proceeded to teach the basics of reading, writing, and arithmetic, and some students even advanced to French. On days they did not go to regular day school, more devout pupils could attend Sunday School lessons.[78] An Alabaman, still trying to grasp the foundations of grammar, proudly stated, "I went to school some at this place."[79] A Florida student broadened his language skills, and by the new year had been "progressing in my French pretty well."[80] F. S. Wade, from Texas, said that his "weight fell from 180 to 160 in a month" at Elmira. However, soon his luck changed after prison officials hired him as a teacher and gave him more food, which quickly gave him "back my twenty pounds of flesh." He concluded that his teaching position "was the best pay I ever got for a job in my life."[81]

Education, skill in a trade, a desire to work—or the lack thereof—laid the foundations for a class structure within Elmira Prison. For many Southerners, the structure was similar to that in the outside world. A small professional class, the businessmen of the prison camp, stood atop the social hierarchy because of what and who they knew, and how much they earned and what they could gain from it. A middling tier developed between the professionals and the lowest class. The middling tier included skilled laborers from carpenters to caretakers, and ran the gamut into the service field of cooks, waiters, nurses, and teachers. Such self-employed workers as barbers, cobblers, and tailors not hired by prison authorities, but still earning tobacco were also found in the middle, particularly at the market place. Numerous independent producers of trinkets also stood in the middle, making the most out of any opportunity to earn credit, and often leaving prison with more than with which they had entered. Below them was a lower class of prisoners, the hunters and gatherers, limited in money, education, and initiative. The underclass lived off the land to sustain themselves. The lowest stratum in the social order were the scavengers, caught in a sickening cycle of prison life, resorting to the bottom of the food chain in a place where rats ranked as a top delicacy.

8

Economics on the Outside

Elmira, a City on a Civil War Contract

In 1860, Elmira was a community of approximately 8,700. The Civil War greatly augmented its growth, not only in population, but also in economic development. Elmira's industries expanded to embrace the city's function as a main military rendezvous in New York that consisted of four training bases. Tanneries sold leather goods to the military and woolen mills fabricated blue uniforms. Hardware stores supplied utensils, cups, and plates, while food contractors made sure their goods were put to use.[1] "Some of the farmers of the vicinity," wrote an observer, "were made comfortably well-to-do by the sale of their produce to the camps."[2] Land and housing leases were negotiated for training grounds, quarters, hospitals, and other spaces required to accommodate the soldiers. Selling horses to the Cavalry Bureau became an important function of the post and a lucrative trade for area dealers; corral stables were built to accommodate twelve hundred animals. Lumber mills provided manufactured wood for the facilities and workers were hired to undertake their construction.[3]

Wartime growth changed Elmira's country town atmosphere. The change became official on April 7, 1864, when Elmira was incorporated into a city with four wards. The city's first few months proved pivotal; military activity within its limits began to diminish. Two training camps shut down early in 1864, and a third was almost vacated. The military gathered, trained, and dispatched 20,796 soldiers from the Elmira Rendezvous during the war, and about half of them were processed during the war's first year. When the soldiers left, so did much of the business required for their care.[4] "Barracks No.1 are quite deserted again," exemplified the "here and gone" attitude stressed by newspapers as men left for the front.[5] No one had anticipated the financial benefits of establishing a military prison in Elmira, nor that it would strengthen the economy.

Elmira underwent a major transformation near the middle of 1864. Many men who rendezvoused in Elmira did not wear Union blue, but Confederate gray. Within months, inmates and prison keepers almost doubled Elmira's population of some thirteen thousand citizens. Its populace grew almost exponentially after the prison and guard camps were both established in Elmira's first ward, where 1,440 citizens had been living.[6]

The old training camp on the Chemung River, designated as Barracks Number 3, was remodeled and turned into a stockade city, an appendage of the community, where services for the prison were demanded in full. In July, when the Southerners began to arrive, readers of local papers should not have been surprised to find that "our mechanics and laboring men are all employed. Not an idle one do we know who is willing to work—During no period have more new buildings been planned and put in the process of construction. The presence of a military rendezvous has also necessitated a large and additional amount of building around the Barracks which have not reached completion, not to speak of the new improvements being perfected as fast as required. The high price of labor and material so far seems to influence only in a degree all kinds of building operations."[7] In August 1864, a month after the prison opened, the *Elmira Daily Advertiser* commented on the economic revival: "The presence of so large a number of military here causes our town to put on the appearance of old times. There will probably be a constant guarding force of over two thousand men here, until the rebel prisoners are disposed of." Furthermore, the paper continued, "The number of officers will be larger than that quartered here last winter. So the prospect of a gay, lively and spirited season for amusements and entertainments seems quite assured for the coming fall and perhaps winter."[8] Two days later, the local press commented, "The true policy for the sure growth of our city seems at last fully inaugurated, namely—the increase of all kinds of manufacturing business, for which there will be a growing demand with the advancing years." The paper could only hope that "these elements of true prosperity, besides, will last and sustain the growth and increase of the town, when all the ephemeral advantages of a military rendezvous shall have been done away by the subjection of the rebellion and the close of the war."[9]

In the middle of October, the *Elmira Daily Advertiser* noted that "Our streets are still thronged with the military, stranger, and citizens. The crowd, if anything, increases, the stir and business everywhere manifested is equal to a city quadruple of our size. . . . So, with the attractions of all sorts about us and the camps and barracks," the paper concluded, "there seems to be a good prospect of a large inflow of strangers and military personages for some time to come."[10]

Newspaper correspondents sent to Elmira detailed not only Johnny Reb's life in captivity, but also the prison's impact elsewhere. On August 17, an enlightening article appeared in the *New York Evening Post*. "The enterprising town of Elmira is one of the government depots for prisoners of war, and the camp now contains between seven and eight thousand rebels. . . . More than two thousand prisoners are yet to arrive, when there will be ten thousand, as many as the camp will accommodate. In a few days from this time the rebels, with their guards, will about equal in number the men, women and children who composed the population previous to the establishment of the rebel depot. Suppose three-quarters of a million rebel prisoners encamped in Westchester county, and you will appreciate the situation here."[11] The metropolitan correspondent did not know specifically who would provide for all of them; he knew only that the prison was "about a mile and a half from the business centre of Elmira" and the "rich farming region furnishes the needed supplies."[12]

On October 7, a *New York Express* reporter wrote: "Elmira is a live town,—a new city if you please. Perhaps it abounds in incidents of real interest beyond any other locality outside of your own great city. . . . It is in short, the most important military post in the Empire state." The Gotham writer continued: "The war has given a great impetus to Elmira. Speculation, too, has had and is still having its widest range. Under this influence it has swelled into the proportion of a city of 16,000 inhabitants. Besides this, it has a floating population of from 10,000 to 12,000. . . . We have to some extent all the characteristics of your great city. Gamblers, pickpockets, fast men and lewd women—the latter are in legion." His most telling comment was the following: "It is here that army contractors fatten and get rich in a day while thousands are wondering where all the money comes from."[13]

Not all the advantages that came with the military's presence in Elmira satisfied everyone. Some carpenters hired by the Quartermaster's Department were unhappy because they were paid with credit vouchers rather than in cash. In fact, most of the department's workers were compensated by vouchers, which could be cashed at local banks, but with a tax. Not being paid in hard money and being taxed on top was bad enough, but the workers felt that their immediate supervisor had made the situation even worse. At the end of October, a spokesman for the carpenters, Eli Monell, wrote to Secretary of War Stanton that they had an agreement with local banking institutions that their tax rate would be adjusted to two percent. Instead, they found that someone had "interfered." Assistant Quartermaster Suydam, they complained, had told the banks "not to cash them for less than five percent."[14] An investigation early in

November found little merit in the carpenter's claims. Quartermaster General Montgomery Meigs informed Stanton that the Elmira carpenters "are liable to and do at times work more than the number of working days in a month, and it is nothing more than fair that they should contribute their legal share towards the support of the Government."[15] The presidents of the Chemung Canal Bank and the First and Second National Banks of Elmira verified that the tax rates they imposed on vouchers had "always" been around five percent.[16]

   Meanwhile, Elmira Prison was gradually taking significant sums of money out of its own fund. In addition to paying quartermaster and commissary expenditures on the pen, the prison fund had been supplying the stockade with extra money, as more expenditures began to pry open the hands of the tight-fisted Hoffman. The prison commissary kept spending at a minimum during the camp's early months, but costs slowly rose as more facilities were required to care for the influx of inmates and the large slush fund helped cover those costs. In September, the fund covered $14,771.21 spent on the prison, and in October $13,026.03. Even when expenses declined at the end of 1864, records from the commissary general's office indicate that as much as $37,566.20 had already been used on Elmira Prison from the fund. These expenditures marked only the beginning of the immense expenditures that continued into the next year.[17]

   The beginning of 1865 brought renewal to the city of Elmira because many of the military contracts had to be extended or rewritten. Commissary Sappington hoped to procure better grades of meat by stipulating larger stock in the new beef contract, which Samuel Hall won with a six-month agreement that began on January 11. The Elmiran was paid almost double the rate of his predecessor—thirteen and seven-eighths cents per pound—because it was agreed that "Cattle Slaughtered for Beef to be delivered under this contract shall weigh Five hundred pounds net after being trimed."[18] This was a promise that Hall could not keep. He scoured the countryside for animals according to the terms, but they were too scarce. The butcher appealed to Sappington, who met with Colonel Tracy. Tracy's legal background told him that he had no authority to change a preexisting contract, so the depot commander wrote to the commissary general of subsistence. "It is represented by Mr. Hall that it is very difficult to get cattle of that size in the country, while young steers & heifers, weighing about 400 to 500 lbs. in good flesh, & much better beef and less bones, than larger animals can be procured. They ask that lighter beef be accepted."[19] Commissary Eaton received word from Gen. A. S. Diven, commander of the District of Western New York, that deemed "the rejection of beef because of the weight injudicious. It should be inspected in reference to the quality, rather than the weight, small cattle if in good condition make good beef, much better than larger, boney cattle."[20] Military authorities had little choice except to modify the contract and incorporate Hall's terms, although his pay rate remained the same.

Hall's fresh beef required salt, so Commissary Sappington wrote out a contract in January for its supply. Virgil Read provided 1,000 bushels, 60 pounds to the bushel at 68 cents per pound, which brought him a modest $680.[21] At the end of the month, Sappington notified his superiors in Washington that he was short on flour because of "the number of troops & Prisoners of War at the post," so he took local bids because he thought, "flour can be obtained here [at] as cheap a rate of the Government as at any other point."[22] Sappington wrote in relative terms—not much came cheap for his department, particularly flour.

Elmira flour mills were extremely busy in 1865. In addition to the amount needed to make bread for prisoners and troops, the camp required, as Commissary Sappington put it, to keep "about 50,000 pounds of [extra] hard bread on hand while the Prisoners were held here in case of any accident to the bake ovens."[23] This supply, along with regular demands, had large repercussions with local flour distributors. On February 2, Jeremiah Dwight agreed to furnish the Elmira Commissary Department with sixteen hundred barrels of flour, evenly divided between two types. He received $10.20 per barrel for eight hundred barrels of wheat flour and $9.70 for another eight hundred barrels of spring wheat flour, a contract worth $15,920 altogether. On the same day, Sappington entered into an agreement with George Worrel for four hundred barrels of extra state flour at $9.60 per barrel. At the beginning of March, J. H. Loring and Co. earned their portion of commissary disbursements. The two proprietors of this local mill, James H. Loring and Edward W. Hersey, obligated themselves to supply sixteen hundred barrels of extra state flour at $9.64 per barrel, which added up to a $15,424 contract.[24] At the end of April, Thomas C. Platt from nearby Tioga County was also awarded a flour contract for sixteen hundred barrels of flour at $7.12½. Platt had grown up in Owego with Colonel Tracy and had personal leverage that other bidders did not. As both men emerged in politics after the war, Platt repaid his close friend with a favor, publicly defending him in the halls of Congress.[25]

Individuals who provided the prison pen with food never endeared themselves to captives. Growling hunger pains led more than one Southerner to consider contractors lowly grafters interested only in making considerable remunerative rewards at their expense. Alabaman J. L. Williams stated, "I think the Government made an honest effort to care for us, but sometimes the Government and sub-contractors were not honest."[26] Marcus Toney "thought for awhile that the government was retaliating on us on account of Andersonville, but afterwards believed it was done by the army contractors."[27] A South Carolinian agreed: "My honest opinion is that they could have treated us much better without much effort. The government may have made the effort, but the agents of the government failed most miserably."[28] Although perhaps failing in quality, food contractors definitely did not fail in quantity. The amount of meat and bread—two staples —doled out to inmates was enormous. Altogether, Sappington provided Elmira prisoners with an estimated 13,000 barrels of flour and 2,396,165 pounds of beef.[29]

As with the commissary, the Quartermaster's Department continued to keep hundreds of individuals in and around Elmira employed in 1865. The logistics of supplying the prison with commissary and quartermaster stores in town kept many teamsters working for forty-five dollars a month, a five-dollar raise over their previous year's pay.[30] Captain Elwell complained regularly to Washington that he lacked proper land transportation for ten thousand prisoners and three thousand guards, and although he admitted that costs were "excessive," he had no other choice but to rent equipment.[31] Private parties rented wagons out at $2.75 a day, and horses at $5 a team. J. S. Baldwin earned himself $365.50 in one month for that purpose, and other Elmirans reaped similar profits. Building up or fixing facilities frequently brought carpenters to the prison and guard camps. Their pay was also increased after the new year, by as much as three dollars per day. General laborers might earn $45 a month, whereas civilian clerks could make as much as $125. Surveyors were paid $50 a month and wood inspectors $100.[32] On the bottom of Elwell's payroll were nine persons hired exclusively as "dirt cart drivers" for removing waste from the prison yard; they received $20 a month. Duties at the depot also required local blacksmiths, and when Cook and Covell won the contract for furnishing the dirt carts, their blacksmith, Miles Trout, built a couple dozen. The two-wheeled vehicles, pulled by horses, carried garbage out of the prison yard on a daily basis.[33] With all the contracts in Elmira, small wonder that lawyers were required "in giving legal advice in regard to leases, contracts and claims against the government." James Dunn charged seventy-five dollars a month for his counseling.[34]

The operational demands of the prison and guard camps kept local businesses active. In addition to providing hardware, Cook and Covell supplied kerosene oil to keep the prison camp illuminated and grosses of lamp wicks and matches for lighting and burning.[35] The masonry firm of Russell and French sold hundreds of dollars worth of lime, brick, and sand for building and disinfecting privies.[36] Record keeping and sending correspondence required an immense amount of stationery and supplies. F. A. Devoe and Son printed sutler orders for the prison, while Presnick and Dudley and the Hall Brothers furnished paper, ledgers, report and prescription books, pens, pencils, erasers, rulers, scissors, rubber bands, envelopes, ink, and sealing wax. George D. Bridgeman and Fairman and Caldwell bound information into voluminous books.[37] The hospital department bought straw and hay in bulk from farmers and used it for bedding patients.[38] Druggists, particularly Ingraham and Robinson, stocked the hospital with medicinal supplies. When the medicine failed to recuperate patients, a more morbid business took over.[39]

Perhaps the greatest opportunity for anyone that prison authorities employed was that of a former slave from Virginia. John W. Jones, held in bondage by the Elzy family in Leesburg, had escaped along the Underground Railroad in 1844. Jones had resettled in Elmira, gained an education at a local school, and advanced to the position of sexton at Woodlawn Cemetery by the time the prison opened in July 1864. At the end of that month, Commissary General Hoffman approved three hundred dollars for leasing a half acre of ground at the local cemetery to bury dead Confederates, and authorized employment of a person to bury them for forty dollars a month. Jones held his modest job at a fortuitous time, for he soon found that the morbid business of death boomed while the prison existed. To help the sexton transfer corpses, Hoffman allowed a wagon to be purchased and modified into a hearse.[40] "The first day that I was called in my capacity of sexton to bury a prisoner who had died," wrote Jones, "I thought nothing of it. . . . Directly there were more dead. One day I had seven to bury. After that they began to die very fast."[41] By 1865, Southern interments were becoming more expensive and expansive as the cemetery began running out of room. On January 1, 1865, Mayor Arnot leased out an additional half-acre of land at Woodlawn, which cost the government $600. Also, undoubtedly to the chagrin of Hoffman, Jones was not paid a monthly fee of $40 but was instead compensated at an individual rate set at $2.50 per burial.[42]

In the meantime, a customized hearse driven by John Donohoe for $60 per month had been pulling up to the morgue for its daily collection. Inmates employed at the prison camp morgue, a sixteen-by-thirty-by-twelve-foot building, prepared their own for burial, constructing pine coffins as fast as they could while corpses piled up in the corners.[43] Clothing and personal items of the

John W. Jones, the escaped slave who became sexton at Woodlawn Cemetery and supervised the burial of Confederate prisoners at Elmira. Courtesy of the Chemung County Historical Society.

deceased were to be left alone, and each cadaver was tagged for identification, which included name, company, regiment, and date of death. These records were transcribed onto the coffin lid, then the papers were bottled and put in the box before it was nailed shut. The straight-shaped coffins were loaded six at a time onto the hearse for removal to Woodlawn, a few miles north of the pen.[44] This "admirable system" provoked one Confederate to state sarcastically that at Elmira "the care of the dead was better than that bestowed on the living."[45]

At Woodlawn, Sexton Jones directed the opening of trenches, most of which were positioned north to south. Caskets were placed in short increments, and a crew of ten to twelve prisoners on graveyard detail helped with the digging. The largest number that Jones buried in a single day was forty-three, which brought more than $100 to him, while his busiest month, March, brought him $1,237.50.[46] This is not to suggest that the sexton did not earn his pay. He meticulously transferred the information on each coffin lid into a large ledger that detailed the position of every Confederate buried at Woodlawn. He made sure that the wooden headboards had the correct information written on them in white lead paint, and then placed them over the appropriate plot. Nine laborers were on the quartermaster's payroll, each paid forty-five dollars per month to set headboards that local carpenter William F. Naefe had built.[47]

Eventually, workers dug more than thirty-six trenches and laid to rest 2,973 Confederates at Woodlawn Cemetery.[48] Incidentally, it would have cost Prison Commissary Hoffman only $480 if the Sexton had been paid monthly. Instead, Hoffman paid him a total of $7,432.50 for prisoner burials. The old slave had adapted quite well to the capitalistic North. Long after the end of hostilities, a personal friend of Jones remembered the significance of the Confederate burials at $2.50 apiece: "The aggregate of these fees was the basis of the comfortable fortune he amassed in the years after the war. He was rated as the wealthiest colored man in this part of the State."[49]

Just as space was needed to put Confederate dead to rest, additional room was required to let Union living sleep. Officers in Elmira were given daily stipends for housing when other quarters were not available. The Brainard Hotel was depot headquarters and furnished rooms for Colonel Tracy, Major Colt, and Captain Suydam. Other hotels in the city housed military guests. However, private homes especially proved hospitable to military personnel, particularly prison authorities, in return for rent checks.[50] Major S. W. Beall rented three rooms from Theodore Edwards for thirty-two dollars a month. Captain R. R. R. Dumars paid only twenty-four dollars for his three rooms from a Mr. Baker. The second chief surgeon of the prison, Anthony Stocker, rented four rooms from Mrs. W. B. Dewitt for thirty-two dollars a month, whereas Adjutant C. C. Barton leased three rooms from her for twenty-four dollars. Many more officers connected with the prison and guard camps lived in private homes and paid similar rates. Clerks and orderlies detailed at the pen received quarters at the government's expense, and even Mayor Arnot got in on the action, renting quarters to the provost guard at twenty dollars a month. Office space was just as valuable, and hundreds of dollars were spent in rent for the Adjutant, Quartermaster, and Commissary Departments. Still, it was hard to beat the monopoly that the Foster family had on their block, which yielded a combined total of $2,590 for 125 acres in space rented for Elmira Prison and Camp Chemung.[51]

Leases and rents, persons and articles hired on contract, expenditures by the commissary, quartermaster, and prison funds—all benefitted Elmirans. Farms, lumber yards, flour mills, meat markets, hardware shops, stationery and drug stores all had to accelerate business to meet military demands. "The merchants are busy morning through night," noticed the *Elmira Daily Advertiser* during the prison's heyday, "all kinds of business seem to be in a flourishing condition."[52] Job growth was not restricted to tasks fueled directly by the quartermaster, commissary, or prison funds. For example, the Brainard Hotel employed an omnibus driver to chauffeur officers up to the pen. Produce vendors, theaters, restaurants, saloons, and less moral establishments overindulged off-duty prison keepers with various forms of entertainment, food, and drink. Commercialization of the prison was taken to a new level with the observatories, which brought more visitors into the city. Simply put, Barracks Number 3 afforded individuals with opportunities they might never have had if it had not been converted into a prison camp. Such opportunities also extended outside of the Chemung Valley.[53]

Although canals had been giving way to railroads for some time in the valley, the inland waterways were revitalized during the Civil War. Delivery of fuel to the depot, particularly coal for keeping the camps warm, kept towpaths crowded. Elmira's main connection to Pennsylvania mines, its supply source, was along the Junction Canal, which connected the Chemung Canal to the Susquehanna systems. Cargo on the Junction Canal increased gradually throughout the war. In 1861, tonnage was 97,331; in 1862, 126,395; and in 1863, 153,059. The year the prison was established, cargo on the Junction, more than half of which was anthracite coal, reached its highest mark.[54] In the middle of November, the *Elmira Daily Advertiser* reported, "Coal is arriving here in large quantities by the Junction Canal, in anticipation of the close of navigation. The gross amount will much exceed the previous seasons."[55] In 1864, 170,849 tons, primarily coal, were transported from Pennsylvania to Elmira. The percentage of anthracite taken from Keystone mines approximately doubled from 1861 to 1864. March floods prevented the canal from matching these figures in 1865, which did not matter to J. D. Baldwin since he sold the majority of his coal, worth about ten thousand dollars, to the prison before the heavy rains fell.[56]

Elmira was a transportation nexus not because of its waterways, but because of its rail lines, the primary attribute that turned it into a military depot. The Erie and Northern Central Railroads intersected at Elmira and reaped large earnings from the army because of their high transportation rates. Not only did the railways move goods in and out of Elmira, but they also transported human freight in a seemingly unending endeavor that saw streams of soldiers coming or leaving the city. In addition to taking soldiers to and from the battlefields, the railroads brought prisoners and guards to Elmira from various places and, after their release, took them elsewhere at government expense. Quartermaster Suydam was in charge of contracting use of the railroads, and despite poor service on the Northern Central and a dreadful mishap on the Erie, the military had no choice but to continue using them at a costly price. For example, from July 1864, when the prison was inaugurated, to the end of July 1865, about the time that it closed, the military incurred $115,000 in charges from the Erie Railroad Company alone.[57]

Quartermaster Elwell never had the luxury of having that type of cash on hand, so the Erie would have to wait at least a year before it settled its debt with the government.[58] Some local contractors were less patient. In March 1865, another complaint about money owed was directed against the Quartermaster's Department. A number of businessmen whose "entire capital is now in the hands of the U.S. Government for lumber, coal, and hardware furnished upon contract on Q.M. orders" were becoming nervous because of the delay in receiving payments.[59] The lumber firm of Hatch and Partridge represented the group and explained the dilemma to Quartermaster General Meigs: "We do not know whether the proper regulations have been made on you or the U.S. Treasury for money to pay this indebtedness but we are persuaded there is incompetency somewhere in the Q. M. Department at this post." The merchants had "no special charge to make with Q. M. Elwell—We are personally acquainted and highly esteem him as a man and a Christian. But so long as we are satisfied that the government has the money wherewith to pay we can but feel that there is great money somewhere, in keeping the credits of the government here."[60] Also in March, Commissary Sappington wrote to Subsistence Commissary Eaton that he had not received cash since December 1864: "The Creditors of the U.S. are very urgent for their money and it would give me great pleasure to satisfy them if the Treasurer could forward the funds."[61] Heavy breath directed down the backs of Elwell and Sappington prompted both men to write their superiors for quicker payments from the Treasury Department.

Prison Commissary Hoffman was having his own funding problems by the spring of 1865. Elmira Prison was starting to absorb even more money from the prison fund, although Hoffman had hoped to save as much as possible as the conflict wound down. Expenditures in January and February were under twenty thousand dollars, but in March a combination of factors led to a disbursement that Hoffman had never anticipated. Facilities from building the winter barracks were still being paid off, which combined with expenses related to the devastation of a flood and its subsequent cleanup resulted in a whopping expenditure of $73,334.16. No fund in any Northern prison came close to covering this figure in any month of the Civil War. For that matter, the value of the expenditures might be better appreciated by recognizing that March expenses at Elmira equaled those of most Union prisons throughout the entire year and a few throughout their entire history, including Johnson's Island in Ohio, Camp Morton in Indiana, and Gratiot Street Prison in Missouri—all three founded in 1862. Moreover, if Commissary Hoffman had tallied the final operational costs for Union prisons at Alton, Illinois; Louisville, Kentucky; Wheeling, West Virginia; Ship Island, Mississippi; Harts Island, New York; and Forts McHenry in Baltimore, Warren in Boston, and Lafayette, in New York, he still would not have had enough money for Elmira Prison in the month of March.[62]

Unfortunately for Elmira, spending on the prison camp would soon stop. At the end of the month the War Department issued General Orders Number 77, which issued the command. Elmira newspapers soon bore headlines that read "Important Order—The Reduction of Expenses by the War Department . . . every possible reduction of military expenses, in view of the conclusion of hostilities, will be made immediately."[63] The act officially prepared citizens for abolition of the rendezvous and the suspension of army activities in Elmira. The army was to purchase only "what is absolutely necessary in view of the immediate reduction of the forces in the field and in garrison."[64] Also, the Commissary and Quartermaster Departments were not only expected to slash spending, but also to downsize the number of their employees quickly. Those who remained on staff were "required for closing the business of their respective departments."[65]

It did not take long for the bad news to affect Elmira's economy. Although newspapers assured readers that "a year will elapse before the complete abandonment of this military post," the potential of losing an immense money-generating enterprise was not received well. Only the prior fall the *Elmira Daily Advertiser* had bragged, "The high price of gold does not seem to effect the pockets of the consumer. The confidence in the stability of the nation is so great that no hesitancy or anxiety actuates the business transactions or pecuniary dealings of trade."[66] At the end of the winter, the paper realized that the war "gave a stimulus to this place, and has caused its growth to increase doubly in material acquirements, and has insured a permanent and steady advance from its previous state, even should the war end today."[67] "Today" was a reality in the spring of 1865, but gold plummeted and buying slackened, while the government started to hand its employees their walking slips. A mild recession looked as if it were taking place: "The prices of provisions are gradually tending downwards in our market," wrote the *Elmira Daily Advertiser* in May. "Prices cannot keep up with the fall of gold and the prospect of the breaking up of the rendezvous."[68]

Downsizing at the depot continued. Officials laid off clerks, laborers, carpenters, teamsters, cooks, messengers, stewards, and other military workers. On May 10, it was reported, "There are now about two clerks at headquarters who are enlisted men. . . . the thinning out, within a few days, has been quite remarkable."[69] Elmirans definitely felt the economic pinch when renters did not renew leases, quartermaster supplies were not bought or borrowed, and the commissary phased out contracts. Residents of the city could see the dismantling of the "stockade city" and its "guard camp suburb" right before their eyes. In July, the *Elmira Daily Advertiser* highlighted the event. "Tearing Down—Already the Saloon buildings along the street, this side of Barracks No.3, are in the process of demolition, or torn down. They have filled their day and must now give way to the new order of things."[70] Also that month, the value of articles purchased by the prison fund dropped dramatically.[71] In August, the local press again verified the changing composition of the city: "There is quite a thinning out constantly going on among the military men at this post. Reductions are gradually taking place, that will restore us in a few months to our former civilian, minus the military aspect."[72]

Gradual reductions had also proceeded at the prison. In April, $28,261.71 was expended on the pen; in May, $20,551.08; in June, $4,379.19; in July, $2,863.64; and in August, a mere $2,714.26. In September and October, the sale of prison camp material continued. Incidentally, the government paid the auctioneer, W. Sheridan, $150 for pitching the sales of government property.[73] In November, the War Department was informed "all the land heretofore occupied as barracks No.3 is no longer required. The following described land, being part of several leases with Messrs. Foster can be surrendered."[74] Officials returned the land to the Foster family after all the government property, which totaled $2,824.10, was sold in December. The amount of money left over in the prison fund amounted $58,151.54.[75]

War had greatly affected Elmira, which was a changed place compared to its condition five years earlier. Soon after the conflict ended and outstanding claims were settled, the economy also seemed to be changed for the better. Debts between individuals lessened and credit, although easily secured, was diminished. Meanwhile, Elmirans paid off their debts more promptly. Pauperism declined in some sections of the city; however, crime rose. The monthly price of farm labor before 1861 was twelve to fifteen dollars, but rose to twenty-four dollars in 1864, and stood at twenty-six dollars by war's end. Even with the drought of 1864, farmland rose in value.[76] One observer noted that the "camps required large amounts of farm produce, meat, vegetables and wood for fuel. . . . Along West Water Street might be seen great wood-piles extending for nearly a quarter mile."[77] Food contractors, supposed to be selling their goods to the military at the lowest bid, never lost much. The market price of flour was nine to ten dollars per barrel, and beef sold as low as ten cents a pound, and both sets of figures compared the price that the military was paying.[78] Consequently, one should not be surprised at Commissary Sappington's assessment after the war: "Citizens were at all times willing and anxious to furnish anything that was required at reasonable prices, and wait the pleasure of the government to pay them, in fact the resources of the country and the faith of the People seemed during this war to be inexhaustible."[79]

Census enumerators help one understand how much the military affected Elmira's local economy. One enumerator wrote that the influence of the war made Elmira "generally more prosperous and contented."[80] Another enumerator noticed that Elmirans had "a great desire to become quickly Rich out of the government by fat contracts."[81] Census Judge Edwin Munson commented on the changing financial and social conditions in the ward that contained the stockade and surrounding guard camp. There was "an increasing tendency to extravagance and display. The large government expenditures at this post with the large number of officials and troops stationed here have doubtless greatly fostered this tendency at this point. The same causes have led to a

largely increased consumption of intoxicants," something more than a few
prison guards could appreciate.[82]

In 1865, Elmira led all Union prisons in funding; no other camp came close
to matching its maintenance fee of $165,225. Not only was this the first prison
camp budget to break six figures in a single year, but Elmira's budget also went
well beyond that total. Comparatively, Elmira Prison doubled, tripled, and
more than quadrupled the budgets of many stockades that operated in 1865.
An examination of some larger Union prisons puts Elmira on top of the list for
expenditures. Camp Douglas came closest, spending $93,995 that year. Then
came Camp Chase, with $52,134 in expenses, followed by Point Lookout, at
$42,436, and finally, Fort Delaware with $30,964. In fact, the twenty-seven
camps under Prison Commissary Hoffman's control in 1865 spent $489,876.29
altogether that year, meaning that about one-third went to Elmira.[83]

All told, the government spent $202,784 on Elmira Prison during its ex-
istence, and some 12,147 prisoners passed through its gates. No prison cost
as much from July 1864 to the following year. Commissary Hoffman's first
prison on Johnson's Island, Ohio, which he hoped would be the only one
required for the war, cost $57,784.69 to care for its 7,627 captives, most of
whom were officers. In central Ohio, a camp converted from training facilities
near Columbus housed 16,335 men through its three-year term as a prison,
and had $128,872.80 spent on it. Camp Morton, a similar prison converted in
1862 from an instruction base on the state fairgrounds a mile and a half from
downtown Indianapolis, received 12,082 Confederates, on whom $43,565.41
was expended. The prison in Alton, Illinois, a former state penitentiary used
by the War Department for 9,330 Southerners beginning in 1862, experienced
expenditures of $33,538.09 by the end of the war. Gratiot Street Prison in St.
Louis, Missouri, once a medical college before becoming a prison early in
the war, never held more than a thousand prisoners, but expended $19,115.93
starting in 1862. Fort Delaware, which a young George McClellan designed as
a river fortress on a ninety-acre acre island to help protect Philadelphia, served
as a pen for Confederates beginning in 1862, held 25,275 prisoners throughout
its existence, and incurred expenses that totaled $122,934.11. Another prison
located on a river was Rock Island in the Mississippi, bordering Illinois and
Iowa. It was established at the end of 1863, confined 11,458 prisoners altogether,
and experienced $96,427.91 in expenditures by the end of the war.[84]

Expenses at only a couple stockades compared to those at Elmira. Point
Lookout, where 42,762 inmates were held during its three-year history, expended $162,416.83. Camp Douglas, established in January 1862 just four miles

from the center of Chicago, spent more than Elmira. However, its spending began in January 1862 and did not end until April 1865, a four-year existence that helped it incur total expenses of $208,230.91 on the 26,060 men it received. Both its prison population and time frame more than doubled Elmira. A closer look finds that the Chicago prison expended $159,543.25 during the existence of Elmira, which spent over $200,000. Moreover, the impact that each had on the local population would be hard to compare. Camp Douglas was located in the main market of the Midwest, where all forms of industry were firmly entrenched. Its population was over 109,000 at the beginning of war, while Elmira's was not even one-tenth that size.[85]

These figures indicate that no other prison camp affected its community as much as Elmira had by the end of the war. The camp helped support the local economy and grew from it, adding stability during a sluggish time. This development did not matter to some locals. More than a few might have wondered if the camp was worth all the trouble for posterity's sake. In addition to leading all Union stockades in expenditures during the year of its existence, Elmira also led Northern camps in another statistic: It had the highest death rate of any pen in the North. Ever since the war ended, Elmirans have lived with the stigma that their Civil War prison was considered the worst of its kind.

9

Johnny Reb's Other Occupations

After morning roll call, a variety of occupations existed for prisoners through-out their day, but first they had to attend to domestic chores. Ward sergeants saw to the orderliness of quarters, making sure that they were swept out and kept tidy for weekly inspections. Prisoners were supposed to keep themselves clean, as well, which they promoted by bathing in the river. When that practice stopped with the onset of cold weather, camp officials did little else to help the prisoners maintain their hygiene. The wash room was exclusively for hospital patients, leaving the only option for men in the regular ranks to wash themselves and their clothes at the water pumps set up around the camp.[1] For many, bathing became an exercise in futility. "With all our care and caution," complained one prisoner, "we could not get rid of the vermin."[2] The vermin, for the most part, were body lice. Men disrobed, then scrubbed, picked, brushed, or beat the parasites off themselves and their clothing until they appeared to be gone. Yet, as James Huffman remembered, "Some fellows did not wash their clothes nor themselves and you could see the graybacks crawling over their clothes on the outside. There were other bitter doses I will not mention."[3] G. W. D. Porter was more frank, writing about how bowel disorders "often subjected the unfortunates to the brutish befouling of cloth-ing and person while standing in ranks awaiting the leisurely completion of a simple routine task."[4] Personal hygiene depended on the individual, said Huffman, because "there were all kinds of mixtures of men and morals in our ward. Some were talking, some swearing, some singing, others playing cards, some laughing and engaged in all kinds of amusements."[5]

Card games were popular, especially poker, as was mumble peg, a contest that involved tossing a pocketknife in the air in hopes it would stick in the

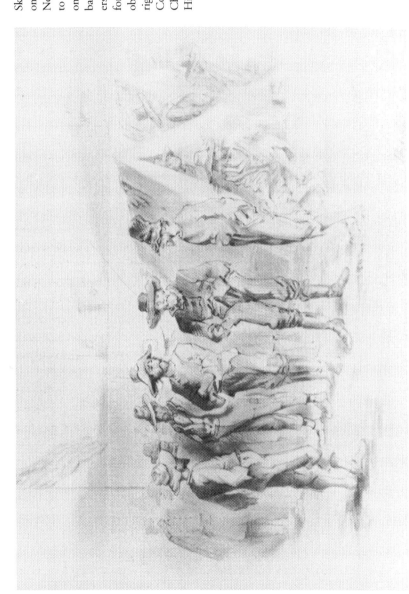

Sketch by Elmira prisoner W. Newman. Notice the flagpole to the left, the sentry on duty in the center background, prisoners at the center foreground, and the observatory in the right background. Courtesy of the Chemung County Historical Society.

ground. Domino, checker, and chess sets were constructed for those seek-ing more mental challenges.[6] Anthony Keiley was a chess enthusiast, taking "refuge" during his imprisonment by frequently checkmating Union officers.[7] Men with artistic talents might procure paper and pencils to draw about their life in captivity. Prisoners were allowed to secure a few fifes and drums so they could play away the hours of boredom. A more formal band was organized under the command of Stephen Moore, who was inspired enough by the band's leader, a German, to grant better instruments for his musicians. The eighteen-member ensemble was obliged to gather each dusk near the flagstaff by headquarters to perform the "retreat" while the flag was lowered. In return, prison officials permitted the band to play ballads with familiar overtones, including where they all wished to be, home in "Dixie."[8]

In September, a library was established, and for the literate, or nearly liter-ate, it became one of the more visited institutions inside the pen. The library's benefactors, the local YMCA and U.S. Christian Commission, plus individuals in the Chemung Valley, donated hundreds of volumes. Its shelves contained loyal papers and leaflets, religious tracts and Bibles, magazines, playbills, childrens' stories, and outdated books.[9] One industrious prisoner requested an edition of *Blackstone's Commentaries* so he could study law and become at least a "partly fledged lawyer by the time the 'cruel war is over.'"[10] The prelaw student would be able to find other Southerners willing to assist him in the skill of deliberating. A debating club was active among Confederates, with about one hundred members enrolled to discuss important questions of the day. Other meetings took place, most notably for the Freemasons Society. Due to the influence of Commandant Moore, one of the camp buildings was designated as their meeting hall.[11]

During the winter prisoners might occasionally enjoy ice skating on Foster's Pond or have fun with some other snow-filled recreation, but most preferred to keep occupied inside. Nightly dances, held at selected barracks, were some of the more favored events during the colder months. Obviously lacking the traditional female partner, Southerners had to become very imaginative. A white handkerchief was tied around an arm of one member of the duet, who then acted the part of the lady, bringing about laughs and heckles on and off the dance floor.[12] Other forms of entertainment were also captured by Southern comedians who acted at opportune moments, as when they were given the unique privilege of seeing real women in their wards. One humorous incident occurred when Moore's son led a few of his young lady friends on a personal tour of the prison. One girl was very impressed by his charm, but she attracted more than his attention. As she strolled through, the unabashed female discreetly raised her silk dress, so inmates could get a peek, realizing full well the appreciative response only confined men could give. "Oh, the nasty, dirty, ignorant, beastly Rebels, how filthy they are," she blurted during their howls, making sure her guide took notice. But the joke, unknowingly, was on her. She sauntered by an unimpressed prisoner name Bish Fletcher, who threw some "Grey Backs" at her; this way, any future admirers might find that the girl was not as pure as she appeared.[13]

Such camaraderie led to close friendships among the imprisoned. Nicknames commonly took the place of formal titles, especially if one had a revealing characteristic in dress or looks. "Buttons" seemed to be a fascinating individual whose long Confederate gray frock was adorned with hundreds of brass buttons he had sewn on, each one signifying an engagement in which he had fought. When walking, his buttons jingled and he appeared to glow in the direct sunlight.[14] "Old Blue Ridge" was an impressive figure who donned a large blue coat, which covered his massive frame much like the mountains he was compared to. "Old Picket" looked for his tobacco chews, "Shocky" was given special treatment since he was known to be a Freemason, and "Promptly" was apparently very punctual. Prisoners would be labeled with monikers simply taken from where they had come.[15] Berry Benson wrote, "At Elmira I was called 'South C'lina' more often than 'Benson.'" A Scottish prisoner, whose name was Smythe, was always called "City of Glasgow."[16] Same nationalities even bunked together. In one ward, 200 of the 207 inmates were of Irish descent, and hence it was termed the "Irish Ward."[17] Despite close companionships, however, Southerners did have to be careful since some mates were less than friendly. An unlawful element was present at Barracks Number 3, some men preying on others to the extent that it was hardly believable they fought on the same side.

Thieving was a common line of work that captives took up. Inmate Miles Sherrill noticed that "there was a great deal of speculation and swindling carried in the prisons; and I am ashamed to say it, yet it is true that sometimes some of our own men were engaged in conspiracy to cheat and defraud their fellow-prisoners."[18] A prisoner given even a small amount of influence, such as that of a ward master, waiter, or orderly, combined with an even smaller conscience, might take advantage. Sherrill said such enviable positions "would ruin some men," and worse, resulted in some growing "fat" while "others starved."[19] Ward Sergeant Marcus Toney admitted he purposely overestimated his barrack ration orders to get extra food.[20] However, this was mostly small-time theft compared to the activities of James M. Gilmore, employed in the mess room. The Mississippi infantryman pilfered up to thirty rations during daily shifts. His accomplice, J. L. Williams from Alabama, helped him sell their spoils, which totaled around ten thousand meals during their tenure in the dining hall. In the spring of 1865, they moved onto other jobs; by that time Gilmore had been made an orderly to help distribute shoes that the Confederacy had donated. He clandestinely heisted thousands of pairs, while Williams sold them for ten cents to a dollar. The Alabaman confessed their undiscovered misdeeds years later with no inkling of shame, stating "you can see we were in the service."[21]

Prisoners drew a fine line between different kinds of stealing at Elmira Prison. Burglarizing Northern property, such as taking extra wood for fuel or forging sutler orders for food, was generally accepted. However, to steal from fellow Southerners was not only unlawful but also considered dishonorable.[22] Early on, prisoners were able to take justice into their own hands. In one case, a prisoner snatched some valuables from a dying comrade. A posse organized and chased the criminal about the pen until he was finally tracked down and turned over to the prison authorities for punishment.[23] Eventually, as inmates were hardened by long-term captivity, such incidents went ignored. Stronger and healthier men got away with stealing from and bullying the sick and weak.[24]

When Southerners could not turn to comrades for support, they sought encouragement through writing, one of their favorite pastimes. A number kept diaries for therapeutic reconciliation. Many more wrote letters to their families, friends, or anyone seeming to be concerned. Relatives were quick to lend their aid, but begging from unfamiliar persons met with resistance. When a sympathetic soul was discovered, his or her name and address were passed along to others. Union officers were also known to drop a few names for less practical purposes. One of their victims, the owner of a local hotel, was delivered thirty "begging notes" in one day. "The joke is considered a good one by the officers," wrote a *New York Post* correspondent, but "the receiver of the letters is not inclined to regard it in that light."[25]

When a prisoner wrote a letter it had to remain unsealed to be read by the examiner before being mailed. If the the writer made any mention of poor treatment in prison, the letter would not be mailed and the author would lose five cents in paper and postage. Furthermore, if letters extended over a single page, they, too, would not reach their destination. Mail that prisoners received had to pass through the same scrutiny. All correspondence that officials approved was stamped "Prison Letter Examined" on the envelope. Wagonloads of mail were carried back and forth from the post office to Barracks Number 3. Like other establishments in Elmira, the post office business dramatically expanded because of the decision to confine Southerners to their city.[26] When the pen opened in July, letters from prisoners averaged about three hundred a day, causing the *Elmira Daily Advertiser* to comment, "It can't be any small task to peruse these manifold effusions of history, love, and personal wants."[27] However, the task got even larger due to the August buildup, outbound mail amounting to more than a thousand pieces every day. Incoming mail also reached the thousands, and by February 1865 a new post office was completed in the city, four times the size of the former building. The express company handled packages sent to Southerners and had to scrutinize them as prison officials scrutized the letters.[28]

No matter the small triumphs, Southerners longed for home. Prisoners many times fell into the abyss of depression, locked up in a strange place far away from family and friends. "Today is Christmas but it seems no more than any other day," wrote a less than cheerful Wilbur Grambling, who preferred to celebrate the holiday in the warmer latitudes of Florida. A few weeks later, the young man was staying busy with school, but he could hardly ignore the wound left from his smallpox shot, a painful reminder that the disease had been "raging" in camp. The Floridian sought the comfort of his diary, but some days nothing could go right: "Weather broken and is quite cold. We have had no coal to keep fire today. No school today. Got the scab knocked off my arm today. Oh it looks quite bad." In early March, despondent that he had not yet been paroled, Grambling confided again: "Almost crazy, I want to go to Dixie so bad. Still live in hope if I die in despair." Two weeks before turning twenty-two years, he sank further: "Oh me! So lonesome can hardly keep back the tears. So long since I have seen any of my associates. Hope my imprisonment won't last always."[29] Fortunately for him, it did not. Even the usually higher spirited William Campbell was occasionally touched by melancholy. Wrote Campbell: "I do not suffer from my captivity but in mind. . . . Sometimes, feelings of sadness creep over me, and the unbridled tear flows."[30] If prisoners strived to pin up their emotions through writing, the effort often failed. A Union guard noticed during his watches that "many of them were diseased, many were slightly wounded, many were feeble and worn out with the campaigning in Virginia, and many more were homesick. . . . They were mentally depressed and the inevitable result followed." That result, he bluntly stated, was dying off like "sheep with the rot."[31]

Prisoners had no choice but to spend much of their time contemplating their own mortality. With a death rate of almost one out of four, they were justified in worrying, being constantly reminded of death. They accepted it as a normal occurrence of captivity, one man stating that with "so many prisoners deaths were necessarily frequent."[32] A callous feeling soon developed among them. Tennessean W. S. Riddle "was horrified one day to see four prisoners sitting in a bunk playing poker, when in a near-by bunk was a dying prisoner. But such is war: A man's sensibilities are dwarfed." Riddle was sent to Elmira with six members in his squad, yet he was the only one to survive.[33] Of the dozen members with James Huffman from Kirby Smith's Company I, 10th Virginia, half were carried out of the stockade in coffins.[34] Just after Miles Sherrill arrived in prison, he was reacquainted with a man he called "Softy" from their days at the Old Capitol Prison. A new nickname was in order since his friend's reception was anything but mild: "Sherrill, you have come to hell at last. Did you see those four horse-wagons going out? They were full of dead men, who died last night." Sherrill did not need much convincing. The North Carolinian found two close relatives in prison, but he was the only family member to leave prison alive.[35] Thomas C. Jones of the 25th Virginia remembered seeing as many as thirty-five corpses "laid out in one day at the deadhouse."[36] That structure, on the opposite side of Foster's Pond, measured thirty-by-forty feet; it held cadavers while preparations were made for their burial.[37] The morgue was a place the prisoners hoped to avoid, but most dreams of freedom died long before they were assembled there.

Confederates had another outlet that might help them escape their fear of death. Soon after the prison opened, Major Colt permitted church services to be held on Sundays. Men of diverse denominations representing the Baptist, Catholic, Protestant, Presbyterian, Episcopalian, and Congregationalist faiths came from in and around Elmira to Barracks Number 3. The prison camp clergy often alternated their visits, but occasionally two were assigned on the same day. No formal church existed, but a nondenominational place was chosen, sometimes inside the dining hall or, for larger crowds, outside in an open area. As many as two thousand prisoners attended these services. Pastors would deliver sermons by yelling out their spiritual praise as the congregation of thousands followed along in boisterous song and prayer. On the Sabbath, fervent words echoed beyond the stockade wall, and even Union soldiers united in refrains heard from a distance.[38] A Southerner remembered how offerings were made "to our heavenly father from devout hearts for His protection and care, and in behalf of all who desired to be prayed for."[39] Sick inmates unable to attend under their own power were carried to the services. Harnessing their strength in a desperate effort, pale figures rose to the forefront, extended their gaunt hands up to the sky, and cried so that all might pray for them.[40]

Prayer meetings were attended with the same religious fervor. In between weekly church services, prisoners gathered in the morning, evening, and if they felt very devout, during the afternoon.[41] Methodist prisoners largely comprised these assemblages, and those who attended extolled the principles of individualism and free grace. They often met on the prison camp "green" and could be seen kneeling in prayer or discussing a variety of social topics. Although these practitioners were more liberal compared to the other religions, a *New York Post* reporter assured readers that they still "do not pray for Jeff Davis."[42]

Those prisoners who adhered to the stricter doctrines of Christianity, notably Roman Catholics, were well represented by the clergy. Father Martin Kavanaugh, priest and rector at St. Peter and Paul's in Elmira, was regularly called to the pen. Mass was performed with the aid of altar boys he brought with him, confessions heard on days prior to observing the Eucharist, and last rites conferred on ill Confederates before they passed on.[43] Higher ranking Catholic authorities also rendered their graces to Elmira Prison. On September 4, 1864, Bishop John Timon of Buffalo came to Elmira and delivered an inspiring sermon during mass.[44] Prior to his appointment as bishop, Father Timon had served as a missionary worker below the Mason-Dixon Line. Having a good rapport with Southerners, the Bishop had one more chance to convert any stray Rebel souls without leaving western New York.[45]

Another pastor held in high esteem was the Rev. Thomas K. Beecher. Not as famous or as extreme as his brother, Beecher was all the same venerated in his hometown of Elmira. Anthony Keiley seemed a bit apprehensive when he learned that the local reverend was a sibling to "the notorious Henry Ward, who cultivates politics, preaching and potatoes, to much temporal advantage, as the world knows." However, after hearing Beecher preach the Virginian surmised, "'Tom' is not as 'sound on the crow' as Ward, and gave us a very practical, sensible, and liberal talk."[46] "Tom" was also noted as being more lighthearted than his brother, and never spoke of the prisoners in harsh terms for fighting on the other side.[47] However, James Huffman recalled, "Others were possessed with devils before they came in. We gave attention and enjoyed good gospels, but had no time to waste on old political hypocrites and would leave." One such preacher opened a sermon by stating, "I want you to all understand that I am a Union man, and my father was a Union man, and

grandfather was a Union man, and my great-grandfather" and by the time
he got any further into his patriotic lineage, most of his audience had left.[48]

The Rev. S. M. Bainbridge, described by one inmate as "a freedom shrieker,"
was rooted in abolitionist sentiment."[49] In a typical sermon, which Anthony
Keiley said was a "long insult to prisoners," some members of the audience
decided to leave. However, Lt. Isaac Richmond was as zealous as their guest
speaker and halted their exit. Before any further escalation, another Union
officer stepped in, reminding Richmond that whether his intervention was
divine or political, he could not force the prisoners to stay.[50] The only retribution Richmond could arrange was a ten-dollar donation that he gave to
Bainbridge the next day, along with a thank you note that concluded, "That's
the religion that suits me." Bainbridge responded to the lieutenant, "I wish it
suited everybody."[51] A perturbed Anthony Keiley responded in his diary: "The
clerical world in Puritan-dom has not changed altogether from the happy days
of Quaker whipping and Papist hanging, whereof the annals of Connecticut
orthodoxy are rife."[52]

More often political motives were kept silent, increasing the pen's spiritual-
ity, which hardly waned. Bibles and other religious publications were the most
requested of all reading material.[53] Religious sects were represented as well as in
the outside world, indicated by a poll taken in the prison in 1865. Of the 1,511
individuals included in the sample, which primarily comprised Virginians and
North Carolinians, 547 were Baptist, 542 Methodist, 242 Roman Catholic, and
110 Presbyterian.[54] Although divided among faiths, the prisoners joined together
to hear preaching from men who might not ascribe to the inmates' individual
beliefs. The reason, wrote a *New York Post* reporter, was because "the devotional
spirit of the rebels is supposed to be strengthened by their confinement."[55]

Inmates at Elmira also religiously practiced customary attempts to escape,
but often their prayers for deliverance went unanswered. The various schemes of
escape resulted in little success. Prisoners must have found this extremely frustrat-
ing, since Elmira Prison had one of the lowest escape records.[56] Altogether, only
seventeen prisoners managed to slip over, under, or through the stockade into
the Chemung Valley and to freedom.[57] The reason for the low figure can be
attributed to a combination of factors. The prisoners were far from their own
lines, which discouraged long travel or outside assistance. Strenuous work was
involved, and usually inmates had to maintain their health in order to succeed.
Finally, men would rather not take the chance of being caught and punished.
Even against poor odds, it did not take long for some to test the guards. One
day after the prison opened, two athletic Confederates got away by scaling the

twelve-foot wall and dropping to the other side. A handful of inmates simply passed through the gates either by walking on their own or being carried out. Most prisoners preferred tunneling, conducted largely in summer and fall, when the ground was easily broken. These were risky ventures by desperate men who felt it was better at least to make an attempt rather than to endure the hardships of prison life.[58] "I obeyed all rules of the prison except one," wrote one of them, "I was ordered to stay, but I did not."[59]

Joseph Womack of Wade Hampton's cavalry was lucky to be selected as a ward sergeant. Womack routinely made out the roll reports and personally delivered them to headquarters. Occasionally, a Union officer with whom he consorted in this duty lent Womack reading material. While perusing the pages of one of these books, Womack later wrote, "my heart jumped to my throat, for there lay, between the leaves, the blank form of a printed pass to go in and out of the prison."[60] However, the valuable bookmarker, inadvertently left inside the volume, missed an important feature: the signature of Maj. Henry V. Colt. Womack found an old sutler's ticket signed by Colt, and began copying Colt's handwriting day after day. After experimenting with his work by forging the commandant's name on a new sutler form, which the store accepted, the sergeant was ready for the real test on the night of October 26. Completing the pass, which allowed him to leave the pen for a couple hours, he put on a stolen Union officer's frock that coordinated well with his blue pants. Womack, with disguised dress and signature, stated "I brushed up both courage and clothes, said 'goodbye' to my messmate, pulled my hat down over my eyes, subsided as far as possible into my coat-collar—for the cold made the disguise more excusable—and thus equipped, started."[61]

Womack briskly marched by headquarters, stepped up to the officers' gate, and confidently knocked. The door opened and Womack handed his pass to the sergeant of the guard, who took it to his superior's office. For Womack, it seemed to take an eternity for the pass to be examined. "Then imagine my ecstasy at hearing the words, 'He is alright, sergeant, pass him out.'" A sentinel marched Womack to the outer limits of the guard patrol, then left him under his own recognizance. In his restrained exuberance he suddenly realized he had forgotten something. He had left his pass at the office and thought his error would surely arouse suspicion. Going back for the paper, currently in the hand of the examiner and being discussed with the guard, Womack appeared—"I remarked to the officer—touching my hat politely—'I have forgotten my pass, sir.' 'Yes,' he replied, 'you might have got in trouble without it;' then handing it to me, we saluted, and separated."[62] The daring gamble won the officer's approval and Womack's escape. The sergeant was again shown on his way, this time never to return, and he jumped on a train traveling south.[63]

Another example of a prisoner wandering outside the prison doors also involved a case of mistaken identity. A young South Carolina prisoner named Bennie Orcutt, who ran errands at headquarters, remarkably resembled Jimmie Dumars, the youth who did the same for his father, federal Capt. R. R. R. Dumars. Being such a frequent visitor to the pen, young Dumars did not have to hand a pass through an inspection window, which officials had installed in the fence since the prior escape. He just had to yell his last name through to the man posted behind, and the door opened. It became apparent that another person knew about this arrangement. One December day when the northern boy did not show up for work, the young Confederate seized his opportunity. As the sun set, the normal time public employees ended their workday and left, Orcutt covered himself in a civilian jacket snatched from the coatroom at headquarters. Cloaked in new attire and dim light, the South Carolinian went up to the gate, faced the window, and carefully pronounced himself as "Dumars." No one knew of his whereabouts thereafter, until Orcutt sent word back to a clerk who was missing his jacket. Orcutt begged forgiveness for his presumptuous act, in a letter postmarked from the South.[64]

Those who could conceal themselves altogether did not outdo inmates who escaped through duplicity. The first such case happened in November and involved a less-than-conspicuous prisoner named Jimmie Jones, better known as "Buttons." Jones claimed to have been infected with smallpox, so he was sent to the smallpox wards across from Foster's Pond. From there, he surreptitiously darted to the nearby morgue, where a friend from Texas named F. S. Wade worked. The Texan found his buddy wrapped up in a blanket and nestled in a coffin, but very much alive. Jones quickly gave Wade a small package of flour and issued the following instructions: "Sprinkle my face and hands with flour, then slightly fasten the coffin lid down, and when the dead wagon comes around, be sure to put my coffin on top of the other dead."[65] The deed was done and, soon enough, the hearse pulled up, picked up almost a load of corpses, and drove off to the local cemetery. Rather than simply jumping from the hearse, Jones wanted to play out the part, hoping it might keep his lone witness hushed during his getaway. The Confederate waited awhile as the old carriage creaked distantly from the stockade, then Jones lifted off the wooden lid and began thumping on it. Not yet getting his riding companion's attention, he hauntingly bellowed out "Come to Judgement." The startled man turned around, thinking this ghost-white cadaver had already risen from the dead, but he decided not to stay long enough to see if the apparition could carry out his promise. After the driver dashed in one direction, Jones rushed in another. Both men escaped, although the driver eventually had to report the incident to prison officials.[66] Thereafter, Melvin M. Conklin of the 151st New York Volunteers, camp detective and spy, was posted at the morgue with orders, he said, to make "sure that every one was dead before being put in a box."[67]

In the spring of 1865, a similar escape occurred, though it involved fewer theatrics and not all the details are known. Contractors were in charge of disposing refuse barrels from the cookhouse, and one inmate persuaded a worker to help him escape from the pen with such a removal. The Confederate cautiously climbed into a full swill barrel, his face propped above the surface to breathe but below the barrel's opening so he could go out unnoticed. Three barrels were taken out one at a time, and during one April morning the Southerner was among their contents. His was the last example of a captive to escape from Elmira, excluding a thrilling mass exodus that took place earlier, in October.[68]

The most common approach to breaking out of Elmira Prison was through tunneling. Throughout the late summer and early fall of 1864 Confederates were digging in one manner or another. Diligent prison policing, due principally to the efforts of Melvin Conklin, foiled almost all burrowing efforts. The young New Yorker mixed well with Confederates, passing himself off as one of them in hopes of gaining their trust and any inside information. He assisted in discovering more than twenty-five tunnels, and his exceptional record was not tarnished very often. Not long before the October exchange, a group of inmates was working hard to do just that. These men were too healthy to be included in the forthcoming departure, so they decided to undertake their own.[69]

Sergeant Berry Benson, a sharpshooter and scout in McGowan's South Carolina Brigade, had attempted to escape by water from Point Lookout, but was recaptured and locked up in Washington's Old Capitol Prison. It did not take long for Benson to grow fidgety in that historic brick relic. However, while planning a break-out there in late July, he and 624 of his mates were moved to the Chemung Valley.[70] Even before entering Elmira Prison, Benson was contemplating ways to escape. As he walked up Water Street to the stockade, he spotted a large walnut tree with branches that stretched almost to the wall and thought that he might climb it and drop to the outside. Once inside, he entertained the notion of climbing out with a friend who was building a ladder with stolen lumber, but that too, was very perilous. He was also ready at one point to take another swim, a hazardous feat in itself, across Foster's murky pond to its edge, where he could sneak out under the fence. However, that plot was also aborted when prison officials hung kerosene lamps inside the pen, keeping it well lit for guards to see clearly within.[71]

Benson considered it his honorable duty to escape from prison and finally concluded that the most practical way to achieve this goal was by tunneling. In August, he led a group of men who started digging under the foundation of a barrack, but in a few days another contingent further along asked them to help dig underneath the second hospital ward. One night while digging, Benson overheard a comrade tell another man that if the authorities discovered this project, they would return to another tunnel, also underway beneath one of their tents. Benson only knew the speaker by appearance, but thought it would be wise to keep him in mind for the future. As their work continued, the inmates found that other prisoners had been tunneling beneath an adjoining ward. The race that commenced, between diggers under the first and second hospitals, did not result in a winner. By the time workers finished the earliest tunnel, under the first ward, almost everyone knew about it. This included Melvin Conklin and a squad of guards, who received the men as they emerged from the tunnel. Conklin had been with them every step of the way, but was instructed to let them continue so that all the perpetrators could be captured. The second tunnel was also discovered. The only consolation for its makers was that they were not caught, unlike their competitors, who were placed in solitary confinement. An entourage of guards armed with pickaxes destroyed both tunnels.[72]

Meanwhile, Benson looked for the man who had spoken about the backup tunnel. He searched for him at church services, meetings, and the market, and finally saw an individual who bore his likeness sitting on the bank of Foster's Pond. As Benson drew closer, he noticed the man discreetly dropping stones into the water, confirming his assumption. Realizing someone was watching, the prisoner stopped, but it was too late; Benson whispering "You'd better be careful; some fellow may see you and tell on you. . . . Here, I'll stand between you and the crowd. Empty your pockets." After a terse denial, the man conceded and slid his remaining stones slowly into the pond, stood up, and told Benson, "Walk with me a little way."[73] He introduced himself as Washington Traweek, a "Jeff Davis" artilleryman from Alabama. Traweek admitted that he was, in fact, tunneling with a party of men, and although he had taken an oath not to tell anyone, he claimed he should be excused since Benson had deduced it alone. Plus, said the Alabaman, "The boys will be glad enough to take you in. We need another hand."[74]

A meeting was convened at the second row of tents, third one in, along the northeastern stockade wall. Benson greeted his five new friends with handshakes and, quickly gaining their approval, placed his right hand on a Bible, swearing on his life not to betray them. Not all his comrades were present, but the party included John Fox Maull, J. P. Putegnat, Gilmer G. Jackson, and William H. Templin—like Traweek, all members of the Jeff Davis Artillery. Alabaman S. C. Malone, South Carolinian J. P. Scruggs, and Glenn Shelton of Mississippi were also participants. Only one more was inducted after Benson. The group astutely picked its members: one a ward sergeant, who kept them abreast of daily inspections, and another a sick sergeant, who provided extra food so they could maintain their health while digging.[75]

Next, Benson was shown the work they had completed so far. Digging from inside the tent was advantageous because the prisoners could work both day and night, keeping themselves and their tunnel well hidden. A sheet used as a bed was pulled away, a three-foot round sod cover camouflaged in the grass pulled off, and board slats used for support taken out, all of which revealed the hole. The entrance was about two and a half feet wide, opening to a shaft that ran six feet deep, then it turned horizontally toward the stockade wall, where a guard booth was chosen as a target. The prisoners had started on August 24, but by the time Benson was admitted, they had dug fifteen feet and had merely fifty more to go. They calculated their distance by sitting around the tent throwing stones at the fence, a sport permitted by the guards, who were intermittently posted twelve feet from the wall. Before one of their heaves, they had attached a string to a rock, hit the stockade, then reeled the string back—the measurement indicated sixty-eight feet.[76]

Tunneling was time consuming because of the length involved and because no traces could be left on the outside. To dispose of the soil, John Putegnat donated a spare shirt, which was cut apart and sewn into little sacks, each of which could carry almost a quart. The dirt sacks would be stuffed into the linings and pockets of coats and pants then emptied into Foster's Pond.[77] Large rocks were hard to remove, as well, but were taken out at night and reburied elsewhere or sunk in the pond. Stones were the easiest to discard; they could be concealed in pockets and tossed away in various places, under prison buildings, and in the ubiquitous rat holes. Benson wrote, "There was no such lavish expenditure in ammunition amongst other hunters as with us." Frequently, there was no quarry at all. Said Benson: "In the dusk an imaginary one might be chased with cries of, 'Here he goes—Kill him!' and a terrific bombardment of stones. Outsiders coming up to join the chase never guessed that there was no rat, but thought simply that he had got away."[78]

The hardest part of the prisoners' task was the actual excavation, digging implements being restricted to knives and bare hands. Daily, the grass cover was taken off and the planks withdrawn. A watchman posted outside the door stopped others from entering, supposedly because a tent mate was washing or changing. To avoid soiled clothing, the workers reversed their apparel before lowering themselves into the shaft. Crawling through the mouth, they found an opening that gradually tapered until only a single body could squeeze through; so tight was the hole that the diggers had to propel themselves with their elbows and toes. Reaching the end in that confined position, air decreasing and sitting in the dark, one picked away at the hard dirt and clay with a knife.[79] Benson, considered the most productive tunneler aside from Traweek, wrote, "In less than a minute, you were panting like a dog—for air. A minute was enough to give one of the most violent, racking headache, and you knew perfectly well in entering the tunnel that you had this to expect." John Maull vomited so much from impure air and lack of oxygen that he could not perform any digging, so he tended to other jobs.[80]

A second man accompanied the lead digger for assistance. After dirt piled up, it was pulled back to the partner, who scooped it up with both arms and moved backward to the mouth of the tunnel to put it in bags. Both jobs were extremely rigorous, so shifts were regulated. One digger remembered—"When the man at the end could stand the suffocation no longer, his head seeming to about burst with pain, his tongue thrust out, breathing fast to keep his blood supplied with the poisoned air, he called to the man behind him to 'back out,' and both backed to the shaft, and a fresh couple went in."[81]

In the second week of September, its work progressing finely, the tunneling party had a scare. Leaving the tent one day, Traweek was confronted by five guards, who told him to report at headquarters. There, Major Colt received him with "Good morning, my young tunneler, they tell me you are engaged in tunneling."[82] The Alabaman played dumb, but Colt was adamant in finding out where it was and who was helping. The indefatigable Melvin Conklin, who had found Traweek's name on a slip of paper under the second hospital, had tipped off Colt. However, Traweek had no idea Colt was looking for participants in the bumbled venture. Refusing to speak, Traweek was placed in a sweat-box, a pressure device much like a straight jacket that captors could crank to momentarily squeeze the wind out of the victim.[83] When Traweek was brought before Colt again to be questioned, he saved enough of his breath to tell his commandant that he would "see him in hell" before admitting anything.[84] The major promptly had him thrown into the guardhouse, an old barracks constructed with cells for solitary confinement. The prisoners' tunneling project remained intact, but they had lost one of their first members.[85]

With the loss of Traweek, Benson assumed the role of leader through the rest of September. As the tunnel lengthened, excavation grew harder, but the South Carolinian was ripe with new ideas for its steady advancement. He felt that raking the dirt to the mouth entailed too much work, so he recommended using a box with long cords on both sides that could be pulled back and forth from each end. When the excavator filled the box at the front, he knocked on its side and the cargo was slowly pulled back, emptied, then retrieved. The system spared much time and effort. Benson's other contribution was even more significant, but came by accident.[86]

The men became worried when they measured the length of the tunnel with their string. They figured that their position should have been about three feet from the fence, but the sound of guards walking above still seemed far away. When the group estimated the tunnel's end using their own noises overhead, they discovered it was not in line with the guard booth. Benson realized he could find the exact location by running a hole to the top. He secured a ramrod, which was heated then pushed through the ceiling. Members on the surface pretended to be conversing in the area they expected the rod to come up, and when the tip broke through the sod one of them placed his foot on the tip, pushed it back down, and marked the spot with stones. The tunnelers were shocked to find that their work had veered to the right, at least ten feet from the booth. The bend, Benson deduced, had developed because all the diggers were right-handed. Because they had to lean on their left sides to dig, they had naturally created the unintentional curve. Better news would develop from their investigation. With an opening already on the surface, they decided fresh air could be admitted through the small hole. Outside, they expanded the hole to about an inch and a half and covered it with a stone; underneath, they enlarged the tunnel into a chamber that allowed the air to circulate. Their "Ventilator" was opened freely at night with no fear of detection, and during the day, when the stone was removed, a few members sat by, ostensibly relaxing, but really allowing fresh air to reach their mates below.[87]

The men compensated for their mistake and again headed straight for the fence. By this time, they worked in unison, at their best. One man dug and filled up the box while another stayed at the widened ventilator chamber making sure each load ran smoothly to a third worker, who received it. Another man guarded the door, while dirt removers carried away the excess. Moreover, the diggers were furnished with additional manpower. Traweek apologized for swearing at Major Colt, who decided his three-week ordeal in the guardhouse was long enough, but would not let him leave without a little advice: "My lad, you were too hasty. If you had been more cautious and taken more time, you would have made your escape. Next time don't be so hasty and you may get out."[88] Although he never admitted it to the major, Traweek used those departing words for encouragement and returned to the tent. He brought with him his cellmate in the guardhouse, Virginian John W. Crawford, the final member of the tunneling party.[89]

On October 5, diggers began to hear the footsteps of guards overhead. The string measure verified that they were almost at the wall. With mounting enthusiasm, the workers planned the exodus for the following night, at around 10:00. Seeing the top of a barn north of the pen, they decided to meet there and then leave in pairs. They began to assemble survival kits, jackknives, matches, ropes, and whatever else they could carry to aid them on their journey. In the market, Benson was even able to purchase a pocket compass that sold for thirty cents. On that Thursday, Benson and Traweek, the quickest diggers, were paired together for the final stage of excavation. Because the men would soon be on their way, the remaining soil would be left in the tent. However, before they got too far ahead of themselves, unforeseen delays cropped up.[90]

Digging had progressed far beyond the ventilator chamber. Traweek and Benson, trying to stave off suffocation, had to take short shifts, one man digging, the other inhaling deep breaths at the ventilator until replacements came. One time, in the process of trading places at the air chamber, the men became lodged against each other. Benson tried to thrust his way up and Traweek tried to push himself down, but they were stuck. It took awhile, but they wrestled themselves free, Benson heading to the front, and Traweek left behind to rest. During Traweek's next shift, he came in contact with a large rock that jutted from the ceiling and hesitated to move it for fear of disturbing the surface. When Benson took his turn, he struggled with it and was eventually able to move the rock without harm. By that time, however, their planned breakout hour had passed and they were moving into Friday morning. Finally, they hit a more promising barrier: a sunken fence post. Benson easily burrowed around it and continued until far enough beyond the wall. They then dug upward, but instead of breaking through, they left a thin crust that would give way with a thrust. Both men returned to the tent to tell the others they were ready.[91]

Anxious to leave, they entered the tunnel's mouth in short intervals. Traweek led the way, with Crawford as his companion. At the end of the tunnel, Traweek gave one good push, and the dirt roof came crashing down, followed by a gust of wind. The opening was directly under the sentinel's walk, and before Traweek peeked his head through a cry came from the guard above—"Half past three o'clock and all is well." Indeed, it was for the tunnelers, as Traweek climbed out of the hole and walked across Water Street toward the barn. Crawford waited, then raised himself up and followed suit. Next was the queasy John Fox Maull. He had been using Crawford's feet as a pillow to ease a wrenching headache, but had temporarily passed out from lack of fresh air until awakened by a cool breeze, his pillow gone and companions behind unaware of the delay. As Maull popped out, he heard "Four o'clock and all is well," then belatedly started for the barn only to find that his predecessors had already gone. Scruggs, the sick sergeant, was next, but with the delay, he decided to make for the mountains. Malone and Putegnat stayed together after they exited, and they, too, felt it was too late for the barn. So instead they headed northeast. In Auburn, they were employed as machinists until they saved enough money to travel home comfortably.[92]

Most of the escapees preferred not to chance an extended stay up North and made for the Pennsylvania mountains and the Potomac River. Benson, the seventh man, was concerned with a few guards he saw huddled around a fire as he crawled out. He veiled himself under the sentinel's platform at the northeast corner of the stockade then walked across Water Street. He listened for the musket fire, which would have sent a minie ball through his back, but the shot never came. However, he did have quite a scare when he ran through a backyard into a garden and was charged by a large, and certainly loyal, watchdog. Benson hopped over a fence and raced toward the highlands, traveling to the South alone, as did the eighth tunneler, Glenn Shelton. By this time, it was getting light. John Maull, leaving the barn, saw the final two party members, Gilmer Jackson and William Templin, heading in his direction. They immediately went west, then turned to cross the Chemung and hiked up the nearby mountains. From their vantage point they witnessed the great commotion caused by their absence.

As guard patrols were deployed and communities near and far alerted, the Confederates made their way through the forests of Pennsylvania.[93] They slept in the woods and in barns—guests of some, chased by others—stealing fruit, vegetables, and poultry from farms and orchards. Walking along railroad tracks and hopping trains, they passed through hamlets such as Canton and larger cities like Williamsport. There, the southerly descent of the Susque-hanna showed them the way and a few borrowed skiffs eased the passage. After reaching the outskirts of Harrisburg, then traveling into south-central Pennsylvania, they crossed over the Mason-Dixon Line, into border state Maryland and beyond. Amazingly, all ten men reached their own lines.[94]

This escape was the largest mass break in Elmira Prison history, and the impressive accomplishment deserved commendation. The group's leader, Washington Traweek, made sure the escapees received recognition from at least one person. Traweek could not resist sending Major Colt a letter from Richmond just to let him know they had made it home safely. Furthermore, the Alabaman expressed appreciation not only for the major's valuable advice, but also for his "kind care and attention while stopping at his 'hotel' in Elmira."[95]

10

Billy Yank as Prison Keeper

The majority of escape attempts led not to freedom, but rather to an escorted walk to the guardhouse. The building, which measured forty-five-by-eighty-by-twelve feet, was divided into cells for solitary confinement. When an offender was taken inside, he was brought down the row of cells and usually imprisoned alone. After the door slammed shut, it was locked, the diamond window closed, and there one remained for hours, days, and perhaps weeks, isolated in the dark. Meals were bland, restricted to soup and bread.[1] Elmira inmates dubbed the cells the "dungeon," but Wilbur Grambling's two day "trial" in the guardhouse was long enough for him to think of another name: a "pretty lousy hole."[2] Tunnelers occupied many cells. Empathetic guards referred to them as the "Engineer Corps," not resenting them as much as those jailed for stealing, fighting, and disobeying prison rules.[3]

Elmira's prison keepers doled out additional forms of punishment for various infractions. The barrel shirt, a heavy vessel with the top and bottom lids removed, was regularly used. Slipped over the head and arms, the barrel lay uncomfortably on the shoulders, limiting movement of the upper torso. A sign was attached to the barrel that announced the crime to everyone, perhaps a worse punishment than the weighty drum itself, since the sign could evoke disdain from the entire community. An armed sentinel paraded those dressed in the barrel shirt two hours every morning and afternoon. "I am a liar," "liar no. 1," "liar no. 2," "liar no. 3," "I am a thief," "stole a cat," and "Dog Eater," were all common epithets attached to those punished long after their humiliating walks.[4] A Confederate who witnessed the humiliation wrote that one prisoner labeled with "'I stole my messmate's rations,' was hissed all around the camp; and deservedly so, because a man who would steal from his messmates in prison deserved the most severe punishment; while the ones who carried the placard 'Dog Eater' had the sympathies of the entire camp, because many of them would have enjoyed a piece of the fresh meat."[5]

Other offenses, such as swearing, drinking alcohol, or attacking those in authority, met harsher penalties. A device more feared than the barrel shirt was appropriately termed "the sweatbox." The long wooden box was about seven feet tall, twenty inches wide, and one foot deep. It stood upright, outside of headquarters, as a constant reminder to the Southerners. When an offender was put inside, the door was shut by a cranking device that made movement not only impossible, but also unbearable as the victim sweated and lost his breath from its tight grip.[6] After Washington Traweek experienced its hold, he wrote: "They claimed to have kept me there three quarters of a minute, but it seemed to me to be three hours and a half."[7] Bucking and gagging could be even more excruciating. The former involved binding a victim to a horizontal rack, like a sawhorse, by the hands and legs. The latter punishment was particularly distressing to one drunk inmate unwilling to reveal his supplier.[8] A wood block was lodged in his mouth, and cords attached to the ends were pulled back and tied around his head so hard "that incisions, or ruptures, were made at the corners of his mouth."[9] Being tied up by the thumbs was another harrowing experience. Each thumb was tied with a separate cord, both of which were then joined to a rope thrown over a tree branch or joist. The rope was then pulled up to raise the arms high above the head until the man was almost off the floor. The captors left him strapped in that precarious position while the thumbs supported his body weight.[10] One Tennessean wrote that "there is no way to relieve the pressure. If he tries to relieve the thumbs, the toes get it; and if the toes are relieved, the thumbs are in trouble." The balancing act stopped either when the victim fainted from pain, or his captors ordered him cut down.[11]

Some of the officers were not reluctant to execute their cruel justice. Although most of the higher-ranking prison camp authorities were well liked, a few subordinates were not.[12] "There was one Major Beall, who I believe, was the meanest man I ever knew," alleged G. T. Taylor.[13] Samuel W. Beall, 1st Veteran Reserve Corps, whom prisoners nicknamed "old peg leg" due to a physical disability, was undoubtedly called worse.[14] As second in command to Commandant Moore, Beall periodically displayed cruelty during his supervisor's absence. Just after Miles Sherrill entered the stockade, wrote Sherrill, "Major Beall, greeted us with the most bitter oaths that I ever heard. He swore that he was going to send us out and have us shot; said he had no room for us, and that we (meaning the Confederate soldiers) had no mercy on their colored soldiers or prisoners."[15] The major, wrote another inmate, "was a source of great trouble and annoyance to the prisoners. He would often visit the camp at midnight in freezing weather, and require the sergeants of the wards to form the men in line, to answer 'roll call.'"[16] The cantankerous and verbally abusive Beall, a veritable insomniac to prisoners, hobbled through camp directing guards to crush mud chimneys or confiscate other useful items, and personally assisted with plundering during his brief military rule.[17]

"Another rarity of the pen," wrote Anthony Keiley, was Lt. John McConnell of the 104th New York Volunteers, "a queer compound of good-nature and brutality. To some of us he was uniformly polite, but he had his pistol out on any occasion when dealing with the majority of 'Johnnies,' and would fly into a passion over the merest nothing."[18] Keiley added: "One Lieutenant R. kept McC. in countenance by following closely his example." His protégé was the diminutive yet devout Lieutenant Richmond. Keiley referred to him as a combination "of fice and weasel, and having charge of the cleaning up of the camp, has abundant opportunities to bully and insult, but being, fortunately, very far short of grenadier size, he does not use his boot or fist as freely as his great exemplar."[19] R. B. Ewan agreed: "Lieutenant Richmond was a disagreeable character who had charge of a gang of prisoners who were digging a drainage trench from the pond to the river. Sometimes the idle prisoners would step on this ditch. If the Lieutenant saw it he would make the prisoners jump back and forth, fast and slow, until his soured nature was satisfied."[20] McConnell was successful in his tutelage; he, too, ordered the sadistic exercise, until one prisoner finally "fell from exhaustion." Anthony Keiley surmised that captives were not "safe from either of them, who however accidentally and innocently, fell in their way, physically or metaphorically."[21]

Elmira prison keepers might go too far in their physical abuse. Just as feared as the cruelty of Lieutenants McConnell and Richmond, was that of Capt. J. H. Borden, 86th Pennsylvania. Characterized as "a fair-haired, light-moustached, Saxon-faced 'Yank,'" he was also personified as the "essence of brutality."[22] A defiant prisoner unwilling to open his mouth to be gagged was causing a stir at the pen, so Borden, serving as officer of the guard, took charge of the situation. He picked up a wooden billet, and with one brisk swing he not only broke the troublemaker's will, but also knocked two teeth out of his bloodied mouth.[23]

Despite these exceptions, prison camp officers were considered gentlemen and behaved that way. The example started at the top with Major Colt and

Lieutenant Colonel Moore, who both displayed genuine acts of compassion and occasionally used their discretion to bend prison rules. During a cold spell, a number of Southerners were caught stealing extra sticks from the wood pile. When they were brought before Major Colt, the commandant stated, "Now haven't I got a nice lot of wood thieves?" A few responded, "Oh, no, Major, we only flanked it," to which Colt answered, "You stole it, you rascals, and the next time you are brought up for stealing I will cut your ears off." They smiled back at their commandant, realizing that he would not punish them under the extreme conditions, and he ordered their release.[24] Stephen Moore demonstrated similar generosity. Two Virginia ladies made the long trip to Elmira, where they ended in Moore's office, one pleading to see her father, the other begging for her husband. It was explained to them that they were not allowed inside without a pass from the commissary general of prisoners. Moore, however, had been touched by their perseverance, especially when their eyes filled with tears, and he devised another arrangement. He told the daughter and wife to sit by his window and rest, adding, "You might see someone you know, perhaps, as there will soon be a detail of prisoners in front of the office to saw wood." After having the kin located, Moore added both men to the detail and the women were allowed a moment with them.[25]

Both officers tried to instill such respect in their subordinates. A member of the 10th Virginia believed that "the Majority of the officers and many of the guards at Elmira were good examples of true manhood." Prisoner James Ford felt that "a few of the petty officers evinced a disposition to be overbearing and tyrannical; not as kindly spoken and courteous as the majority were wont to be."[26] One of Colt's adjutants, Capt. Charles Barton, was described as a "smart and rather consequential young gentleman, as adjutant's are wont to be, . . . but upon the whole, Barton was a good fellow, notwithstanding he considered Abe Lincoln a Chesterfield, and accounted Grant . . . in about equal proportions, of King Solomon and Alexander the Great."[27] Captain R. R. R. Dumars, 161st New York Volunteers, was informal enough with prisoners that they called him not by his initials, but referred jokingly to him as "Captain Radway's Ready Relief."[28] Captain Whiton, a "cute, active ex-bank officer, who supervised the cookhouse," was the recipient of a formal thank you letter endorsed by twenty-two prisoners: "While differing most essentially upon points of political interest you do not forget—though the difference is so great—that there are grounds upon which we can meet and unite without a compromise. Your generosity now, as on many other instances, can only incite us to like deeds of kindness, when fortune so favors us that we may be in a condition to reciprocate."[29] Similarly, prisoners kindly remembered Capt. Benjamin Munger, who continuously tried to upgrade living conditions through his inspection reports: "Wherever he is, and whatever he does," wrote an old inmate, "Captain Ben Munger has the good-will of every prisoner who ever drew rations at Barracks No. 3, on the banks of the Chemung."[30]

The manpower required to maintain the prison camp had a tremendous effect throughout the Chemung Valley. Union personnel numbered in the thousands, which combined with Southerners already there, doubled the small city's population. Daily, some forty officers and more than three hundred enlisted men were required to keep watch inside and outside the pen in five separate squads. A "main gate" detail assigned to the entrance had two lieutenants, two sergeants, six corporals and seventy-five privates. The "rear guard" consisted of similar numbers, whereas the "camp guard" included one lieutenant, two sergeants, three corporals, and more than fifty privates. An "outside patrol" and "reserve picket" each had a captain and lieutenant, four sergeants, six corporals, and about ninety privates. Elmira prison keepers were detailed in twenty-four-hour shifts, divided into reliefs usually two hours on duty and four hours off.[31]

Inside the stockade, guards were posted at intervals near the twelve-foot wall. Due to their presence, no structural boundary existed to warn Rebels they were too close to the fence. As a general rule, prisoners could not pass a guard's beat or go any nearer than six feet from the facade. The same could be said for outside the fence, and if anyone went too near the stockade he risked being shot. On the walkway above, guards were positioned about forty feet apart. In foul weather, they went into their sentry booths, staying dry while keeping close watch through the portholes on either side. From 9:00 P.M., the scheduled time for taps or lights out, each guard was required to announce every half-hour his position number, the time, and an "all is well," in succession around the entire wall until his voice faded into the night.[32]

Guards left differing recollections concerning their tours of duty. Joseph Requa of the 54th New York National Guard stated "it was not very hard for [when] I was on patrol outside the fence all I had to do was lay around all day at the guard station and at night walk 2 hours and lay around on the ground and then walk again." He was more pleased with his new post at headquarters because, as he told his wife, "they pick out the best looking soldiers for headquarter guard."[33] In comparison, a Union private complained that "the long period of twenty-four hours—which is often twenty-six by the delay in the mounting of the guard—had to be spent amid those miserably cold storms with which we have been visited for some time, while the Johnnies were snugly stowed away under cover." Furthermore, he assured the reader, even though the men were allotted four hours off during their tour, "little rest could be had while the heavens are discharging floods of rain."[34] Other guards complained of the monotonous watches and the hardships they faced because of the elements. Men were susceptible to colds, flu, and fever, while ailments typical of camp life, such as dysentery and diarrhea, were also common. Medical officers were attached to the regiments so they could treat and relieve individual complaints.[35]

Some sentries believed that their living conditions at Camp Chemung were similar to those of men confined in Barracks Number 3. One guard protested that the shelter, food, and clothing given to Southerners were comparable, if not better than his; "our Government takes far too good care of them."[36] Members of the 19th Veterans Reserve Corps objected that "they [were] not receiving their just rights and dues." They griped over lack of fuel and straw, and "even in that land of plenty they receive no vegetables, and [complained] that by some strange process of reasoning the War Department has decided that they do not need as much food as men in the field."[37] Conversely, seasoned veterans might remind their peers how easy they had it, compared to both captives and men at the front. A 4th U.S. Artilleryman wrote, "Prisoners, it was alleged, were allowed the same rations, excepting coffee and sugar, that their guards received. They did not get it."[38] A Pennsylvania soldier wrote that Elmira "is a fine city and our duties here will not be attended with all the dangers and exposures incident to those of the front."[39] A Rochester journalist reported that the guards' "food is well prepared as we know from inspection. . . . There is nothing wanting from for the health or comfort of the men here encamped that can be supplied, unless it is shelter for those on guard duty from the heavy dews at night, which fall upon them like a shower, saturating their clothing."[40] Apparently, some soldiers were more tired of army life than of any real deprivations.

When the prison commissary afforded lumber and approved funding, Quartermaster Elwell built up Camp Chemung with better facilities as the new year progressed.[41] By spring 1865, the *Elmira Daily Advertiser* called the camp a "little suburb to the city."[42] It eventually consisted of guard barracks, officer quarters, administrative buildings, mess halls, kitchens, hospitals, a wash house, privies, guardhouses, a carpenter's shop, a pay office, a wood office, and stables.[43]

Most guards stationed at Camp Chemung were unfit for duty at the front. Many of them came from what had been termed the "Invalid Corps," men who had sustained injuries, but still wanted to serve their country. By the time prison guards were needed in the valley, they had earned themselves the more complimentary title of "Veterans Reserve Corps." At Elmira, the 1st, 16th, and 19th Veterans Reserve Corps were all represented.[44] Another group initially restricted from fighting was African-American soldiers, who acted as prison keepers to the chagrin of more than one Southerner.[45] Their tours of duty were kept to a minimum, but not few enough for one Georgian captive who alleged that they were actually freed slaves purposely sent to Elmira so they could "guard their former masters."[46] No matter to one African-American sentinel, whose duty at the prison made him feel, along with some Confederates, that he was "on the upper rail now."[47]

The New York National Guard and the state militia contributed men to serve as guards, and as prisoners increased in Elmira, so did militiamen. However, these men were not considered regulars and were defamed as "Governor Seymour's pets."[48] Nevertheless, they served in the valley when no one else was available. They were composed of the A and B Batteries of the Rochester Union Grays Artillery; the Dewitt and Dumont Guards, the 50th New York National Guard from Ithaca; the 54th from Rochester; the 56th from Brooklyn; the 58th of Mount Morris; the 77th from New York City; the 98th from Ulster County; and the 99th and 102d, both from New York City. U.S. regular troops were also called into service at Barracks Number 3, including Battery A of the 4th U.S. Artillery, plus companies of the 2d, 12th, and 14th U.S. Infantry.[49] By numbers, most guards were Veterans Reserve Corps members or state militiamen, followed by regulars. Officers were usually recovering from wounds. City patrols included men from Camp Chemung, whereas soldiers stationed at Barracks Number 1, like Pennsylvania Bucktail regiments who trained recruits, were also required to guard prisoners and regularly escorted them for exchange.[50]

The provisional guard could be called out at a moment's notice, as on the night of October 13, six days after the infamous tunnel escape. Around 11:00 P.M., the beat of drums that sounded off an apparent emergency at the pen awakened the camp. Men quickly rose, grabbed their muskets, and fell into ranks. Officers had their men march double quick to the main gate, where they were met by regiments in the outlying grounds in fifteen minutes flat, all ready for a surprise mass escape. The men soon realized that the alarm was only a practice drill, but they continued through their movements, discharging guns and cannon so that at least the captives realized they were prepared to meet them.[51]

Drill became part of the prison keeper's daily life at Camp Chemung. Dress parades were held regularly, and for special events military reviews moved to Elmira's public streets. Spectators came from miles to see their home guards in action, one reporter from Rochester reminding "friends anticipating a visit here, bear in mind to stop at the 'City Hotel,' from which they will find a 'buss' in waiting to convey them to and from the camp."[52] The *Elmira Daily Advertiser* reported, "Our streets are still thronged with the military, strangers, and citizens. The crowd if anything, increases, the stir and business everywhere manifested is equal to a city quadruple our size. The constant incoming of soldiers to our rendezvous draws a large number of their friends and acquaintances from a distance."[53] At Camp Chemung, observers watched units drill at the command of men on horseback, who raised dust during their evolutions and wheelings and tried to maintain disciplined lines, their muskets pointed high with bayonets affixed. Their steps did not always conform to the music of regimental bands, but "vacant coat sleeves, a halting walk and scars and wounds revealed the honorable services of many."[54]

With the exception of drill and performance, guards had much time to spare. Exclusively for officers, hops and dances were organized almost weekly. Elmira's Ladies Hospital Aid Society sponsored many, and tickets sold at a dollar per person, each event raising hundreds of dollars. Hotel dining rooms or officer mess rooms and barracks at Camp Chemung were converted into gala dance halls.[55] These evenings epitomized the romanticism of the Civil War, making memorable evening for the officers and, as the *Elmira Daily Advertiser* judged, "a large representation of Elmira's beautiful daughters."[56] Patriotic flags, regimental banners, and ornamental sabers hung on walls and long tables held a variety of meats, breads, cakes, and coffee. Guests also enjoyed a delicacy no festive setting would be without. As one attendee wrote: "Oysters were supplied in unstinted measure to all the lovers of that favorite bivalve."[57] Musical tastes favored quicksteps and reels and waltzes as the night wore on.[58] Finally, recalled a participant, "the tables were cleared and the long room was prepared for the mazy dance, in which gay uniforms and female loveliness mingled with great zest and pleasure up to a late hour."[59]

Enlisted soldiers had to amuse themselves with different types of pastimes. Prison guards played baseball. Camp Chemung had a field where teams played exciting games on Saturdays in front of enthusiastic crowds. Friendly rivalries developed between some of the regiments, the most significant between the 54th Rochester and 56th Brooklyn. On September 3, one of their matchups turned out to be a late summer classic, except for the pitching. Bets sided with the more athletic Brooklyn team, which the odds favored at two to one. However, that day the Rochester shortstop hit safely in all four at bats, which drove in four runs and led his club to a thirteen to twelve victory.[60]

Like the Confederates they guarded, Union men spent much of their time in camp writing letters. They asked for fruits, vegetables, and when the weather got cold, boots, shirts, and gloves.[61] Other times they wrote to comfort loved ones. "My Dear Mary little Mary, Monday night 9:00 and all is well. I thought I would write a little. We have got our bed ready but I long so much for the time when I can go to bed with your arm around my neck. . . . I can scarcely know how to wait until our time is out. I could not go to bed without writing you or thinking I want to see you so much."[62] Guards were permitted furloughs for short visits home. An officer wrote his wife, "Tell Clara Papa will come to see her before long. I think that I can obtain a 7 day leave . . . keep up your courage all will be well."[63] In the meantime, soldiers had their pictures taken at photograph studios, mailing their likenesses home to make up for their absences.[64]

Many guards used their army pay to buy additional food and clothing, which could be purchased at the Demorest sutlery a business that never held the same monopoly as Demorest's shop inside the prison. Soldiers could purchase goods in the free market in the city. They brought back fruits, vegetables, meats, cheeses, sugar, and butter, and pooled their money to accommodate themselves better in camp. Seasonal dishes were available, camp cooks getting pumpkins in October for pies they sold at twenty cents apiece. Foraging on their own made products cheaper for soldiers.[65] The New York City regiments had quite a reputation for not respecting the property of Chemung Valley's farmers, stealing whatever food they could pick for themselves. Remarking on the recent harvest, a state census enumerator complained, "Orchards, Gardens and Poultry yards were mostly Script by Governor Seymours Militia 'Friends' Sent from New York and Brooklyn to guard the Reb Prisoners confined here—we hope we may never see them here again."[66]

Some soldiers set an example to follow while stationed at Elmira, particularly William Perry of the 149th Pennsylvania. The infantryman was regularly rewarded with passes to go downtown. "Came off guard this morning at nine o'clock, received a pass and attended church in the city. . . . [F]ound the congregation remaining seated but soon saw it was a Methodist meeting after notwithstanding."[67] The pious Perry usually went to Sunday school, as well as prayer and temperance meetings.[68] His conduct was, as he said himself, atypical.

"It is quite a relief to be here but I sometimes almost wish we had been left at the front when I witness the looseness of character and the baseness of many of our men now that access to liquor and other sources of evil is had. Those with whom we have associated with prove to be drunken sots or miserable wreckless characters in many cases bringing reproach on themselves and us."[69]

If William Perry had an opposite, he was John Holland, whose duties included guarding Southerners after the war ended, while they were being discharged to go home. Vices were even more readily available to him since discipline became very lax as the camps were broken up.[70] After his first day stationed at Barracks Number 3, he "got up feeling all Hunk a dory. . . . I went to the brewery drank Beer until 9." However, the next morning, he "got up with a severe Head ache and felt about half sick went on and got a drink of bitters was detailed for guard."[71] Holland's diary entries were habitually laden with comments like "was on a bender the night before," "Came back to town and got on a Bum with several of the Boys and Bumed all afternoon . . . went to bed about half gone."[72] Other problems soon surfaced: "Elmira N.Y. Bks 3. Was relieved of guard at 8. Went to town and got on a drunk. 3 P.M. was paid two months Pay and one installment total was sixty five dollars & 30 cents. Went to town and got hack and went to Horse Head on a spree. Put up at a hotel for the night. Had a great time with a heap of fun."[73] Possibly, the repercussions of this fun-filled evening did more to Holland than land him in the guardhouse for leaving camp. A week after his "spree" he entered in his diary "the 'gonhera' began to Break Out." Soon, Holland was writing, "did not feel well all day was troubled with the 'Gona,'" which left him "rather unwell . . . severe pains in Back & Groins." At the end of his diary Holland made another troubling admission: "Was Flat Broke and went to debt for Whiskey for the first time in four years."[74]

The number of guards arrested for being drunk on and off duty might have left some observers wondering how officials kept escapes to a minimum. William Barr of the 19th Veteran Reserve Corps, posted as a sentry inside the pen, was "such in a state of intoxication as to render him incapable of performing his duty." Private William Cunningham was found guilty of the same offense, and both men lost $6 pay per month for the next half year.[75] Jesse Reynolds, a private in Company A of the 1st Veterans Reserve Corps, as stated in the military court proceedings, "having been regularly detailed as a member of the guard over rebel prisoners, did become so drunk that he was unfit and unable to perform his duty." Worse, he left his post without permission, so officials also charged him with "absence without leave." Reynolds was found guilty and sentenced to a twenty-dollar fine, confined in the guardhouse for a month, and required to carry the barrel shirt for four hours each day.[76]

Some guards were also quite reckless off duty. Such was the case with Cyrenus Ross of Co. H, 19th Volunteer Reserve Corps, who was supposed to be resting at his quarters in Camp Chemung preparing for guard watch the next morning. Instead, on December 6, 1864, around 10:00 P.M., the inebriated private prematurely concluded a drinking binge by stopping at the saloon of L. B. Buel. As he acquainted himself with some local patrons, Ross told them "every citizen is a damned scoundrel," and furthermore, he would "show them," by proceeding to draw his revolver. Fortunately for Ross, and for the civilian targets who dove for cover while he scattered shots around the bar, he was so intoxicated he missed everyone. Ross was apprehended and taken to the officer of the guard, who ordered him to retire for the night so he could be ready for service the next day. However, Ross replied, "I will be damned if I do any more duty, that god damned Lieutenant of mine has turned me over to the civil authorities." Drunkenness, disobedience to an officer, and absence from camp and duty, all led to the greatest dishonor of any prison keeper. In front of his peers, the officer of the guard stripped Ross of his uniform, shaved his head, and drummed him out of Camp Chemung.[77]

Proprietors of local establishments put up with soldiers' conduct in return for their business. Going into town for many men was their most exciting experience at Elmira. Gambling parlors were filled. There they could play card games and bagatelle, something similar to billiards.[78] Restaurants offered men opportunities to enjoy meals other than those prepared on an open fire. Sullivan's eatery on Water Street was such a place, its owner attempting to "feed all the farmers and soldiers in the country."[79] Hotels, like the Hemlock, Delavan, and Brainard also served food, as did boarding houses.[80] Guards attended theaters, playhouses, and auditoriums, taking in plays, minstrels, and circus acts. Joseph Requa and Dan Norton of the 58th Rochester, for example, were "going down town this evening to the theatre."[81] One evening John Holland was in rare form; instead of drinking his night away he remained sober and "went to town to see the Tight Rope performance," then he walked "to 'Ely Hall' to see the 'Zouave' Troupe 'Perform' which was a very good performance." Holland was more critical of the Bishop and Florence minstrels, "a perfect Humbug," and a rendition of Cross of Gold, "a Perfect farce."[82] As Holland proved, the guards paid many visits to Elmira's watering holes. Buell's, Nolte's, Quin's, Ready's, Franklin's, and Arbours' saloons offered wine, whiskey, and beer.[83] The Cold Springs Brewery, a large three-story facility, was the main supplier of lager, which sold at $11 a keg. The brewery produced "200 to 300 barrels of ale, all of which has found immediate sale at home, and the demand is greater than the firm can yet supply."[84]

For many entrepreneurs, proximity to Camp Chemung was paramount for starting a business in food and beverage. A row of temporary establishments was built on the same side as the prison, down Water Street, so they could entice military customers by an easy walk. The *Elmira Daily Advertiser* called the businesses "landmarks of a large, brisk and thrifty trade with soldiers. . . . Many of their owners and occupants have made small fortunes," the paper continued, and "it is astonishing to what extent the presence of so much military has given rise to so many mushroom accommodations by way of saloons and eating houses. The sum of money spent upon them must have been very large; for aside from the dry and rather monotonous rations dealt out to soldiers, these afforded them the means, as long as the monthly pay lasted, of gratifying their taste in delicacies and tit-bits, at a good round profit."[85] Some of these merchants, according to the *Elmira Daily Advertiser*, conducted "business honorably to a host of customers, others dishonorably and demoralizing to all." Notwithstanding, the local press concluded, "They have helped besides to make up and supply the little community, that has grown up around Camp Chemung—They have aided in building up this pleasant little suburb to the city."[86]

An older profession also flourished in the city. The presence of drafted men at Barracks Number 1 and prison guards at Number 3 provided ample opportunities for women to find work in Elmira, which was dubbed the "Queen City" for a predominance of pretty ladies. Some of these ladies, apparently, fell from grace.[87] Anthony Keiley perhaps overstated this fact in his diary: "More than one of the officers of the post assured me that there were one thousand prostitutes in Elmira, . . . and from more than one surgeon I heard statements of the proportion of their soldiers who suffered from venereal taint, which surpassed any thing in the recorded military statistic of the world."[88] Exact figures can never be known, but the long list of women arrested for prostitution was tabulated in the city's recorders court. Lena McCoy, Rosanna Salmon, Mary Steele, and Rebecca Blaisdell were some of the madams who ran houses of ill repute. Business was very good and fines fairly low, some violators being penalized as little as twenty-five dollars for operating a "disorderly house."[89] Elmira's patrol guard made regular stops at these institutions, including that of Joseph Sherwood, whose residence was "looked upon as a notorious haunt for soldiers running around." One night culminated in the proprietor not letting the patrol guard inside his house to collect some military patrons, and Sherwood fired a weapon on the guards, only to be slightly wounded himself in return.[90] Patrick Quin, a saloon keeper near Barracks Number 3, did not mind these perils, and expanded his business by having rooms used for additional purposes. He, too, was charged with running a "bawdy house."[91]

Whether women worked independently or for an employer, among the various risks that came with the job was that of being arrested. Fanny Havens, Mary Preston, Jenny Hogan, Eugenie Doty, Amanda Guiles, Mary Hayes, Frances Hill, and Jenny Barnes were just some of the prostitutes who found themselves in the Chemung County jail. In the spring of 1865, the *Elmira Daily Advertiser* commented, "The police are rapidly ridding the city of loose women. They will hardly be able to stay here unless they stay in jail."[92] However, the jail could not hold all the "disorderly characters, which infest the town." Later in the spring the paper stated "the jail is overflowing and it is absolutely needful to clear the present occupants out, that there may be room for more."[93] Repeat offenders were moved, and the "risqué" Phoebe LeJoy, Hattie Forshay, Mary Provoe, Anna Lysch, Elizabeth Preston, Sara Seward, and Kitty Langdon were all sent to the Rochester Penitentiary for four months because they were continually caught for prostitution.[94]

Other societal nuisances, such as fighting or vandalism, also kept the provost guard busy. Not long after the August buildup in guard force, problems became quite apparent. At the end of the month, the *Elmira Daily Advertiser* reported a "disturbance" that took place near the railroad crossing on Water Street between soldiers of the 22d Veterans Reserve Corps who had escorted prisoners from Washington and troops of 102d New York National Guard.[95] In mid-September, another "collision occurred," primarily because an officer in the 77th New York National Guard deployed an unscrupulous patrol guard. A party of New York City soldiers under his command robbed civilians of their money and valuables. The main perpetrators were quickly arrested, and the *Elmira Daily Advertiser* tried to calm public fear by printing, "Hereafter no patrol will be allowed to be sent out of Camp Chemung without an order of the commanding officer."[96] Members of the 77th had already gained notoriety in Elmira by kidnapping the son of a local minister who was chopping firewood near his home on Water Street. The militiamen had petitioned the youngster to join their ranks, and when the boy declined the guards took him by force and, with a little more persuasion, he unwillingly signed enlistment papers. The youth was released the next day after the details of the episode were made clear to Depot Commander Eastman, who condemned the soldiers' behavior.[97]

After these occurrences, Brig. Gen. Alexander S. Diven, commander of the Military District of Western New York, took stronger measures to control his soldiers. General Diven reaffirmed his authority in General Orders No.2.—"The great mischief resulting from soldiers being at large, in the town and the vicinity of the camps, requires that the regulations prohibiting men from leaving camp without written permit from the Commanding Officer of the camp be vigorously enforced." Furthermore, "The commanding officer of the Rendezvous and camp of Rebel Prisoners, at Elmira, will establish a sufficient and effective patrol guard, who shall patrol the streets of the City of Elmira, and the vicinity of the various camps, and arrest all men in uniform who have not a sufficient pass, furlough, or discharge."[98] The local government also did its part in trying to control unruly soldiers for at least one day of the week. Mayor Arnot pushed through a city ordinance that closed all saloons and prohibited the sale of liquor on Sundays. Yet the military and the mayor did not intimidate the soldiers, or for that matter, saloonkeepers. Men still sneaked out of camp, alcohol was still served to them on the Sabbath, and the rowdiness continued.[99]

On January 3, 1865, the *Elmira Daily Advertiser* reported that "a riot took place on Railroad street, on Friday night caused by some soldiers of the 1st V.R.C., who, having imbibed most too freely, concluded to smash some glass. . . . First attacking the saloon of P. Ready, they completely demolished every pane of glass and every sash in front of the building, broke all the decanters and severely injured Mr. Ready." When city policemen arrived, the rioters resisted arrest until the patrol guard also arrived and arrested seventeen soldiers.[100] Also in January, Patrick Quin, the owner of a saloon near Barracks Number 3 that doubled as a bordello, was charged with "inciting soldiers to burn the barn of James McCann, which was set on fire the night of the 4th."[101] In February, "Quite a row occurred between the proprietor of a saloon opposite the Elmira Hotel, and some soldiers last evening. The soldiers were ejected and the contention was continued out in the street, but was promptly quieted by the timely arrival of a squad of the provost guard."[102] Provost guards served to maintain order in Elmira, but as noted with the 77th, they might do the opposite. Incidents occurred with other state militiamen found drunk while on patrol who harassed citizens on the street and in their homes. In the spring of 1865, Tracy reminded them, "Any member of the Provost Guard of this

City found in any drinking saloon or house of ill-fame except while in the discharge of duty will be summarily arrested and confined by the provost guard, . . . and the name and the offence of the man will be reported to these headquarters."[103] At times, the contradictory system itself failed because of the patrol's questionable character, undoubtedly making Elmirans wonder who policed the military police.

A military court was established to hear cases of Union soldiers, many lower-ranking men, who committed infractions inside and outside the prison yard. William O'Neil and C. B. Smith, privates acting as ward sergeants, were caught hiding soap bars supposed to be given to Southerners, "but sold the proceeds for their own private use." O'Neil and Smith both pled guilty and had to forfeit a portion of their pay.[104] Private Alfred Pugh, Co. E., 12 U.S. Infantry was the company cook. He sold coffee stolen from the mess to a Mrs. Ruppberry, supplying her right across from the prison. Pugh was sentenced to lose $24 in pay and kept at hard labor for a month.[105] For leaving his guard detail at Barracks Number 3 for two hours, Pvt. John Vean, 102d New York National Guard, was punished in front of his regiment. Privates Alexander Hamilton and Pallock Arthur, of the same regiment, were charged with "violation of the 50th article of war," each deserting their post after guard mounting and being absent until the next day. The military court found them guilty, and each had to wear a ball and chain for twenty days while confined.[106] Marcus Swarlfiger in Co. H of the 12th U.S. Infantry, "duly mounted as guard did willfully neglect to load his gun when ordered to do so by officer commanding the guard." Swarlfiger's plea of innocence not only cost him $40 in pay, but also led to a sentence that required him to "carry a log 4 hours each day for 20 days and perform police duty for the same amount of time."[107]

Up to this point, infractions committed by guards never involved the most serious crime of all, or at least no one knew about it until the afternoon of March 19, 1865. Around 3:00, Jerimiah Wager and Alexander Thomas, guards from Company A of the 19th Veterans Reserve Corps, stumbled upon a corpse a mile and a half northwest of the prison, in woods behind the Sly farm. The deceased was Amaza Mulock, a sixty-three-year-old tree pruner who frequented Camp Chemung. His body could still be recognized; although he lay at the same spot for three months the long winter had delayed decomposition. Next to the body was the apparent murder weapon—a broken musket that looked as if it had been used to deliver severe blows. The guards quickly returned to camp and notified Commandant Moore, who had the body brought back to Barracks Number 3 so medical officers could examine it. They concluded that the left side of the cranium had been compressed against the brain, causing death within minutes, and that the nose and cheekbone had also been broken. Just as telling were Mulock's pants pockets—turned inside out—which indicated robbery.[108]

The military turned the case over to the civil authorities, an investigation ensued, and a soldier in Company E., 12th U.S. Infantry, stationed at Camp Chemung, became the leading suspect. Additional information and witnesses connected the soldier with the victim near the time of death, and suspicion increased because of a weak alibi. Three days after discovery of the body, an inquest found Henry E. Gardner responsible not only for robbery, but also for murder. The jury determined that on December 29, 1864, the twenty-four-year-old private had lured Mulock, who was carrying a substantial amount of money, into the forest, where the act was committed. Gardner's court date was set for April 9, 1866, a year after the war. Two days later, a jury found Gardner guilty of murder and sentenced him to hang on June 1. An appeal delayed matters for almost another year, but the decision held and the convicted felon was scheduled to die on March 1, 1867.[109]

On that cool Friday, Gardner was brought to the first gallows in Chemung County constructed for an execution. More than three hundred tickets had been distributed for people to watch in a reserved area directly in front of the structure. Further back, and all around the scaffold, spectators jostled for positions that might command some view. People hung their heads out windows in businesses and homes, whose roofs also filled, while others climbed up trees, making for a crowd estimated in the thousands. Sheriff E. W. Howell escorted Gardner from the jail, passed a coffin built for his modest measurements, then proceeded on to the gallows. After Gardner climbed the steps, a noose was placed around his neck. The prisoner stood unflinching and composed over the trapdoor as he looked out into the multitudes that came to see him hang. Suddenly, Gardner broke his silence while the crowd hushed and he proclaimed that they all should "learn to love Christ, and live honest and holy lives!" "Now hurry," he begged Sheriff Howell, who bid him farewell, Gardner returning the gesture with a "Good-Bye!"[110] The trapdoor opened and Gardner plummeted as moans echoed from the audience. Something went wrong, however, for two braids of the rope broke, which left Gardner's toes skimming the ground. A deputy dashed for the rope and with a heave lifted the struggling prisoner back up, where he was left suspended. Fifteen minutes afterward, "Chemung's First Cain" was pronounced dead. Perhaps there was even more retribution for Gardner's murderous act. It was later found that

Gardner's neck did not instantly snap from the jolt of his freefall, but instead the noose slowly strangled him.[111]

Gardner's corpse was quickly placed in the casket and taken to Woodlawn Cemetery, where perhaps a few Southerners he once guarded were also buried. His remains did not rest long. Earlier, when Gardner had realized his fate, he had decided to donate his body to a local doctor, Patrick H. Flood. The physician helped the soldier financially during his court case and proved to be a good investment, at least for the doctor. Flood preferred to make it look as though Gardner was buried so he would not be criticized for his scientific pursuits. The evening of the execution, the doctor exhumed the corpse under the cover of darkness and removed it to his home on Water Street for embalming. Dr. Henry Flood, a member of the next generation of doctors in the family, took the corpse after his father's death and considered reinterring it at the cemetery, although one source indicated that "he will probably keep it as a ghastly relic of the first execution in Chemung County."[112] Indeed, years after the hanging Gardner was still reputedly standing, preserved in an upright pose in an Elmira apartment, "so near a window that those passing by could touch it if the window were open. It is a ghastly sight."[113] Chemung's "First Cain" was among many firsts introduced in Elmira during the Civil War, leaving a haunting reminder that certain social expenditures were paid in return for monetary benefits gained from the military.

II

March Showers, April Flowers, & the End of the Civil War

With all his concerns during the Chemung Valley winter, Depot Commander Benjamin Tracy was also giving a warning for the spring. He wrote to Henry W. Wessells on January 9, 1865, "I am convinced that a mistake was made in locating the prison camp. It is divided by a pond of waters, about twenty five (25) acres being north of this pond, on high ground, and fifteen (15) acres south, on low ground, which overflows in times of high freshets." Colonel Tracy continued: "A fence similar to the present one was washed away from this place, a few years since. All old citizens agree that probably this fence cannot be maintained here in the spring."[1] Chief Surgeon Anthony Stocker, who first pointed out to Tracy the camp's precarious position, suggested enlarging the prison yard to the west. The barracks built to accommodate the 19th Veterans Reserve Corps could be used as prison quarters, and new facilities built for the guards on higher ground. Either way, both officers urged that the low ground that comprised the pen be "abandoned" by spring.[2] However, for unexplained reasons prison authorities in Washington ignored the recommendation. Perhaps it was lost during the transfer of Hoffman, who replaced Wessells at the end of the month. In any event, the matter remained unresolved through February.

Spring arrived early in 1865. It finally appeared to be a merciful sign from Mother Nature, giving Southerners an easier climate. However, Tracy thought otherwise when premature spring freshets, which drained into local streams and rivers in the middle of March, enhanced the early thaw. Runoff from the highlands of Pennsylvania pushed into New York via the Tioga River and intensified when it met at the flooded Coshocton from the north, which funneled its way down into Chemung Valley. The normally calm Chemung turned unruly, its banks unable to contain the overflow. On Wednesday, March 15, waters reached the stockade and showed no signs of subsiding. That night at 9:00 P.M., Tracy held an emergency session at Barracks Number 3 with Stephen Moore and his staff. They decided that the three hundred men closest to the swollen river, those laid up in the smallpox wards on the flat, had to be relocated to higher ground. Tracy petitioned hardware and lumber merchants in town for supplies and equipment required for the evacuation. Tools, nails, lumber, tar, and rope were gathered and tacked into rudimentary river craft.[3]

At 1:00 A.M. Thursday, the removal of smallpox patients began, with Southerners impressed and serving as the primary brawn of the rescue, which Tracy and Moore supervised. The powerfully crested Chemung did not ease the operation, and workers became drenched in sweat and rain. The workers spent the early morning hours releasing rafts by rope out to the smallpox wards for patients to board, then hauling them back. The work was so strenuous that relay teams changed with every trip and were rewarded with whiskey for their efforts. After the teams towed the patients to safety they were housed in the barracks of the 19th Veterans Reserve Corps. Fortunately, they were removed just as the Chemung engulfed the flat, sweeping away the stockade wall.[4]

The next day, St. Patrick's Day, prisoners in the regular wards awakened to find they were surrounded by "a wilderness of water."[5] The flood had reached its high water mark, rising above the twenty-foot slope, up onto the upper part of the prison all the way past the appropriately named Water Street. Almost every patch of ground stood under water. Southerners were left isolated in their quarters, but even though a fence no longer enclosed the stockade they did not test the dangerously cold Chemung. In the barracks, built a few feet off the ground, men were forced up to the second and third tiers of bunks to stay above the water, which topped as high as four feet inside. Yet the captives were not totally discouraged because the patter of rain on their roofs stopped, which indicated the end of the deluge. Prison administrators relaxed when they watched the muddy waters stabilize, making it unnecessary to remove any men except for the sick in the hospitals. Throughout the day, a fleet of rowboats visited flooded barracks, checking on the men and bringing them food.[6] I. N. Kale stated that the flood "made us climb to the second bunk like possums. I saw the Yankees sail through out wards in little skiffs, in at one door and out the other."[7] John King was happy to see the prisoners "confined to the higher bunks for a day or two with nothing to eat or drink but the dirty river water. . . . [M]en came into our wards through doors in row boats, passing near where we were 'roosting.' They gave us something to eat. My, but it tasted good!"[8] Many hospital patients were removed to dry ground, although removal was a hazardous procedure that could worsen their condition. One onlooker wrote, "In transferring the sick from the hospitals to the boat often they fell into the cold water. A poor fellow came out of the hospital next to our ward. . . . Trembling and tottering with weakness, as he stepped on the plank, the boat vaciliated and the poor fellow staggered, threw up his arms and went headlong into the water. I feared he would drown, but he was rescued and shivvering was taken away in the boat."[9] Years later, a North Carolinian could joke that he had also fallen into the flooded Chemung "and was baptized all by myself, in ice water, and that is the reason why I am a Baptist still."[10]

The deluge became known in local annals as the "St. Patrick's Day Flood," the worst flood recorded to that date. In addition to its destruction of prison camp property at Barracks Number 3, the flood immobilized the city, miles of water flooding out stores, businesses, and homes. Dams and canals spilled over, roads and rail lines were washed out, and bridges crumbled under the extreme force of the river. Uprooted trees and farm animals, including a cow and horse, were seen floating down river, trapped in the Chemung's current.[11] On Saturday, March 18, the floodwaters receded, falling even faster than they had surged. By evening, all the sick prisoners had been brought back to the camp and men moved freely in and out of their odorous barracks. Dead eels and debris lay all around, sidewalks were torn apart, tents carried away, and pieces of building torn off.[12] "Perhaps you can form some idea of the sediment or mud left all over the camp," wrote James Huffman, "in the building and under the buildings and everywhere you would turn your eyes."[13] The worst damage was done to the stockade wall; the flood turned 2,700 feet of it into driftwood, requiring sentries to stand guard where the fence once stood.[14]

On March 21, Tracy reported on "our embarrassment occasioned by the recent inundation of the Chemung River." He assured Hoffman: "There was no loss of buildings and none of stores, except a very small quantity stolen by prisoners during their removal."[15] Tracy also mentioned that the 2,700 feet of stockade would be rebuilt immediately, but the task actually became a costly project that was delayed because he lacked lumber.[16] He seemed most pleased by the handling of the situation because, he wrote, it was "accomplished with great promptness; with no escape of prisoners, and, what is still more remarkable with but slightly increased loss of life."[17] This was verified by Lt. James R. Reid, who noted that the flood caused but "slight increase of mortality among the patients."[18] Prisoner accounts were just as vague in details about fatalities but suggested they were higher than what prison officials reported. James Huffman recalled, "The sick were taken out in boats and a great many died before they returned."[19] John King almost stumbled over "several blankets near my feet. Looking closer I discovered a number of dead men concealed under them."[20] Exact numbers that died went undetermined, but such a traumatic episode would likely have debilitated suffering men and contributed to their deaths. One prison guard said that the "effects of the flood were plainly visible upon the health of the men for some time."[21] A later observer concluded that their "exposure doubtless increased the mortality for that month."[22] Indeed, of the 7,102 men imprisoned in March, 491 died, 40 on a single day, numbers that were never surpassed in the prison's history.[23]

Flooding also resulted in long-term inconveniences for prisoners and notably hampered their exchange. The Northern Central Railroad remained inoperable for at least two weeks.[24] An "elated" James Huffman, thinking he would be exchanged in March, mentioned that he "was all ready and we were waiting for the Government train, when a warm rain set in and melted all the snow in the Pennsylvania and New York mountains." When he heard that the "railroad down this river to Harrisburg was torn to pieces," his dreams were dashed: "This flood foiled my hopes and my exchange never came."[25] Before the flood, prisoner exchanges had been running smoothly. In February, 701 prisoners joined a prison population that totaled 8,996, but by month's end 1,491 were released. A contingent of prisoners was exchanged every week in March prior to St. Patrick's Day. On March 2, 500 prisoners were given their paroles, the same number on March 6, and on March 12, 518 were delivered on the Northern Central. From that date to the war's end, no more prisoners would be transferred on the basis of the exchange system. Attrition from death then added to the general depletion of the population. February saw the largest number of deaths, 426, until that record was shattered in March. Deaths and the exchange of prisoners in February and March reduced by half the camp population, which numbered 5,054 on April 1.[26]

The weather changed in April, as did appearances inside the camp. In addition to rebuilding the stockade wall, Commandant Moore saw that buildings were repaired, cleaned, and aired out, while the grounds improved and plans were made for growing flower gardens.[27] Prison Inspector James Reid reported in early April that the general health of prisoners was "improving with the mild weather."[28] However, the same could not be said about their mates fighting in the Army of Northern Virginia. On the afternoon of April 3, a message was wired to Elmira that foreshadowed things to come—"Richmond Taken."[29]

Elmira was immediately thrown into a frenzy. People rushed into stores and shops, hotels and homes, spreading the news all around the city. Businesses closed early and workers went home to prepare for a grand celebration, courtesy of Colonel Tracy. After consulting with the mayor, Tracy announced "the entire military force at this post, except that required to perform actual guard duty, should parade at 5 P.M."[30] Troops at Barracks Number 1 were marched to the center of town while Stephen Moore led his men from Camp Chemung and all met at the corners of Main Street. The soldiers, some fifteen hundred strong, marching to brass bands occasionally drowned out by ringing church bells, paraded through Elmira into the evening. "Along Lake, Main, Church, Water, South Water, and other streets," reported the *Elmira Daily Advertiser*, "houses were illuminated from cupola to cellar, and sent forth into the gathering shades of darkness resplendent lights indicative of the widespread joy and rejoicing."[31] Festivities convened in front of the Brainard Hotel, depot headquarters. Just two weeks earlier water had covered this street; now it was filled with thousands of people. From the balcony civilian and military dignitaries gave their salutations, congratulations, and prognostications about dealing the "final blows upon the great Rebellion."[32] In between the oratories, bands played patriotic music and continued even after the last speech was given. The next day, the prison released twelve Southerners after they took the oath of allegiance, the largest number to that point.[33] It was also apparent that other Southerners were thinking what a Tarheel inmate was writing in early April: "I suppose the end is near."[34]

On April 10, prisoners once again heard a medley of church bells. It was rumored throughout the camp that their beloved Gen. Robert E. Lee had surrendered his army at Appomattox Court House the previous day.[35] A few days later they accepted it as fact. "Seems to be settled that Gen. Lee and Army has surrendered to Grant," bemoaned a Floridian. "Some seem to rejoice while others lament the capture of so noble an army."[36] Most inmates, at least in their accounts, seemed to take the latter viewpoint. A Tennessean declared, "This is a dark day for us, and the officers celebrated by getting drunk," while an Alabaman regretted, "We knew now the war was over."[37] Shortly after the surrender, the Rev. Thomas Beecher came to prison and consoled the defeated Southerners with an afternoon sermon. Rain had poured throughout the day, which further dampened spirits as the camp again turned into a quagmire. The reverend at least attempted to raise the prisoners' spirits, reminding them that not all was lost. "Now, boys, the war is over and you will soon be with your friends. When you are dismissed and return to your quarters, should you fall down in the mud, don't get up and say, 'Well damn the Yankees!'"[38] Laughter rolled through his congregation. Beecher left the prisoners with the prophetic message that they all "should be contented, as Paul, the Apostle, was contented, in and out of prison."[39]

The hope of an early discharge waned when the inmates received more disturbing news at the end of that memorable week. Early Saturday morning, April 15, "pandemonium had broken loose," wrote Marcus Toney, when it was reported "President Abraham Lincoln assassinated by a Rebel."[40] Most prisoners expressed regret, but one commented: "It is a good thing; Old Abe ought have been killed long ago!" The guards who overheard him took him to headquarters, where he was ordered to be hung by the thumbs.[41] After that display, other Southerners hid their sentiments. By nightfall, prisoners began genuinely to fear for their lives, and prison keepers were described as "excited" and "very vigilant."[42] The prisoners were being watched, a Virginian noted, as though they "were accused of the crime."[43] Inmates speculated on how they would be executed: either shot, bayoneted, or for quicker measure, bombarded by the artillery. Nothing out of the ordinary occurred that night, except for a quietness unusual for the prison camp.[44]

The same could not be said regarding the situation outside the prison, for a peculiar cloak and dagger twist had one of the individuals allegedly involved with plotting Lincoln's assassination prowling around Elmira. The night Lincoln was shot, John Surratt was in Elmira, sent by Confederate espionage authorities from Canada. His mission was to reconnoiter Elmira Prison and determine the practicality of liberating prisoners. Southern secret agents had long believed that Elmira could be targeted from north of the border. One scheme involved an entourage of armed men trekking down to the valley, impersonating new Union recruits, but instead of going to Barracks Number 1, they would enter Barracks Number 3 and overpower prison keepers. Neither this plan, nor any other covert attack, came to fruition, which ultimately left Surratt in Elmira when he heard the president had been shot. He immediately returned to Canada, then fled across the Atlantic.[45]

A week after the assassination, the body of Abraham Lincoln arrived in Elmira. Arrangements were made for the fallen president to be taken by train to his home in Illinois, following a route that took him to the Chemung Valley. Once again, soldiers from Barracks Numbers 1 and 3 combined their forces, this time not in celebration, but in remembrance. Elmira prison keepers, marching in the order of the 19th and 1st Veterans Reserve Corps, 12th U.S. Regulars, and Colonel Moore and with his officers, led the long procession. Next were the 150th and the 149th Pennsylvania Bucktails from Barracks Number 1, then Depot Commander Tracy and his staff, followed by pallbearers who escorted the black hearse. Behind the funeral car came government and clerical officials, while mourners on foot and in carriages filled the rest of a two-mile calvacade estimated to include about ten thousand people. The funeral party stopped at the public park on the steps of the Congregational Church, where Lincoln was eulogized before the casket continued its journey to Illinois. Not far from this scene, back at headquarters, sat a pardon for an Elmira inmate named James Hall. The Virginian's release had been endorsed "A. Lincoln," signed on the eve of the president's death. Hall was the last Confederate captive that Lincoln ever pardoned. When Colonel Tracy learned of this, he framed the document as a lasting tribute to Lincoln's merciful nature.[46]

Despite the apparent end of hostilities, Stephen Moore attempted a makeover of the prison. New sinks were dug, sidewalks planked, and streets graded. However, it was greenery that most interested the commandant. Lawns were cultivated, trees planted, and sod beds laid for gardens. Flowers concentrated on the prison's main thoroughfare sprouted in bright colors. To maintain the grounds, the commandant hired a large number of prisoners, including a Louisiana Cajun landscaper who supervised care of the gardens.[47] Perchance or by purpose, on April 24 Tracy allowed the editor of the *Elmira Daily Advertiser* to visit inside the stockade.[48] Two days later, the paper reported, "For nearly a year the portals to these grounds have been closed against the general public. When we say, therefore, that the first things which greeted our eyes on passing the gate were elegant drives, beautiful lawns and handsome walks, and tasteful flower gardens, our surprise may be well imagined. The idea of a prison never associates itself in the mind with such scenes as these, but they are, a monument of skill, enterprise, and cultivated refinement of the officers in charge of the camp."[49]

Also on April 24, the War Department gave the first indication that the army post would soon be disbanded. The *Elmira Daily Advertiser* carefully prepared its readers: "It seems to be the present intention, that this military rendezvous shall be given up, but the needful details of business in carrying out the order must occupy some time, yet."[50] Barracks Number 1 would serve strictly as a gathering point for soldiers to be mustered out of service and would close in about three months. As for the Confederates in Barracks Number 3, they were being persuaded to take the oath.[51] The *Elmira Daily Advertiser* predicted that "six months will probably be required to clear out the prisoners of war at Barracks No. 3, including the sick in the hospitals, many of whom will not be able to travel until that time has elapsed."[52]

The day the order came down from Washington, prisoner officials called the inmates into ranks and read a memo to them from Edwin Stanton. The War Department was compiling names of men willing to take the oath of allegiance. Those who had consented before Appomattox would be given priority over the rest, and those refusing would remain captive.[53] Wilbur Grambling entered into his diary on April 24 that "great excitement" existed because clerks were writing names of those "willing to take the oath, and those who won't take the oath." As for Grambling, he emphatically declined, remarking "I am still a R E Reb." It took only a couple days for the homesick Floridian to change his mind, condemning himself as "weak enough to do so."[54] An adamant Louis Leon "took the cursed oath" because the "cause is lost; our comrades who have given their lives for the independence of the South have died in vain."[55] This held especially true in prison. Despite the number of deaths dropping to 276 in April, the death rate in Elmira was higher than in any other Union pen for that month.[56]

In May, other Southerners were coming to grips with the reality of defeat and agreed to the oath. However, even the men who gave their allegiance to the United States were not immediately released. William Campbell wrote to his sister on May 9: "The old oath takers will be released first & those who have expressed a willingness do to so afterwards, I am of that number, having come to that decision after the surrender of Lee & Johnston. It will however be fully five weeks before I leave my prison. Continue to write."[57] Some obstinate inmates, like Marcus Toney, resisted the oath for another month, but admitted that resistance just "delayed the release of the boys."[58] Such inmates, however, were in the minority, and by mid-May paroles were moving faster.[59] On May 17, a newspaperman followed a party of released men to the railroad depot: "All professed a love for the good old Union and had seen fight enough and experienced suffering sufficient to last many a day. Like other detachments previously sent away, they drove quite a trade in trinkets. . . . Rings and fans such as they have manufactured in their confinement are elaborate and ornate, and valuable momentos to be kept to show to children and children's children. Their trades must have furnished them considerable amounts of pocket money, which will not come amiss in their distant journeys homeward."[60] By the end of May, 1,144 men had made that trip.[61]

On June 1, 3,610 prisoners remained in Barracks Number 3. Most of those who had taken the oath prior to the fall of Richmond were gone, and those who remained expressed their willingness to sign.[62] Military regulations at the pen were extremely lenient, which had a positive effect. A June holdover noted that "the prison rules were now relaxed, and visitors could come and go with all liberty; and the prison was kept pretty lively in the daytime and the boys did a fine business selling rings and other trinkets, and took in quite a lot of shinplasters and five- and ten-cent pieces of silver."[63] The inmates saved their earnings and made preparations for the long trip after being informed they would go next. Before leaving, captives got haircuts and shaves, and had clothes made or patched, anything to make themselves more presentable for traveling.[64] When its time came, a squad was assembled at the cookhouse, and its members told to raise their right hands and repeat "I, _____, do solemnly swear, in the presence of Almighty God, that I will henceforth faithfully support, protect and defend the Constitution of the United States, and the Union of the States thereunder; and that I will, in the like manner, abide by and faithfully support all laws and proclamations which have been made during the existing rebellion with reference to the emancipation of slaves: So help me God."[65] After the recital, prisoners were given two days of rations and their parole papers. Their remaining comrades saluted their departure as they lined along the main road. "I will never forget the march from the cookhouse to the big gate," wrote a solemn John King. "All the prisoners who were left behind congregated near the street as we went out. No battle scarred veterans ever marched to victory prouder than the ragged, poorly fed, miserable 300 which passed through the big gate never to return. Many of the poor fellows left behind waved us farewells, but for few ever met again."[66]

When marched outside the prison, inmates were free to go on their own. Some stayed in the Chemung Valley, employing themselves as farmhands. Most headed south, given transportation home by railroad or steamer compliments of the U.S. government. Those who had money quickly sought service from Elmira merchants' downtown.[67] Marcus Toney's itinerary included a restaurant, a clothier, and a barbershop. While he and twenty-seven of his comrades waited at the railroad depot to embark, a photographer approached with a pitch: "Boys, you should take a picture home to show the folk how you looked the day you got out of prison. I will charge you only a quarter."[68] Toney approved; he was the only one of his group who could afford the cost and was already dressed for it since he had recently purchased a new hat and duster. They all huddled together, including a man whose jaw was bandaged from having lost his teeth to scurvy and another too debilitated to stand, and the homely group was set in tintype. Thanks to Toney's generosity, it became the only picture taken of inmates just released from Elmira Prison. Those in the photograph were among the 2,509 paroled in June, leaving just 1,047 in Barracks Number 3.[69]

By July 1865, Benjamin Tracy had resigned as depot commander, and he moved on to New York City, where he resumed a career in law and public service that lasted long. His replacement was Col. John R. Lewis, 1st Veterans Reserve Corps, who had been in command at Camp Chemung.[70] A July 1 prison camp inspection commended, "The improvements in the grounds projected and carefully carried out by Lieutenant Colonel Moore commanding are tasteful and worthy of great praise. This officer has energetically given great attention to this and is deserving of special mention for the success attained over great difficulties arising from the nature of the obstacles overcome."[71] Stephen Moore, given instructions to begin clearing out Barracks Number 3 in July, put a crew of convalescent inmates to work. Buildings were vacated, grounds cleaned, and equipment collected, which took much of the month. Guards patiently awaited their discharges, while prisoners were rapidly leaving. On July 3, 100 left; on July 5, 342; on July 7, 321; and three days later, 226. Also on July 10, Commissary Hoffman recommended that the 140 remaining Rebels be transferred to a post hospital in the city.[72] The very next day, the *Elmira Daily Advertiser* reported: "We understand that Barracks No. 3 are to be immediately broken up. . . . Improvements have been going on up to the time of the discharge of the last of the prisoners of war; these have made the place a small eden, but just as the grounds and grass plats are putting on their attractive appearance, the hand of change comes to undo all that has been done."[73]

At the end of July, the operational departments within the prison camp were being dissolved and records turned in at headquarters. The commissary, adjutant, hospital, and labor departments progressively released their work forces. One prison employee left his position in the treasurer's office with a bonus, discovered by the departmental head, Lt. Joseph Groves. While reading over the final accounts, Groves found that his chief clerk, inmate Joseph Allen, had been purposely over calculating credit books. Allen's scheme allowed him to pocket money from fellow Southerners in return for inflated credit. By the time Groves figured out, Allen was gone with $72.40. The Quartermaster's Department would help make up the lost money.[74]

In early August, Assistant Quartermaster S. P. Suydam advertised throughout town that an enormous "Public Sale" would take place at Barracks Number 3. "Many of the articles are in good condition," he announced "and will be sold without reserve."[75] This sale offered citizens a legitimate opportunity to buy prison property at substantial markdowns, some as much as half the original cost paid to area merchants. On Friday August 11, at 10:00 A.M., Elmira's prison gates opened and customers came in to examine various items scattered inside buildings and across the lawns. There were 3,000 pounds of stovepipe, 284 coal and wood stoves, 346 pounds of rope, hundreds of shovels, axes, spades, chimneys, and lamps, plus an assortment of hatchets, hammers, dustpans, levels, and gauges. Other items included pails, wheelbarrows, coal scuttles, oil cans, barrels of coal oil and kerosene, and the 117 large illuminating reflectors that burned kerosene. The commissary provided five large cooking stoves, enormous cauldrons, pots, scales, 1,500 tin cups, 2,000 knives and forks, 2,000 plates, and 37 breadbaskets. From the hospital came counters that pharmacists could use as shelving. Rag dealers could take their pick of cloth, although they initially feared transmission of disease. Furniture, bedding, and even the barracks were available for the taking at low prices.[76] A local man purchased the deadhouse and used it for a storage shed. Barracks and officer's quarters were moved off the lot to nearby streets and became family dwellings. Other structures were utilized as barns and eventually garages well into the next century.[77]

While the sale of property continued, other items from the deadhouse and hospitals were piled together and burned.[78] Before its ignition, another six hundred Southerners were received at Barracks Number 3. The *Elmira Daily Advertiser* seemed as surprised as anyone: "We had supposed prisoners of war had generally been discharged, but it appears the government is not disposed to turn this last bunch loose yet. . . . They are probably intended to be fattened, roasted alive and served at a Radical barbecue. We fail to see what other use they can be put by Stanton."[79] The secretary of war also directed that anyone left in Barracks Number 1, along with patients at the general hospital, including Rebels, be moved to Barracks Number 3. The barracks had become the only remaining camp at the military rendezvous, a multipurpose bastion that housed a variety of men, including Confederates. War Department records end in July and no statistics are available for August, but the transformation evidently brought the dissolution of Elmira Prison. The final man discharged from Barracks Number 3 left in late September, but the sale of property continued until the entire stockade was dismantled and everything gone in December.[80]

Notwithstanding Mother Nature's attempt to wash away the stockade, Stephen Moore's passion to cover it up with flowers, and a final dismantling by rummage sales that yielded about three thousand dollars, Elmira Prison's legacy would long continue. Even after nothing remained except what had existed before the Civil War, an empty lot occupied only by Fosters Pond, headboards at nearby Woodlawn Cemetery displayed nearly three thousand reminders that almost one quarter of the more than twelve thousand Southerners sentenced to Elmira remained in the Chemung Valley forever. These calculations were well publicized by Southerners during Reconstruction.

12

The Aftermath & the Legacy

The seed of the trouble sown at Point Lookout was cultivated at Elmira,
and the cemetery reaped the harvest
　　—Elmira Prisoner Marcus Toney[1]

Elmira's death rate was the highest of all Union military prison camps. Of the
12,147 prisoners confined there, about 2,961—or 24 percent—perished. Most
astonishing was the fact that the prison only existed for a short period. The
monthly sick and death returns give specific insights into their demise.[2]

		SICK PRISONERS	DEAD PRISONERS[3]
1864	July	177	11
	August	394	115
	September	563	385
	October	640	276
	November	666	207
	December	758	269
1865	January	1,015	285
	February	1,398	426
	March	823	491
	April	647	267
	May	509	131
	June	218	54
	July	—	16

In comparison to other Northern prisons, Elmira held a most undesirable position. The mortality rate at Camps Alton and Rock Island, in Illinois, was 14 percent. Camp Chase had a 13 percent death rate; Camp Morton, 10 percent; and Fort Delaware, 9 percent. Johnson's Island, which unlike Elmira imprisoned mostly officers, had a minimal death rate of .03 percent. Because of the large number of prisoners confined in Point Lookout, which totaled more than 40,000, its mortality rate slipped to .06 percent.[4] Elmira compared most to Camp Douglas, which was also built to muster and train Union soldiers, but became a prison camp. Fifteen percent of those held in Camp Douglas would "Die in Chicago."[5]

Not long after the Civil War, the Surgeon General's Office examined the causes of sickness and fatalities among Confederate prisoners. Its conclusions were published in *Medical History of the War of the Rebellion*, the official account. Army doctors in the office studied various cases of disease, illness, and deaths, which they calculated in annual ratios for every thousand inmates. They deduced that Elmira "stands forth as the most insalubrious of these prison-camps. . . . Not only had it a high-mortality rate, 441.1 annually per thousand of strength, but the percentage of fatal cases, 28.8, was more than double that of any other depot."[6] The office's investigation of medical files revealed that, for every 1,000 men, 21.2 died from continued fever, 9.9 malarial fever, and 58.9 eruptive fever. Scurvy seemed to be less life threatening: only 3 of every 1,000 soldiers succumbed to the vitamin deficiency, although it could have increased susceptibility to other afflictions. Cold weather certainly intensified respiratory problems: deaths from pneumonia and pleurisy accounted for 117 per 1,000. Bowel disorders were the largest killers: diarrhea and dysentery accounted for 211.5 of every 1,000 deaths. Altogether, doctors diagnosed 4,379 Elmira prisoners with diarrhea and dysentery, and 1,394 perished, most from chronic diarrhea.[7]

The yearly death rates per thousand in all Union prisons was: Alton, 55.0; Camp Douglas, 44.1; Rock Island, 98.0; Camp Morton, 46.7; Johnson's Island, 9.8; Fort Delaware, 45.4; Point Lookout, 46.4; and Elmira, 241.0. Medical examiners who studied Elmira also concluded that, in addition to respiratory and bowel problems, "Large mortality was undoubtedly referable to over-crowding, insufficient hospital accommodation and insufficient protection from the cold of a northern climate." In addition, they echoed Marcus Toney's statement that "the main influence underlying all these and raising them into strong relief, was the broken-down condition of the men at the time of their commitment."[8] Although the medical officials admitted that Elmira had gained "unenviable notoriety" from these figures, it was comparisons with a Southern prison that brought Elmira's extensive death record before the public eye.[9]

In early January 1876, Representative James G. Blaine of Maine, Republican House minority leader, set off one of the most controversial debates in Reconstruction politics. Republicans feared that a Southern resurgence might restore former Confederates to political positions as high as the executive office, so he attempted to curb it with an amendment to the Amnesty Bill, which sought to restore the political rights of Southerners. Blaine demanded that the bill exclude Jefferson Davis, former president of the Confederacy.[10] "It is not because of any particular and special damage that he above others did to the Union," Blaine said, "or because he was personally or especially of consequence." Blaine wanted to exempt Davis because he was responsible, "knowingly, deliberately, guiltily, and willfully," for the "gigantic murders and crimes at Andersonville."[11]

Blaine held Davis accountable for almost thirteen thousand deaths at the infamous Georgia prison. After speaking the word "Andersonville," Blaine was promptly interrupted by a colleague, who yelled out "And Libby," referring to the officers' prison in Richmond.[12] Said Blaine, "Libby pales into insignificance before Andersonville," which he likened to "Dante's Inferno and Milton's Hell." The Georgia "den of horrors" ranked with other world-class acts of barbarity: "And I here, before God, measuring my words, knowing their full extent and import, declare that neither the deeds of the Duke of Alva, in the low countries, nor the massacre of Saint Bartholomew, nor the thumb-screws of the Spanish Inquisition begin to compare in atrocity with the hideous crime of Andersonville."[13] Applause echoed from galleries to the floor and Blaine hoped for similar approval throughout the North. However, Blaine never counted on a reply to his statements about Andersonville.[14]

Georgia representative Benjamin Hill had been waiting for an opportunity to vindicate his state. For Hill, the issue went beyond local matters, since Democratic colleagues regarded him as not only a representative of Georgia, but also a defender of the entire South. Jefferson Davis was Hill's political ally and personal friend, and disparagement of Hill's home state moved him to respond in a way that it might have pleased Preston Brooks.[15] On the morning of January 11, Hill began his speech with a disclaimer: "Mr. Speaker, the House will bear witness that we have not sought this discussion," but the "gentleman of Maine" was responsible for reopening "this discussion of the events of our unhappy past."[16] Hill argued that Andersonville was located in an advantageous place and that Confederate prison keepers gave plenty of food to its occupants. He attributed the high death rate to the Union war policy, which blockaded medicine, burned clothing factories, and halted exchanges.[17] "Now, sir, I do not wish to unfold the chapter on the other side," but in his hand was "a letter written by one who was a surgeon at the prison at Elmira, and he says:"

> The winter of 1864–65 was an unusually severe and rigid one, and the prisoners arriving from the Southern States during this season were mostly old men and lads, clothed in attire suitable only to the gentle climate of the South. I need not state to you that this alone was ample cause for an unusual mortality among them. The surroundings were of the following nature, namely: narrow, confined limits, but a few acres in extent and through which slowly flowed a turbid stream of water, carrying along with it all the excremental filth and debris of the camp; this stream of water, horrible to relate, was the only source of supply for an extended period, that the prisoners could possibly use for the purpose of ablution and to slack their thirst from day to day; the tents and other shelter allotted to the camp at Elmira were insufficient and crowded to the utmost extent; hence small-pox and other skin diseases raged through the camp. . . . The diet and other allowances by the Government for the use of the prisoners were ample, yet the poor unfortunates were allowed to starve. But "why!" is a query which I will allow your readers to infer and draw conclusions there from. Out of the number of prisoners, as before mentioned, over three thousand of them now lay buried in the cemetery located near the camp for that purpose—a mortality equal if not greater than that of any prison in the South. At Andersonville, as I am well informed by the records at Washington, the mortality was twelve thousand out of, say, forty thousand prisoners. Hence it is readily to be seen that the range of mortality was no less at Elmira than Andersonville.[18]

Congressman Thomas C. Platt instantly broke the hush of the House when he jumped out of his seat. "Will the Gentleman allow me to interrupt him a moment to ask him where he gets that statement?"[19] Hill left the author anonymous, reiterating that he was a Union surgeon who had served at Elmira Prison and had his letter published in the *New York World*. Platt, who had ascended from local politics in Tioga County to become a major cog in the New York state Republican machine, responded: "I live within thirty-six miles of Elmira, and . . . those statements are unqualifiedly false."[20] "Yes" said Hill, "and I suppose if one rose from the dead the gentlemen would not believe him." Platt asked Hill if he felt the statements were true, to which the Georgian responded, "Certainly I do not say that they are true, but I do say that I believe the statement of the surgeon in charge before that of a politician thirty-six miles away."[21] As for the reliability of his source, Hill said "He is a wonderful witness. He is not even equal to the mutilated evidence brought in yesterday. But, sir, it appears from the official record that the confederates came from Elmira, from Fort Delaware, and from Rock Island and other places with fingers frozen off, with their toes frozen off, and with their teeth dropped out."[22]

The next morning, January 12, Benjamin Tracy, now a successful Brooklyn attorney and close political associate of Thomas Platt, picked up his morning newspaper, where he found Hill's widely printed speech.[23] Tracy wired Platt that he would speak on his friend's behalf. Platt asked for the House floor later that day because "I hold in my hand a telegraphic communication from General B. F. Tracy, late commandant of the military post of Elmira, and I beg permission to read that communication. Platt began,

The facts justify your denial of cruelty, inhumanity, or neglect in the treatment of prisoners at Elmira. There was no suffering there which is inseparable from a military prison. First, there was no deadline. No prisoner was ever shot for attempting to escape. Second, the food was ample and of the best quality. Thousands of dollars were expended in the purchase of Vegetables, in addition to the Army ration. No congressman in Washington eats better bread than was given daily to the prisoners. The beef was good, and of the same quality and quantity as that distributed to our own soldiers guarding the camp. Third, the dead were not buried in trenches, but the remains were placed in neat coffins and buried in the public cemetery at Elmira. Fourth, there was no better supplied military hospital in the United States than the hospital in the prison camp. Fifth, all the prisoners were comfortably quartered in the new wooden barracks, built expressly for them. From the time I took command in September, all the saw-mills in the vicinity of Elmira were kept constantly running to supply lumber for buildings, & c. The barracks for prisoners were first built, and in the extreme cold weather of winter the prisoners were all in barracks, while the soldiers guarding them were still in tents. I was criticised for this in the Army and Navy Journal, I think it was, at the time, by an officer of our army. Sixth, the camp and all the buildings were well policed, and kept scrupulously clean. Seventh, the mortality which prevailed was not owing to neglect or want of sufficient supplies or medical attention, but to other and quite different causes.

B. F. Tracy

Late Commandant Military Post Union[24]

Next, Congressman James Garfield of Ohio read an urgent telegram from another former Elmira official, Quartermaster John Elwell, who resided at that time in Cleveland: "To General Garfield, House of Representatives: By authority of the Secretary of War I furnished 15,000 rebel prisoners at Elmira with the same rations—coffee, tobacco, coal, wood, clothing, barracks, medical attendance—as were given to our soldiers. The dead were decently buried in Elmira cemetery. All this can be proved by democrats of that city."[25] Evidently, both Tracy and Elwell had short-term memories; during the war, each had documented inadequacies in food, clothing, lumber, and medical treatment. Meanwhile, news of the controversy spread to New York state. Stephen Moore, who had become proprietor of the Groves Springs Hotel on Keuka Lake, northwest of Elmira, sent a letter to the *Elmira Daily Advertiser*.[26] It was from a former prisoner and was subsequently published in the newspaper on January 17: "I tender you my humble and sincerest thanks for your great kindness to myself, and to all the Prisoners who were ever under your command."[27]

Two days later, the *Elmira Daily Advertiser* assured its readers, "Of course no one believes the words that Congressman Hill uttered in relation to the treatment of prisoners of war at this depot. There are too many witnesses living to put the stamp of falsehood on what he said." The newspaper then printed two favorable inspection reports, borrowed from Stephen Moore and "taken at random from the file." To no surprise, each report was taken after Moore's spring cleaning of the stockade. Among the wording of the report prepared after P. W. Stanhope's inspection of May 6 were the statements "Conduct, orderly," "Quarters, neat," "Bedding, blankets sufficient," "Food, quantity of vegetables in addition to prison rations," "Water, abundant," and "Sinks, fair"—"I take pleasure in calling the attention of the commanding officer to the taste and energy displayed in the improvements of the grounds now in progress." The other report was taken on July 1, 1865, not long after the camp closed.[28]

In far-off Maine, another retired prison official entered into the debate. In the same pompous style that had displeased more than one of his superiors, Surgeon Eugene F. Sanger wrote to the *Portland Press* that because "Hill's shameless defense of Andersonville in the House of Representatives, by attempting to show that Southern prisoners of war were treated as cruelly at Elmira, as Federal prisoners at Andersonville, should not go unrebuked, . . . I feel called upon to respond."[29] The old surgeon gave a brief history of the pen, the problems of congestion, limited acreage, poor drainage system, and especially, hospital administration.

> Few realize the hindrances to rapid and efficient action in such a work, where everything must be obtained according to the inevitable red-tapeism and routine of army regulations, every demand going through by a circuitous route to the Commissary General of Prisons at Washington for approval, and repeatedly returned for further explanations. People at home have not the remotest idea of the herculean labor required to build a well regulated hospital of 500 beds, with its outside relief to more than 1,500 to 2,000 ailing in quarters, wards, sinks, wash rooms, drainage, laundry, dietary, cuisine, bakery, apothecary shop, medical staff, clerical duties, hospital furniture and bedding, and a retinue of nurses, ward masters, all to be looked after, and for which the surgeon-in-chief was immediately responsible. Such was the work laid out and accomplished during the fall of 1864.[30]

As with Tracy and Elwell—or for that matter Blaine and Hill—Sanger was not completely honest. However, he was the first of Elmira Prison officials to blame a peer publicly. "The will of our camp, from the Colonel commanding to the lowest subordinate, was to do everything in our power for the well-being of those prisoners. Unfortunately after the retirement of Colonel Eastman, U.S. Army, on account of sickness, the colonel of a negro regiment was assigned to us who manifested more interest in the hygiene of camp than the din of war and who liked the smoke of the frying pan better than the smoke of battle. Camp hygiene is a great study, which during the war was left by our bravest and ablest generals, to the medical staff. It would have been better at Elmira, but notwithstanding this drawback."[31] Apparently, no public rebuttal came from this "drawback," Benjamin Tracy, if he were even aware of Sanger's comment. As to why Elmira had achieved ignominy, Sanger believed, "First, contrary to war department instructions, a female reporter was let in, who was disappointed in the valiant bearing of our Johnnies and because she did not find the neatness of a gentleman's parlor." Second, "A Petersburg editor had a hack at us. . . . Being a jolly fellow and quite a favorite at the officers quarters, he begged of me to let him out with the exchange of the sick. . . . I included this editor, and if he was not fit or willing to fight within sixty days,

Wartime bust photograph of Bvt. Brig. Gen. William Hoffman, whose thriftiness did not help alleviate the suffering of Elmira prisoners. Courtesy of the Roger D. Hunt Collection, USAMHI.

he traveled for us with his pen as soon as he got home, descanting upon the horror of Elmira. . . . Copperhead Journals were not slow in copying these malicious attacks."[32] Unbeknown to Sanger, that "jolly fellow" was at that time the mayor of Richmond. Anthony Keiley's accusations were just the beginning of many more criticisms that mounted specifically against Sanger and continued long after his death.

One individual who remained quiet during the Elmira-Andersonville controversy was the commander of Union prisons, William Hoffman. Perhaps he felt it was pointless to get involved or perhaps he wanted to conceal his frugal ways. Growing up in a large family with little money, Hoffman had little choice in his early years except to be close with a dollar. After West Point, he had embarked on a military career on the outposts of the frontier, where expenditures were kept to a minimum, which reinforced his penchant for penny-pinching. However, Hoffman was obsessed with saving money.[33] His biographer conceded, "His preoccupations with thrift and the temporary nature of the camps contributed to inadequate prison conditions."[34] Consequently, money remained in prison funds across the North—money that could have better served prisoners rather than reverting back to the government after the war. The total afterward stood at $1,853,353, even before adding the sales of prison camp property.[35] With Elmira, as with the other prison camps Hoffman supervised, the "strictest economy" was intended. But, Hoffman failed at Elmira. To Southerners, he failed because of the high mortality rate; and because of the largest amount of spending on a prison in a single year at Barracks Number 3, Hoffman failed himself.

In the meantime, as during their imprisonment, Confederate dead buried throughout the North were neglected after the war. The once neatly kept grounds of Woodlawn Cemetery became overgrown, and deteriorating headboards lay atop graves. The remains of about twenty men had been taken back home to rest in the South, which left plots only partly filed. After the war, Sexton Jones was to be paid $50 annually to maintain the section for Southerners. However, after Jones failed to receive the full amount, he withheld his services. A little northwest of the Confederate graves were two rows of Union headboards, mostly from the prison guard, and even some of those lay on the ground. For the time being, the numbered headboards could still be read.[36] Fortunately, the situation eventually improved. Not long after Hill's speech, the War Department and the city of Elmira entered into negotiations over making the burial grounds into a national cemetery. The city finally agreed in December 1877 to devote a two and one-half acre lot for such purposes in return for fifteen hundred dollars. This arrangement was the first step that the federal government took to honor Elmira's Civil War veterans.[37]

At the turn of the twentieth century, few people paid attention to the old prison site. However, members of the Grand Army of the Republic, Baldwin Post Number 6, under the auspices of Melvin Conklin, the former prison detective, believed that at the very least the borders of the pen should be remembered. In 1900, two granite blocks, each measuring a foot square, were placed along Water Street as markers to show where the northern corners of the stockade had once stood. Each stone was engraved "Military and Prison Camp, 1861–1865. Erected by Baldwin Post, No.6, G.A.R., 1900."[38]

Six years later, the U.S. government finally turned its attention to the Southern dead buried in the North. On March 9, 1906, Congress approved an act "To provide for the appropriate marking of the graves of the soldiers and sailors of the Confederate army and navy who died in Northern prisons and were buried near the prisons where they died."[39] The act empowered the War Department to find the burial places of Confederates, report on their condition, and prepare accurate identification of the deceased in triplicate, including grave number, name, rank, regiment, and state. The information was to be filed at the local cemetery, with the quartermaster general, and at the War Records Office. White marble headstones inscribed with appropriate information would replace wooden headboards and fences originally built to preserve grounds that might eventually be purchased for government supervision. In addition, the secretary of war received authorization to appoint an individual to perform these tasks, which also included verifying proper identification and attempting to locate unmarked graves.[40]

On June 13, 1906, Grave Commissioner William Elliot reached Elmira. The day afterward, he went to Woodlawn Cemetery and was delighted to find the grounds maintained well, largely because of its status as a national cemetery. Relatives had already constructed eight headstones over Confederate graves. Elliot found that the fastidious record keeping of Sexton Jones facilitated identification of most burials. Some concerns still existed regarding assertions made by locals that Woodlawn did not hold every deceased prisoner at the camp, but that officials had interred some in and around the stockade. Elliot could not substantiate these claims. For the next four weeks he visited Woodlawn daily, working on these and other matters, which included the task of finding a contractor to stake out the plots before the marble tombstones arrived.[41] Doane and Jones Lumber in Eldrige Park, New York, received that assignment, and began placing 2,963 wooden markers at a total cost just under $70 for labor and material. Meanwhile, Elliot had the old headboards collected and burned. By July 10, a stake marked every burial site and Elliot was ready to travel on.[42]

The following day around noon Elliot caught an Erie Railroad train to investigate burials at Shohola. He retraced the deadly path of the Erie with the help of Shohola postmaster E. R. Kalbfus, who helped him locate the burial spot. Much brush and undergrowth covered the site and it had to be cleared. Realizing the impossibility of identifying each body put into the mass grave, Elliot gave up and moved on.[43]

The marking of headstones at Elmira exemplified other expenditures connected to the old prison camp. Because of comparisons to Andersonville, it seemed proper that Elmira shared its post-prison contracts with a Georgia-based marble firm. In June 1907, the federal government awarded the Blue Ridge Marble Company in Nelson, Georgia, a contract to furnish the marble tombstones, each priced at $2.90 and measuring 39-by-12-by-4 inches. In early August, Elliot began to solicit proposals for "setting up 2,932 headstones for the dead Confederate prisoners of war in Woodlawn National Cemetery at Elmira, N.Y."[44] The headstones weighed approximately two hundred pounds each, and Elmira was to receive three hundred weekly until all were delivered to the Northern Central Railroad depot. From there, they needed to be taken to the cemetery. Elliot sought local bidders for that task, and Melvin Conklin, Elmira's retired postmaster, suggested some prospective firms.[45]

Woodlawn Granite Works of Elmira put in a bid for 65 cents a headstone, which totaled $1,905.80 for the work. Elliot deemed the price too high. Melvin Conklin, evidently still dabbling in government detective work, found that the City Granite and Marble Works on West Church Street might come down to as low as 25 cents per headstone. Elliot only offered 20 cents, so no deal was struck. In late September, with no other serious offers, Elliot finally acquiesced, offering Charles E. Rainey, owner of City Granite and Marble Works, 25 cents for each stone, which totaled $733 for the job.[46] On October 2, 1907, a contract was drawn stating "that the said Charles E. Rainey will set up in the Confederate Section of Woodlawn National Cemetery 2932, more or less, marble headstones . . . to be set as to show twenty (20) inches above the ground when set, and to be left plumb, alined and well tamped."[47] The entire project, when finished, left an impressive sight. Woodlawn National Cemetery glowed with rows upon rows of white marble headstones, lined up together as if standing at attention for a final roll call. Every former Confederate state and a few border states were represented. Virginia claimed 550 headstones, South Carolina 387, Georgia 314, Alabama 235, Tennessee 76, Louisiana 64, Florida 30, Mississippi 10, Texas 6, Arkansas 1, Maryland 3, and Kentucky and Missouri each 1. North Carolina accounted for almost half the markers, 1,233. At least seven prisoners could not be identified and were defined with the customary "Unknown."[48]

In May 1909, William Oates, who had replaced Elliot, visited Shohola and with the aid of one Postmaster E. R. Kalbfus ventured out to King and Fuller's cut. Oates described the setting: "The land there is very rough and rocky. It is worth but little, but the man who owned it was too unpatriotic, narrow-minded and stingy to allow the unfortunate men who had lost their lives to be buried on his land, and hence the dead prisoners were put four in a box and the dead of the guard were put one in a box. All the boxes were then taken down below the steep bluff into the swamp on the second bank of the Delaware River and there buried."[49] The burial site was not visible from the tracks or the river, and had been tucked away for years with nothing left to inform Erie travelers that they had just passed through the most dangerous railroad curve of the Civil War. Oates wrote to the secretary of war that measures should be taken so that the memory of the dead soldiers could be made more visible: "The Blue and the Gray—the Federal and Confederate—each doing what he conceived to be his duty, ended their earthly career in the unlooked-for calamity of a great disaster, and there they sleep by the side of each other in the swamp of the Delaware."[50] Unfortunately for their families, they would have to sleep there a little longer. In July, the War Department directed Oates to wait "until fiscal year 1911 for Congress to make a propriation" to reinter the remains into a national cemetery.[51]

During the interim, the government considered contract proposals for the Shohola exhumation. In July 1910, C. I. Terwilliger and Son, undertakers of Port Jervis, about thirty miles from Shohola, made an offer. For $450, they could deliver the remains to Cypress Hills National Cemetery in Brooklyn. William Oates, to his credit, recommended that the men be buried in Elmira, which had a fine national cemetery, because that would have been their destination. His suggestion was approved. In September, representatives from Terwilliger and Son met with a Mr. Vogt, who told them that seventy-two individuals were buried at the site. On October 22, 1910, Postmaster Kalbfus informed the Quartermaster Department that C. E. Sills, who owned the land on which the soldiers had been buried, did not object to excavation of his property as long as the graves were refilled and that he had agreed that the digging could start immediately. Incidentally, Terwilliger and Son, which competed against a bid from Edwin M. Skinner of New York City, lowered its price to $275.[52]

In early 1911, Congress approved the money for the exhumation at Shohola, and the digging was scheduled to begin in late spring. On April 8, the Quartermaster Office awarded the contract to Terwilliger and Son because it was "the lowest responsible bidder at $275."[53] On Monday morning, June 5, the undertakers commenced digging equipped with proper exhumation permits obtained from county officials, which accumulated to $36. A Union veteran, who had witnessed the burials in 1864, pointed out the estimated gravesite to Capt. Charles M. Fenton, the officer in charge of the project. Fenton watched Terwilliger's workers dig through the soft soil until they struck the remains about six feet down. The coffins existed no more, only the thumbscrews that held them together remained, along with bricks used to prop up heads. The workers found these remnants mostly at one end of the trench, which indicated that the soldiers were buried separately. Each bone was picked out by hand and boxed, then separated as well as possible into Union or Confederate categories. Records indicate the workers found only sixty remains, and it was very likely that Delaware River floods had washed some away.[54]

It took three days to dig up the bones, which workers put in white pine boxes then stored in four larger cases for shipment. The first case weighed 310 pounds and contained Southern bones; the second case weighed 335 pounds and included the remains of Northern guards, who were placed in box 9. The other cases contained Confederates, the third weighing 375 pounds and the fourth 325. After workers exhumed the bones, they returned the site to its natural condition. On the afternoon of June 8, officials shipped the cargo to Woodlawn Cemetery, and the next day, Saturday morning, the remains of prisoners from Point Lookout and members of the 11th Veterans Reserve Corps were reinterred with their fallen compatriots. In addition to the $275 fee, officials paid $36 for disinterrment permits at Shohola, $12 for railway transportation to Elmira, $3 to haul the bones to Woodlawn, and $24 to open the graves, all of which totaled $350. The government was not done spending. In late October, it appropriated $600 for construction of a monument to the accident victims. On May 27, 1912, the Shohola Monument was raised with two bronze tablets that listed the names of the crash's victims. Fittingly, the Confederate tablet faces south, while that of the Union guards looks north. Unbefitting, a rain storm canceled the Shohola Monument's dedication ceremony.[55]

Years passed with only slight remembrances of Elmira Prison. Now and then, pieces of the past would resurface. Two years after Shohola Monument was built, Almond Gould was working under his home, on a short road that bore his family name between Water Street and Foster's Pond. While excavating a cellar, his pick suddenly struck a wooden object wedged in the dirt. Gould unearthed a large pine box and opened it, only to be greeted with a horrendous odor as the contents instantly crumbled. After catching his breath, Gould found a corpse, most of which had disintegrated except for some bone fragments, strands of clothing, shoes, and a few personal belongings. The bones were buried in lime, which indicated that the individual had died of a contagious disease, probably smallpox. Rumors had circulated that not all prisoners were buried in Woodlawn, particularly during an epidemic, and to the chagrin of the commissioner of graves the stories were apparently true.[56]

In 1925, a considerable February snowfall blanketed the Chemung Valley. Morgan Guinnip was using for storage two small buildings that his father had purchased from the camp and moved northwest to his property. One of the shacks was believed to be the odious deadhouse during the war. However, heavy snow seriously jeopardized its structural integrity during the winter, when the roof caved in and the walls buckled. The structure, which had stood for all those years containing the unpleasant memories of prison life, finally gave way to time.[57]

In 1937, the United Daughters of the Confederacy built a monument at Woodlawn Cemetery. The imposing monument, set with a large bronze relief of a Southern soldier gazing toward the cemetery, reads, "In Memory Of The Confederate Soldiers In The War Between The States Who Died In Elmira Prison And Lie Buried Here." The statue depicted a healthy middle-aged man, fully clothed with hat in hand and good shoes—features atypical among Elmira inmates.[58] By the 1940s, some of the buildings removed from the prison lot had been repaired and remodeled. D. Clarence Espey owned an old barrack, which he redesigned on the interior and to which he added a front porch. What had once quartered soldiers, was rented out as a summer cottage along the banks of the Chemung.[59]

In January 1955, a few other relics of the venerable prison camp were recognized, including some old cast-iron stoves originally bought for prisoners. An Erin, New York, businessman, James H. Rodbourn, had purchased three of the huge stoves. One had been moved to Rodbourn's general store. Melvin Conklin had been a frequent customer there, and warmed by the stove, had been known to ask the owner, "J. H. R., a lot of Rebels got warm by this stove; do you suppose it would be safe for me to get warm by it?"[60] Rodbourn donated the second stove to the Erin Methodist Church. Rodbourn installed the third stove in his store in Swartwood, New York. As time went on, the stoves at both general stores became worthless. However, in 1955 the stove at the Methodist Church, although in need of some maintenance, was beginning its fiftieth year of operation in the auditorium—almost one hundred years after it was first bought. Although some parishioners sneered at the antiquated stove's appearance, its value went beyond nostalgia—it still worked.[61]

The centennial of the Civil War renewed debate about Elmira Prison. Local historical societies held forums on the prison camp and articles were published that excused or attacked the pen. Indeed, little had apparently changed from a century earlier, including the absence of any significant memorial at the old prison yard.[62] In 1984 James E. Hare, a history teacher from Horsehead, New York, and Elmira councilman, put forth a proposal that Hare's students had inspired. Two of his eighth graders had presented a project on the prison that included a model of the stockade, and Hare hoped to build on their enthusiasm to create a memorial on a larger, lasting scale. Hare envisioned a monument that would include a six-foot high concrete wall wrapped around in the shape of a horseshoe and a case in which to display photographs, a map, and summaries of the camp's history and those involved with it. Three flag poles would be set into the edifice: the United States flag centered in the middle, slightly higher than the New York state and Confederate flags.[63]

The Elmira Civil War Monument movement gained support with publication of a story in the *New York Times*. Chemung County historian Thomas Byrne told the newspaper, "It will fill a void that should have been filled many decades ago." Perhaps one reason why construction of the monument took so long was because some locals would have rather forgotten Elmira's Civil War past. Byrne addressed that issue by commenting, "Elmira is visited regularly by descendants of the Confederate prisoners, and the monument is partly for their sake. They want to take their kids to step on the grass where great-grandpa was a prisoner. We want to treat them kindly."[64] Another local historian, Alfred Hilbert added, "They come in here with blood in their eyes because they say their great-grandfather was mistreated here and we killed them. But when they see the cemetery and see the graves are well cared for, they change their tune."[65]

Woodlawn caretaker Frank Williamee stated that "an average of five visitors a day come to see the graves of their Confederate forebears."[66] Southerners helped with donations for the monument, particularly after reading the article in the *New York Times*. However, it was local businesses, community organizations, volunteer groups, and philanthropists in Elmira that made the largest contributions, which were estimated to total around ten thousand dollars. Elmira's business community was finally paying back Confederate inmates who had brought local entrepreneurs prosperity. Yet the payment came in a form one might value more than money. The city's repayment was a memorial in their honor.[67]

On August 25, 1985, Elmira Civil War Monument dedication day, almost five hundred persons gathered on the land that Barracks Number 3 once occupied. They crowded onto Winsor Avenue, south of Water Street, which would have been inside the eastern part of the stockade. Southerners from Virginia to Georgia, including the president general of the United Daughters of the Confederacy, were present. Representatives from their Northern counterpart, the Daughters of Union Veterans, also made the trip from as far away as Illinois. Soldiers dressed in blue and gray could again be seen around the city, reenactors trying their best to authenticate the event.[68]

For the community, the event celebrated an achievement—for their own effort—and represented an observance for American soldiers. James Hare led the introduction, Deacon William Dougherty gave the invocation, and Mayor Stephen Fesh Jr. welcomed all visitors from within and outside of Chemung Valley. "A Litany of Dedication" was presented under the direction of the Rev. Frederick L. Turner, and the audience was asked to follow from their programs. The Reverend Turner spoke to the large crowd: "In humility and in penance we pray—For the wounds and suffering of the Civil War fought in good faith by North and South." The crowd responded, "Forgive Holy Father." The Reverend proceeded, "For the horror of this Prison Camp in Elmira, New York," and again the response was "Forgive, Holy Father." "For the continued hatred and prejudice that separate your children even now by race, creed, and nation"—"Forgive, Holy Father." "In caring love we pray," said the Reverend, "For the relatives of all those who suffered and died in the Civil War Camp of Elmira, New York," to which the people chanted from their programs, "We Pray For Your Help, Loving Father." "For the descendants of all those who fought, bled and died in the Civil War, both of the South and of the North"—"We Pray for Your help Loving Father." All voices then joined together for the final refrain of the litany; "Praying For Forgiveness, Intercession, And Dedication We Offer This Memorial To The Glory of God. May this Civil War Monument Heal The Past, Stimulate The Present, And Be Hope For The Future."[69]

Notes

INTRODUCTION

1. Thomas E. Byrne, ed., *Chemung County . . . Its History* (Elmira, N.Y.: Chemung County Historical Society, 1961), 16, 28–29.

2. The word Chemung in Native American language denotes "place of the horn," which refers to a large mammoth's tusk found by the riverbank. Thomas E. Byrne, *Chemung County 1890–1975* (Elmira, N.Y.: Chemung County Historical Society, 1976), 4; Thomas E. Byrne, "Chemung Valley: War Path of 1778," *Chemung Historical Journal* 24.1 (Sept. 1978): 2813–15; Oscar Jewell Harvey, *History of Wilkes-Barre* (Wilkes-Barre, Pa.: Raeder Press, 1909), 2:984, 1018–19; Philip S. Klein and Ari Hoogenboom, *A History of Pennsylvania* (University Park: Penn State Univ. Press, 1980), 101.

3. Towner, *History of Chemung County*, 53–54; Byrne, *Chemung County 1890–1975*, 9, 11, 60.

4. Towner, *History of Chemung County*, 26.

5. Thomas E. Byrne, *Chemung County*, 11, 60–65, 36–37; Walter Henry Ottman, "A History of the City of Elmira, New York" (Ph.D. diss., Cornell Univ., 1900), 78, 70, 120.

6. Thomas E. Byrne, *Chemung County*, 5; idem., *Chemung County 1890–1975*, 15–16; Towner, *History of Chemung County*, 163–64.

7. Thomas E. Byrne, *Chemung County*, 20–22. New York State census for Elmira, 1865, Steele Memorial Library, Elmira, N.Y., U.S. Census 1850, 1860, Chemung County, N.Y.; Ottman, "History of Elmira," 162.

CHAPTER ONE

1. *Albany (N.Y.) Atlas and Argus*, Apr. 19, 1861.

2. James M. McPherson, *Battle Cry of Freedom: The Civil War Era* (New York: Oxford Univ., 1988), 324; The editor of the *Elmira Advertiser* tried unsuccessfully to name the depot "Camp Cameron." *Elmira (N.Y.) Weekly Advertiser*, May 11, 1861.

3. *Elmira (N.Y.) Weekly Advertiser*, Apr. 20, 1861.

4. Elmira contract book 1861, entry 442, RG 393, National Archives, Washington, D.C. (hereafter cited as NA); *Elmira (N.Y.) Weekly Advertiser,* Apr. 27, May 25, 1861.

5. Elmira contract book 1861.

6. Elmira contract book 1861.

7. *Elmira (N.Y.) Weekly Advertiser,* May 18, 1861; Ottman, "History of Elmira," 165; Thomas E. Byrne, *Chemung County,* 28; Elmira contract book 1861; Carl Morrell, "Elmira's Elusive Northside Civil War Barracks," Chemung Historical Journal 41.1 (Sept. 1996): 4559; *The War of the Rebellion: A Compilation of the Official Records of the Union and Confederate Armies,* 128 vols. (Washington, D.C.: GPO, 1880–1901), ser.2, vol. 4:67–75, (hereafter cited as *OR*).

8. *OR,* vol. 4:68–73; Barrack Inventory, The Elmira Rendezvous 1861–1865, Prison File, TS, Chemung Historical Society, Elmira, N.Y.; Morrel, "Elmira's Civil War Barracks," 4557–59.

9. Elmira contract book 1861.

10. *OR,* vol. 4:67–69; Barrack Inventory.

11. *Albany (N.Y.) Atlas and Argus,* May 3, 1861.

12. Ibid.; Thomas E. Byrne, *Chemung County,* 28–29; *Elmira (N.Y.) Star-Gazette,* May 17, 1993.

13. *Elmira (N.Y.) Weekly Advertiser,* July 6, 1861.

14. Ibid., July 6, Aug., 21, 1861; *OR,* vol. 4:67–75.

15. *OR,* vol. 4:67–75, 266; Morrel, "Elmira's Civil War Barracks," 4557–58; William C. Davis, ed., *The Image of War: 1861–1865,* vol. 4: *Fighting For Time* (New York: Doubleday, 1983), 4:400; Towner, *History of Chemung County,* 224–25, 235, 241.

16. *New York Times,* Jan. 14, 1863; *Elmira (N.Y.) Star-Gazette,* May 17, 1993; Towner, *History of Chemung County,* 261; Barrack Inventory; Thomas E. Byrne, *Chemung County,* 28; Ottman, "History of Elmira," 170.

17. Davis, *Fighting For Time,* 400–401; William B. Hesseltine, *Civil War Prisons: A Study in War Psychology* (Columbus: Ohio State Univ. Press, 1930), 24.

18. *OR,* vol. 4:266–68.

19. Davis, *Fighting For Time,* 400–401; Hesseltine, *Civil War Prisons,* 74–76, 82–82, 93, 109, 113, 228–30; *OR,* vol. 7:607.

20. Hesseltine, *Civil War Prisons,* 226–32; *OR,* vol. 7:615, 8:240.

21. OR, vol. 7:793.

22. Towner, *History of Chemung County,* 242, 252, 256; Ottman, "History of Elmira," 199–200, 258, 282; Thomas E. Byrne, *Chemung County,* 68; *Elmira (N.Y.) Star-Gazette,* May 17, 1993.

23. Towner, *History of Chemung County,* 245; *OR,* vol. 7:146.

24. *OR,* vol. 7:146.

CHAPTER TWO

1. *OR,* vol. 7:152.

2. S. Eastman to W. Hoffman, Jan. 10, 1863, Letters Received, box 45, entry 11, RG 249; *OR,* vol. 7:152.

3. *OR,* vol. 7:152. For more examples of Hoffman's frugality, see Davis, *Fighting For Time,* 397, 398, 399, 402, 406.

4. List of Buildings Erected at Elmira, N.Y., MS, box 561, entry 225, RG 92; *OR,* vol. 7:157.

5. C. McKeever to S. Livingston, May 25, 1864, J. J. Elwell to M. C. Meigs, Oct. 1, 1864, Letters Received, box 561, entry 225, RG 92; Text Record of Contracts, vol. 16, entry 1238, RG 92.

6. Report of Persons and Articles Hired, Elmira, N.Y., entry 238, RG 92.

7. Report of Persons and Articles Hired, Elmira, N.Y.; List of Buildings at Elmira, N.Y.; *OR,* vol. 7:424–25; Marcus B. Toney, *The Privations of a Private* (Nashville, Tenn.: M. E. Church, South, Smith, and Lamar, 1907), 93; Francis T. Miller, *The Photographic History of the Civil War,* vol. 4, *Prisons and Hospitals,* ed. Holland Thompson (New York: Review of Reviews, 1911), 77, 79, 81.

8. *OR,* vol. 7:394.

9. Ibid., 394, 106, 424–25; S. Eastman to W. Hoffman, July 3, 1864, Letters Received, box 561, entry 11, RG 249.

10. James Marion Howard, "A Short Sketch of My Early Life," TS, Chemung County Historical Society, Elmira, N.Y., 13; John R. King, *My Experience in the Confederate Army and Northern Prisons* (Clarksburg, W.V.: United Daughters of the Confederacy, 1917), 32; Louis Leon, *Diary of a Tarheel Confederate Soldier* (Charlotte, N.C.: Stone, 1913), 67.

11. Anthony M. Keiley, *In Vinculis; or, The Prisoner of War* (Petersburg, Va.: Daily Index Office, 1866), 116; Walter D. Addison, "Recollections of a Confederate Soldier of the Prison Pens at Point Lookout, Md. and Elmira, New York," MS, Thomas Jefferson Green Papers, Southern Historical Collection, Univ. of North Carolina, Chapel Hill, 3.

12. Keiley, *In Vinculis,* 120; Leon, *Diary of a Tarheel,* 67; King, *My Experience,* 32; Toney, *Privations,* 90–93; Addison, "Recollections," 3.

13. Toney, *Privations,* 90–91; Addison, "Recollections," 3–4.

14. Addison, "Recollections," 3–4.

15. Ibid., 3–5; King, *My Experience,* 32; James Huffman, *Ups and Downs of a Confederate Soldier* (New York: William E. Rudge's Sons, 1940), 93.

16. Toney, *Privations,* 32.

17. Leon, *Diary of a Tarheel,* 67.

18. Keiley, *In Vinculis,* 120.

19. Ibid., 124–16; King, *My Experience,* 32; Toney, *Privations,* 90–91; Leon, *Diary of a Tarheel,* 67.

20. Allegedly, prisoner Emanuel Miller, gifted in carpentry, constructed the entrance for Elmira Prison. Tom Byrne to Weiss, Mar. 1, 1989, Prison File, Chemung County Historical Society, Elmira, N.Y.; Clay W. Holmes, *The Elmira Prison Camp: A History of the Military Prison at Elmira, N.Y., July 6, 1864, to July, 10, 1865* (New York: Knickerbocker Press, 1912), 27; Keiley, *In Vinculis,* 129; Thomas E. Byrne, "Elmira's Civil War Prison Camp: 1864–65," *Chemung Historical Journal* 10.1 (Sept. 1964): 1282; Towner, *History of Chemung County,* 267; *Elmira (N.Y.) Daily Advertiser,* July 4, 1864, July 12, 1865.

21. Susan W. Benson, ed., *Berry Benson's Civil War Book: Memoirs of a Confederate Scout and Sharpshooter* (Athens: Univ. of Georgia Press, 1992), 131; Henry V. Colt pension file, NA.

22. *Elmira (N.Y.) Daily Advertiser,* Sept. 18, 1865; Keiley, *In Vinculis,* 131–32; Henry V. Colt pension file.

23. *Elmira (N.Y.) Daily Advertiser,* July 12, 1864.

24. Ibid., July 11, 12, 13, 1864, July 11, 1865; Keiley, *In Vinculis,* 129.

25. Marcus Toney wrote that Point Lookout prisoners frequently suffered from "night blindness. . . . This peculiar condition was attributed to the nature of are surroundings. There was nothing green for the gaze to rest upon as a relief from the glare reflected from the sand and the white walls of the tents." Marcus Toney, "Prison Life," *Annals of the Army of the Tennessee and Early Western History* 1.6 (Sept. 1878): 272. As for the drinking water at Elmira, Virginian Thomas Jones wrote, "We had very good water and there was plenty of that." Thomas C. Jones prison file, Chemung County Historical Society, Elmira, N.Y. Keiley, *In Vinculis,* 130; Huffman, *Ups and Downs,* 95–96; King, *My Experience,* 33–34; Benson, *Civil War Book,* 127; Holmes, *Elmira Prison Camp,* 23–24; A. E. Stocker to B. F. Tracy, Dec. 31, 1864, Letters Received, box 140, entry 11, RG 249; U.S. War Department., *Medical and Surgical History of the War of the Rebellion,* part 2, vol. 5, *Medical History* (Washington, D.C.: GPO, 1879), 56. *OR,* vol. 7:465.

26. *OR,* vol. 7:465.

27. Ibid., vol. 7:450–51, 465–66; *Elmira Prison Camp,* 29–30.

28. *OR,* vol. 7:465–66.

29. Ibid., 488–89; *Elmira (N.Y.) Daily Advertiser,* July 18, 1864; *New York Times,* July 16, 1864; *(Port Jervis, N.Y.) Tri-States Union,* July 22, 1864; Joseph C. Boyd, "Shohola Train Wreck," *Chemung County Historical Journal* (June 1964): 1253–55; Edward H. Mott, *Between the Ocean and the Lakes: The Story of Erie* (New York: Tickner, 1899), 441.

30. *(Port Jervis, N.Y.) Tri-States Union,* July 22, 1864; George J. Fluhr, *Shohola—History of a Township* (Lackawaxen, Pa.: Alpha, 1992) 38–39; *(Honesdale, Pa.) Wayne County Herald,* July 21, 1864; Mott, *Story of Erie,* 442.

31. Mott, *Story of Erie,* 442; Fluhr, *Shohola,* 39; Howard B. Snyder, "The Wreck of the Prison Train: A Factual Narrative Based on Observations of Persons on the Scene at the Time," TS, Chemung County Historical Society, Elmira, N.Y., 2; *(Honesdale, Pa.) Wayne County Herald,* July 21, 1864; *Elmira (N.Y.) Daily Advertiser,* July 20, 1864.

32. Mott, *Story of Erie,* 442; *(Honesdale, Pa.) Wayne County Herald,* July 21, 1864; Boyd, "Shohola Train Wreck," 1255; *OR,* vol. 7:489. See also, informational note 36.

33. Mott, *Story of Erie,* 442. Evans recalled more of the shocking details: "Perched on the reared-up end of the tender, high above the wreck, was one of our guards, sitting with his gun clutched in his hands, dead!" Also, a young railroad worker noticed "one poor fellow's skin had turned very dark. I was curious to know what happened to him," and the guard told Evans, "Well son, if you must know, I was squeezed between two masses of wreckage." The youngster "learned afterwards he died from it." Snyder, "Wreck of the Prison Train," 3.

34. Boyd, "Shohola Train Wreck," 1255; *Elmira (N.Y.) Daily Advertiser,* July 20, 1864; *(Port Jervis, N.Y.) Tri-States Union,* July 22, 1864; *Wayne County Herald,* July 21, 1864.

35. Boyd, "Shohola Wreck," 1255–56; Fluhr, *Shohola,* 40; Mott, *Story of Erie,* 441–42; *(Honesdale, Pa.) Wayne County Herald,* July 21, 1864; *(Port Jervis, N.Y.) Tri-States Union,* July 22, 1864.

36. Due to the mutilated condition of the bodies, it was hard to ascertain exactly how many actually perished. Further complicating matters were five who reportedly escaped, but perhaps some of that number died and could not be recognized when buried. Evidence did suggest that one sixteen-year-old escapee took refuge with a Shohola family that needed a farm hand to help tend the harvest, while another Confederate who fled made his home in nearby Matamoras, Pennsylvania. In any event, the buried men were eventually exhumed and taken to a more appropriate cemetery in 1911. *OR*, vol. 7:489; Fluhr, *Shohola*, 40–41; George J. Fluhr, "Miscellaneous Papers," TS, Shohola Railroad and Historical Society, Shohola, Pa.; Boyd, "Shohola Train Wreck," 1255–58; Mott, *Story of Erie*, 442; *(Honesdale, Pa.) Wayne County Herald*, July 21, 1864; *(Port Jervis, N.Y.) Tri-States Union*, July 22, 1864; Burial of Confederate Prisoners, file 2158, entry 89, RG 92.

37. *(Port Jervis, N.Y.) Tri-States Union*, July 22, 1864; *(Honesdale, Pa.) Wayne County Herald*, July 21, 1864.

38. *(Port Jervis, N.Y.) Tri-States Union*, July 22, 1864.

39. Ibid.; *(Honesdale, Pa.) Wayne County Herald*, July 21, 1864; *(Honesdale, Pa.) Republic*, July 21, 1864. The Erie Railroad Company accepted some responsibility by paying undisclosed damages for guards hurt in the accident. *OR*, vol. 7:489.

40. *(Honesdale, Pa.) Wayne County Herald*, July 21, 1864; *(Port Jervis, N.Y.) Tri-States Union*, July 22, 1864; *OR*, vol. 7:489. On September 1, 1993, the Shohola Railroad and Historical Society held a ceremony and unveiled a state commissioned historical marker that honors those who lost their lives in the accident. The "Civil War Prison Train Wreck" tablet is located at the Caboose Museum in Shohola Village. Also, the old hotel where the injured men were taken still operates. Inside Rohman's Inn, a plaque denotes its claim to importance in the area's local history. Fluhr, "Papers."

41. *Elmira (N.Y.) Daily Advertiser*, July 15, 16, 18, 1864; Holmes, *Elmira Prison Camp*, 30.

42. Boyd, "Shohola Train Wreck," 1258–59; *Elmira (N.Y.) Daily Advertiser*, July 18, 1864; Keiley, *In Vinculis*, 155–56.

43. *(Port Jervis, N.Y.) Tri-States Union*, July 29, 1864; G. Kent Strickland, "The Search For Thomas," *The State: Down Home in North Carolina* 54.6 (Nov. 1986): 20–22. G. Kent Strickland and his family had originally thought that his great-grandfather, Thomas Strickland, had died at Drewry's Bluff, Virginia. Upon further research, they discovered that he was killed in the Shohola accident.

CHAPTER THREE

1. *Elmira (N.Y.) Daily Advertiser*, July 20, 21, 22, 29, Aug. 2, 1864, July 25, 1865; *OR*, vol. 7:568–69; Toney, *Privations*, 94; Tapley H. Stewart, "Reminiscences of Tapley H. Stewart," TS, Robert W. Woodruff Library, Special Collections, Emory University; Keiley, *In Vinculis*, 162–63.

2. *OR*, vol. 7:568–69.

3. Ibid.; *New York Times*, Aug. 3, 1864; *New York World*, Aug. 3, 1864.

4. *New York World*, Aug. 3, 1864.

5. *New York Times*, Aug. 3, 1864.

6. McPherson, *Battle Cry*, 756; *OR*, vol. 7:502, 594.

7. *New York Times,* Aug. 3, 1864; Elmira (N.Y.) *Daily Advertiser,* July 25, 1865, Aug. 3, 4, 22, 1864; *Rochester (N.Y.) Daily Union and Advertiser,* July 20, Aug. 2, 4, 1864.

8. *Elmira (N.Y.) Daily Advertiser,* Aug. 11, 17, 22, 1864, Aug. 8, 1865.

9. Ibid., Aug. 22, 1864.

10. Ibid., Aug. 6, 25, 1864; Records of the Quartermaster General, Elmira, N.Y., box 561, entry 225, RG 92; *OR,* vol. 7:560.

11. *Elmira (N.Y.) Daily Advertiser,* Aug. 10, 13, Dec. 2, 1864; *Rochester (N.Y.) Daily Union and Advertiser,* Aug. 6, Sept. 13, 1864, Jan. 14, 1865; *New York Times,* Oct. 9, 1864; Report of Persons and Articles Hired, Elmira, N.Y.; Records of the Quartermaster General, Elmira, N.Y.

12. *Elmira (N.Y.) Daily Advertiser,* Aug. 10, 1864.

13. Ibid., Aug. 18, 1864; U.S. War Department, *Medical and Surgical History,* pt. 2, vol. 8:502.

14. U. S. War Department, *Medical and Surgical History,* vol. 8:502

15. *Elmira (N.Y.) Daily Advertiser,* July 27, Aug. 23, 1864; Report of Persons and Articles Hired, Elmira, N.Y.; Records of the Quartermaster General, Elmira, N.Y.; U.S. War Department, *Medical and Surgical History,* pt. 2, vol. 5:56; Keiley, *In Vinculis,* 152. Holmes incorrectly wrote that the hospitals were erected entirely by inmates. Holmes, *Elmira Prison Camp,* 44.

16. John J. Elwell Pension File; J. J. Elwell to S. Eastman, April 15, 1864, Letters Received, N.Y., box 561, entry 225, RG 92; Annual Report to the Quartermaster General 1864, box 6, entry 225, RG 92; Inspection Report to the Quartermaster General at Elmira, N.Y. July 19, 1864, box 561, entry 225, RG 92.

17. *Elmira (N.Y.) Daily Advertiser,* Aug. 10, 1864; Post Returns at Elmira, N.Y., box 130, entry 199, RG 109; Records of the Quartermaster General, Elmira, N.Y.

18. Requisitions, July 26, 1864, box 561, entry 225, RG 92.

19. J. J. Elwell to M. C. Meigs, Sept. 9, 1864, Letters Received, box 561, entry 225, RG 92.

20. *Elmira (N.Y.) Daily Advertiser,* Aug. 4, 10, 1864.

21. Ibid., Aug. 4, 1864. About two thousand feet of hemlock were purchased for hospitals from Jacob Briggs at the price of $280. To extend the guard walk, prison authorities purchased 5,502 feet of hemlock boards from William Viall for $82.53. Statement of Prison Funds, July–Aug. 1864, Letters Received, box 46, entry 11, RG 249.

22. *New York Evening Post,* Aug. 24, 1864; *Rochester (N.Y.) Daily Union and Advertiser,* Aug. 12, Sept. 13, 1864; *Elmira (N.Y.) Daily Advertiser,* July 29, Sept. 6, 1864; John Kaufhold, "The Elmira Observatory," *Civil War Times Illustrated* (July 1977): 31–32. Eastman wrote Hoffman at the end of August, stating that the Quartermaster's Department was able to lease most of the property in front of the prison for the guard encampment "excepting the small piece on which an observatory is erected." S. Eastman to W. Hoffman, Aug 28, 1864, Letters Received, box 46, entry 11.

23. *Elmira (N.Y.) Daily Advertiser,* July 11, 1864; *New York Evening Post,* Aug. 24, 1864; *Rochester (N.Y.) Daily Union and Advertiser,* Sept. 13, 1864. Before the Upper Observatory was built, the *Elmira Daily Advertiser* reported that locals were intrigued with Southerners,

even with an obstructed view through "cracks and knotholes": "People from the country are hardly willing to go home after their shopping is done, without a peep at the varmints, and those of the town, during the cool evening dews, don't fail in securing a like privilege."

24. *Elmira (N.Y.) Daily Advertiser,* Aug. 10, 1864.

25. Keiley, *In Vinculis,* 158.

26. *Rochester (N.Y.) Daily Union and Advertiser,* Aug. 12, 1864.

27. Ibid., Sept. 13, 1864.

28. *Rochester (N.Y.) Daily Union and Advertiser,* Sept. 13, 1864; *Elmira (N.Y.) Daily Advertiser,* Sept. 6, 1864.

29. *Elmira (N.Y.) Daily Advertiser,* Aug. 30–Sept. 6, 1864; Holmes, *Elmira Prison Camp,* 35; Keiley, *In Vinculis,* 158.

30. *Rochester (N.Y.) Daily Union and Advertiser,* Aug. 12, Sept. 13, 1864.

31. *New York Evening Post,* Aug. 24, 1864.

32. *Elmira (N.Y.) Daily Advertiser,* Aug. 1, Sept. 9, 1864.

33. G. W. D. Porter, "Nine Months in a Northern Prison," *Annals of the Army of Tennessee and Early Western History* 1.4 (July 1878): 159.

34. Huffman, *Ups and Downs,* 105.

35. Keiley, *In Vinculis,* 158.

36. J. B. Stamp, "Ten Months Experiences in Northern Prisons," *Alabama Historical Quarterly* 18 (1956): 496.

37. Frank Wilkeson, *Recollections of a Private Soldier in the Army of the Potomoc* (New York: Knickerbocker Press, 1887), 227–28.

38. Synopsis of Instructions Pertaining to the Management of the Depot, Elmira, New York, box 9, entry 289, RG 94.

39. Holmes, *Elmira Prison Camp,* 35–36. For continued observatory business in the spring, see King, *My Experience,* 43.

40. Keiley, *In Vinculis,* 157-158; King, *My Experience,* 43.

41. Keiley, *In Vinculis,* 150–53, 158.

42. Holmes, *Elmira Prison Camp,* 290, 301–3.

43. Keiley, *In Vinculis,* 158.

44. Ibid., 158–59. Clay Holmes met Keiley after the conflict and relied on him for much of his history due to the Virginian's "truthfulness of statements made concerning the prison camp." Holmes, *Elmira Prison Camp,* 300.

45. Keiley, *In Vinculis,* 158; F. S. Wade, "Getting Out of Prison," *Confederate Veteran* 34 (1926): 379.

46. Undated newspaper clipping in Prison File, Chemung County Historical Society, Elmira, N.Y.

47. E. F. Sanger to J. K. Barnes, Aug. 6, 1864, Eugene F. Sanger, Personal Papers of Medical Officers and Physicians, RG 94; "Military Order of the Loyal Legion of the United States," Circular no. 8, series of 1897, number 146, "Companion Eugene F. Sanger," Bangor Historical Society, Bangor, Maine.

48. *Bangor Daily News,* scrapbook of clippings, 1934, Bangor Historical Society, Bangor,

Maine; "Military Order Tribute to Eugene F. Sanger"; *History of Penobscot County, Maine* (Cleveland, Ohio: Williams and Chase, 1882), 769; *OR,* vol. 7:465; W. J. Sloan to E. F. Sanger, Aug. 3, 1864, Eugene F. Sanger, Personal Papers of Medical Officers and Physicians; E. F. Sanger to J. K. Barnes, April 8, 1865, Letters Received, box 561, entry 225, RG 92.

49. *OR,* vol. 7:604.

50. Ibid., 604–5, 1004–5.

51. Ibid., 603–4.

52. On Oct. 23, Hoffman wrote that "the whole work should not cost over $120." *OR,* 603–4, 1003–5, 1025.

53. Ibid., 1005.

54. Ibid., 605, 1004–5, 1025; U.S. War Department, *Medical and Surgical History,* pt. 2, vol. 5:56.

CHAPTER FOUR

1. *OR,* vol. 8:997–98; ibid., vol. 7:560, 691–92.

2. Ibid., vol. 7:692.

3. Ibid., 691–92.

4. Ibid., 786.

5. *OR,* vol. 7:677, 682; Keiley, *In Vinculis,* 173; James I. Robertson Jr., "The Scourge of Elmira" in *Civil War Prisons,* ed. William B. Hesseltine (Kent, Ohio: Kent State Univ. Press, 1972), 88, 90. A late summer inspection also that mentioned "Many of those in quarters are unable to attend sick call, and in some cases had not been visited by a surgeon in four days." *OR,* vol. 7:677.

6. King, *My Experience,* 40.

7. A. Rifleman, *Prisoner of War or Five Months Among the Yankees* (Richmond, Va.: West and Johnston, 1865), 100; *OR,* vol. 7:682; Frank L. Byrne, "Prison Pens," 406; Robertson, "Scourge of Elmira," 88; J. Michael Horigan, "Elmira Prison Camp—A Second Opinion," *Chemung Historical Journal* 30.3 (Mar. 1985): 3456.

8. The vegetable reduction included cutting the amount of potatoes in half, from thirty to fifteen pounds for every hundred men. Meanwhile, sutlers were temporarily limited to selling items such as soap, combs, toothbrushes, and towels, writing supplies and stamps, and tobacco and matches, plus material and tools for mending clothing. Hesseltine, *Civil War Prisons,* 188–201; *OR,* vol. 7:72–75, 150–51, 574.

9. *OR,* vol. 7:682.

10. *OR,* vol. 7:183, 666, 683, 785; Leslie G. Hunter, "Warden for the Union: General William Hoffman (1807–1884)" (Ph.D. diss., Univ. of Arizona, 1971), 25–26, 82–85; *Elmira (N.Y.) Daily Advertiser,* July 6, 1864; *New York Evening Post,* Aug. 17, 1864; Amount of Expenditures, box 1, entries 16 and 77, RG 249. An example of savings from the prison fund can be taken from October, when 257 barrels of flour, costing $9.75 each, reverted $2,505.75 back for other spending. Grease was also sold from the cookhouse, which in September put $80 into the fund. October 1864, Savings of Prison Bakery at Barracks No. 3, box 46, entry 11, RG 249; Sept. 30, 1864, Ledger of Disbursements of Prison Funds, vol. 1, entry 97, RG 249.

11. In 1895, Tracy was awarded the Congressional Medal of Honor for carrying his unit's battle flag during the second day of the Wilderness Campaign. Stewart Sifakis, *Who Was Who in the Civil War* (New York: Facts On File Publications, 1988), 660; B. F. Tracy to W. Hoffman, Letters Received, Oct. 9, 1864, box 9, entry 289; *Elmira (N.Y.) Daily Advertiser,* Sept. 20, 29, 1864; *OR,* vol. 7:878; Benjamin Franklin Cooling, *Benjamin Franklin Tracy: Father of the Modern American Fighting Navy* (Hamden, Conn.: Archon Books, 1973), 7, 20–23, 26–28, 33–34. The *New York Evening Post* inaccurately reported that Eastman "was suspected of being a Democrat, and hence superceded" by Colonel Tracy. *New York Evening Post,* Oct. 15, 1864.

12. *OR,* vol. 7:878.

13. The prisoners lacked soft bread, but received fourteen ounces of hard bread instead; if beans were distributed, rice or hominy was not. Amount of Expenditures, Regulations from the Commissary General's Office for all prison stations, Apr. 20, 1864.

14. *New York Evening Post,* Aug. 17, 1864.

15. *Elmira (N.Y.) Daily Advertiser,* Dec. 2, 1864.

16. *Rochester (N.Y.) Daily Union and Advertiser,* Sept. 13, 1864.

17. *OR,* vol. 8:76–77.

18. Ibid., 52–53. The mail inspector did not examine the Brunsan letter, which was not the customary procedure. Instead, it was secretly sent out by a ring of Union soldiers working on the inside. Consequently, a commissioned officer, an assistant surgeon, and two enlisted soldiers were apprehended before they mailed even more inmate letters. Ibid., 76–77.

19. Keiley, *In Vinculis,* 146, 145.

20. Miles O. Sherrill, *A Soldier's Story: Prison Life and Other Incidents in the War of 1861–65,* (Raleigh, N.C.: Edwards and Broughton, 1911), 10.

21. John N. Opie, *A Rebel Cavalryman With Lee, Stewart, and Jackson* (Chicago: W. B. Conkey, 1899), 319; Addison, "Recollections," 7; Porter, "Nine Months," 161; King, *My Experience,* 36.

22. "Statement of a United States Medical Officer," *Southern Historical Society Papers* 1.4 (1876): 297–98.

23. Toney, *Privations,* 98.

24. G. T. Taylor, "Prison Experience in Elmira, N.Y.," *Confederate Veteran* 20 (1912): 327; Howard, "Short Sketch," 14.

25. Clay Holmes exemplified the Elmira Prison defender, dedicating his study to Elmirans "Who Loyally Displayed The Highest Christian Spirit In Their Treatment Of The Confederate Prisoners Of War." The author also had a family member "who languished for months at Andersonville." Nevertheless, his research included a vast amount of primary material by inmates, officers, and other valuable information from contemporaries. Holmes, *Elmira Prison Camp,* v–vi, 10, 91–96, 348–50.

26. King, *My Experience,* 29.

27. Opie, *Rebel Cavalryman,* 315, 317, 319.

28. Toney, *Privations,* 98–99; Holmes, *Elmira Prison Camp,* 325–40.

29. Luther B. Daskin was hired as the head baker, and Edward Garrat became his assistant. Statement of the Prison Fund, Oct. 1864, box 87, entry 11, RG 249; N. J. Sappington

to A. B. Eaton, June 28, 1865, General Correspondence, box 10, entry 17, RG 192; Holmes, *Elmira Prison Camp,* 64, 92, 344–45; Records of the Commissary General of Subsistence, box 17, entry 77, RG 192; N. J. Sappington to A. E. Shiras, July 13, 1864, Letters Received, box 201, entry 10, RG 192; N. J. Sappington to A. B. Eaton, Jan. 27, 1865, Letters Received, box 201, entry 10; *Elmira (N.Y.) Daily Advertiser,* Aug. 7, 1864.

30. Benson, *Civil War Book,* 132; Toney, *Privations,* 98; King, *My Experience,* 29; Stewart, "Reminiscences," 2; List of Buildings at Elmira, N.Y.

31. Benson, *Civil War Book,* 132.

32. King, *My Experience,* 29; Keiley, *In Vinculis,* 146–47; Benson, *Civil War Book,* 132–33; Holmes, *Elmira Prison Camp,* 338.

33. King, *My Experience,* 29; Benson, *Civil War Book,* 132; Keiley, *In Vinculis,* 147, 154–55.

34. Keiley, *In Vinculis,* 154-55.

35. Ibid.

36. Ibid., 155.

37. Records of Contracts with the Commissary General of Subsistence, Elmira, N.Y., July 11, 1864, box 10, entry 77, RG 192; Holmes, *Elmira Prison Camp,* 89, 96–97; N. J. Sappington to A. E. Shiras, July 13, 1864.

38. N J. Sappington to A. E. Shiras, July 13, 1864.

39. Contracts, July 11, 1864, box 10, entry 77, RG 192.

40. The terms of Rogers's contract stated that the fresh beef should be "of a good and marketable quality in equal proportions of fore and hind quarter neck shanks and kidney tallow to be excluded." Specifically, from the head down, the cattle were to be cut below the fourth spinal joint and sectioned, front quarters four inches atop the knee joint, the back quarters six to eight inches above the hock joint. Contracts, July 11, 1864; N. J. Sappington to A. E. Shiras, July 13, 1864.

41. Holmes, *Elmira Prison Camp,* 89–91, 96–97.

42. Ibid., 90; *Elmira (N.Y.) Daily Advertiser,* Oct. 4, 1864.

43. N. J. Sappington to A. B. Eaton, Oct. 31, 1864, Letters Received, box 201, entry 10.

44. N. J. Sappington to A. B. Eaton, Oct. 31, 1864.

45. N. J. Sappington to A. B. Eaton, Oct. 31, 1864.

46. A. B. Eaton to N. J. Sappington, Nov. 5, 1864, Commissary General of Subsistence Letter Book, vol. 54 entry 1, RG 192.

47. *OR,* vol. 7:1185.

48. Ibid.

49. N. J. Sappington to A. B. Eaton, Oct. 31, 1864; N. J. Sappington to A. B. Eaton, Dec. 7, 21, 22, 28, 1864, Letters Received, box 202, entry 10, RG 192.

50. N. J. Sappington to A. B. Eaton, Dec. 7, 1864. Sappington contended the "test applied by Capt. Munger that of boiling the meat to obtain the quantity of bone resulted I think rather in favour of its quality." N. J. Sappington to A. B. Eaton, Dec. 28, 1864.

51. N. J. Sappington to A. B. Eaton, Dec. 28, 1864; *Elmira (N.Y.) Daily Advertiser,* Dec. 2, 1864. Clay Holmes asserted that Elmirans suffered more than prisoners for want of fresh beef. Holmes, *Elmira Prison Camp,* 90, 96–97.

52. *Elmira (N.Y.) Daily Advertiser,* Dec. 3, 1864.

53. In the winter of 1864, the amount of potatoes was expanded to thirty pounds and onions fifteen pounds per every hundred rations for three out of every five days, which better controlled scurvy. N. J. Sappington to A. B. Eaton, June 28, 1865, General Correspondence, box 10, entry 17, RG 192; Subsistence Contracts, box 18, entry 77, RG 192; Oct. 12, 1864, Commissary General of Subsistence Letter Book, vol. 54; N. J. Sappington to A. E. Shiras, July 13, 1864, Letters Received, box 201, entry 10; Oct, 8, 1864, Quartermaster General Records, box 9, entry 289; *OR,* vol. 7:878, 1173.

54. N. J. Sappington to A. B. Eaton, Dec. 28, 1864.

55. *OR,* vol. 7:1185; N. J. Sappington to A. E. Eaton, Dec. 21, 22, 1864.

56. N. J. Sappington to A. B. Eaton, Dec. 22, 28, 1864.

57. Nicholas J. Sappington, Pension and Service Files, NA; N. J. Sappington to A. B. Eaton, June 28, 1865.

58. N. J. Sappington to A. B. Eaton, June 28, 1865.

59. The labor shortage was because "the number of enlisted men at present here is very small and it requires every man to do guard duty over the prisoners of war." N. J. Sappington to A. E. Shiras, July 13, 1864; Post Returns at Elmira, New York, July–October, 1864.

60. Holmes, *Elmira Prison Camp,* 345; *Elmira (N.Y.) Daily Advertiser,* July 18, 1864.

61. Ottman, "History of Elmira," 161.

62. *Elmira (N.Y.) Daily Advertiser,* July 29, 1864.

63. Halliday replaced the musty flour with fresh meal. N. J. Sappington to A. B. Eaton, Dec. 22, 28, 1864; *Elmira (N.Y.) Daily Advertiser,* July 18, 1864; Commissary General of Subsistence Letter Book, vol. 43; Subsistence Contracts, box 18, entry 77, RG 192. Briden and Briggs and D. D. Reynolds and Co. also provided hops for the prison bakery. Monthly Statement of Prison Fund, December 1864, Letters Received, box 140, entry 11, RG 249; Monthly Statement of Prison Fund, July 1864, Letters Received, box 46, entry 11, RG 249.

64. In July, D. D. Reynolds received $43.65 for supplying Elmira inmates with salt and potatoes. In August, Levi Coke sold $133.41 worth of potatoes, hops, and salt for use in the prison bakery. During October, Coke earned $48 for potatoes, whereas Andrew Hawthorne sold $638 worth of potatoes and onions. Jackson Goldsmith sold $66.51 in potatoes, L. B. Gardner received $396.31 for potatoes and onions, and Noah Turner earned $33.05 for potatoes, all in November. In December, F. J. Bundy sold $173.69 worth of potatoes, Andrew Hawthorne $890.43 worth of onions, and J. H. Loring $189 worth of whiskey. Contracts at Elmira, N.Y., box 18, entry 77, RG 192; Commissary General of Subsistence Letter Book, vol. 43; Records from Monthly Statements of Prison Fund, July–Dec. 1864, Letters Received, boxes 46, 87, 142, entry 11, RG 249.

65. N. J. Sappington to A. B. Eaton, June to October 1864, Letters Received, Cost of the Ration at Elmira N.Y., boxes 200, 201, entry 10, RG 192; Records from Monthly Statements of Prison Funds, July, 1864 to May, 1865, Letters Received, boxes 46, 87, 142, entry 11, RG 249.

66. Records from Monthly Statements of Prison Funds, July to December 1865, Letters Received, boxes 46, 87, 142, entry 11, RG 249.

67. Wilkeson continued, "I repeatedly saw the Confederate prisoners draw their provisions, and they never got more than two thirds rations." Wilkeson, *Recollections,* 225. Reductions in prisoner rations could account for the disparity between food for guards and inmates.

68. N. J. Sappington to A. B. Eaton, July 1864 to July 1865, Letters Received, Cost of the Ration at Elmira, N.Y, boxes 201, 202, 231–33, entry 10, RG 192.

69. Letter Book of Contracts at Elmira, N.Y., May to December 1864, vols. 51–54. Sappington's time was dedicated largely to negotiating contracts for prisoners' food, as indicated in his annual report to the Commissary of Subsistence: "My duties during the past year have been confined almost exclusively to providing Subsistence for a large Depot for Prisoners of War at Elmira N.Y." N. J. Sappington to A. B. Eaton, June 28, 1865.

70. Wilbur Wightman Grambling, Diary and Account Book, Mar. 27, 1865, TS, Chemung County Historical Society, Elmira, N.Y.; Benson, *Civil War Book,* 133.

71. Benson, *Civil War Book,* 133.

72. Ibid., 133–34; Grambling, Diary, Mar. 27, 1865; Toney, *Privations,* 99.

73. Toney, *Privations,* 99.

74. Benson, *Civil War Book,* 134.

75. Ibid., 134; Toney, *Privations,* 100.

76. Benson, *Civil War Book,* 134.

77. Toney, *Privations,* 100–101.

78. King, *My Experience,* 42; Wade, "Getting Out of Prison," 379.

79. Toney, *Privations,* 101; Opie, *Rebel Cavalryman,* 322.

80. Keiley, *In Vinculis,* 146.

81. Ibid.; Leon, *Diary of a Tarheel,* 68. See page 128 for a picture of prisoners buying rats.

82. Keiley, *In Vinculis,* 146; Leon, *Diary of a Tarheel,* 68; Benson, *Civil War Book,* 134; Toney, *Privations,* 101; King, *My Experience,* 42.

83. M. J. Haley, "Report from an Andersonville Prisoner," *Confederate Veteran* 15 (1907): 58.

84. Ibid., 58; Wade, "Getting Out of Prison," 379; Addison, "Recollections," 10; Stamp, "Ten Months," 496.

85. Wade, "Getting Out of Prison," 379; Toney, *Privations,* 100.

86. Holmes, *Elmira Prison Camp,* 318, 333, 335; King, *My Experience,* 42. The two Southerners were punished by being marched around the camp in a "barrel shirt," an open-ended vessel that fit snugly over the head. A sign stating "Dog Eaters" was nailed to each barrel. Holmes, *Elmira Prison Camp,* 318; King, *My Experience,* 42; Toney, *Privations,* 99–100. For more examples of punishment at Elmira Prison, see chapter 9.

87. Huffman, *Ups and Downs,* 100.

88. Opie, *Rebel Cavalryman,* 318–19.

89. Huffman, *Ups and Downs,* 100.

90. Ibid.; Opie, *Rebel Cavalryman,* 318–19; Addison, "Reminiscences," 10.

91. Holmes, *Elmira Prison Camp,* 326.

92. Addison, "Recollections," 10.

93. Keiley, *In Vinculis,* 146.

94. Holmes, *Elmira Prison Camp,* 335; King, *My Experience,* 46.

95. Stamp, "Ten Months," 496.

96. King, *My Experience,* 45.

97. Keiley, *In Vinculis,* 178.

CHAPTER FIVE

1. *OR,* vol. 7:891.

2. Ibid., 891–92.

3. Ibid., 996; Keiley, *In Vinculis,* 178–81.

4. Keiley, *In Vinculis,* 185.

5. Ibid., 185–86.

6. *OR,* vol. 7:1094.

7. *Elmira (N.Y.) Daily Advertiser,* Oct. 12, 1864.

8. Keiley, *In Vinculis,* 181–82. A number of Petersburg, Virginia, militiamen, including Anthony Keiley, not part of the established Confederate army were also paroled and sent home. *Elmira (N.Y.) Daily Advertiser,* Oct. 13, 1864.

9. *Elmira (N.Y.) Daily Advertiser,* Oct. 11, 12, 1864; Keiley, *In Vinculis,* 189–91; *OR,* vol. 8:182, 892–93.

10. *OR,* vol. 8:893.

11. Ibid., 892–93.

12. Ibid., 894.

13. Ibid.

14. Keiley, *In Vinculis,* 192–93.

15. *OR,* vol. 8:893.

16. Ibid.

17. Keiley, *In Vinculis,* 194.

18. *OR,* vol. 8:894.

19. Ibid.

20. Ibid., 892.

21. Ibid., 182; vol. 7:997.

22. Ibid., vol. 7:1093–94.

23. For other references to the Tracy–Sanger dispute, see Cooling, *Tracy,* 31, 33; Miller, *Prisons and Hospitals,* 69–70; Horigan, "Elmira Prison Camp," 3453. The article defends Sanger's tenure at Elmira and scrutinizes Secretary Stanton.

24. *OR,* vol. 7:997; U.S. War Department, *Medical and Surgical History,* pt. 2, vol. 5:56; "Map of the Confederate Prisoner of War Camp, Veterans Reserve Barracks and Artillery Encampment," Chemung Historical Society, Elmira, N.Y.

25. Keiley, *In Vinculis,* 139–40; Opie, *Rebel Cavalryman,* 320–21.

26. King, *My Experience,* 37.

27. *OR,* vol. 7:1094; U.S. War Department, *Medical and Surgical History,* pt. 2, vol. 5:56; Keiley, *In Vinculis,* 140; Stamp, "Ten Months," 494–95; Addison, "Recollections," 6; Huffman, *Ups and Downs,* 101–2.

28. *OR,* vol. 7:997.

29. Ibid., 996–97, 1065.

30. Ibid., 997.

31. Ibid., 1092–94.

32. Ibid.

33. Ibid., 1134–35.

34. Ibid., 1159; Cooling, *Tracy,* 22–23, 30, 33; *Elmira (N.Y.) Daily Advertiser,* Nov. 19, 1864.

35. *Elmira (N.Y.) Daily Advertiser,* Nov. 22, 1864.

36. Tracy's prominent postwar career included serving as secretary of the navy under President Benjamin Harrison. Cooling, *Tracy,* x, 12, 13, 22; Keiley, *In Vinculis,* 141.

37. Keiley, *In Vinculis,* 141; *OR,* vol. 7:1094, 1135–36.

38. Keiley, *In Vinculis,* 175.

39. Addison, "Recollections," 6.

40. Ibid.; Robertson, "Scourge of Elmira," 91. Dr. Van Ness asked that his one-hundred-dollar-per-month contract with the military be dissolved so he could leave Elmira, a request that was granted on December 5, 1864. He reentered the army in March 1865. Ira Van Ness, Personal Papers of Medical Officers and Physicians.

41. Keiley, *In Vinculis,* 139, 175. In Keiley's opinion, the prison camp medical department operated "as part of the education of young doctors assigned to us, for as soon as they learned to distinguish between quinine and magnesia they were removed to another field of labor."

42. Ibid., 143, 151–52.

43. Ibid., 174–75.

44. Huffman, *Ups and Downs,* 97; Addison, "Recollections," 6–7. See also Robertson, "Scourge of Elmira," 91.

45. Keiley, *In Vinculis,* 138, 141, 144–45; Holmes, *Elmira Prison Camp,* 118.

46. Keiley, *In Vinculis,* 138.

47. Clay Holmes, the preeminent defender of Elmira Prison, could not do the same for Sanger when he "received verification" of the doctor's addiction "from citizens who personally knew him." Holmes also hinted that Sanger's "personal excesses" might have contributed to the rift between him and Tracy. Holmes, *Elmira Prison Camp,* 117–18.

48. Ibid., 328.

49. Eugene F. Sanger, Personal Papers of Medical Officers and Physicians. Holmes was unable to find out why Sanger left Elmira, or anything about his career afterward: "A shade of mystery hangs about the final exit of Surgeon Sanger. . . . Inquiry at the War Department elicits the following reply under date January 17, 1912: 'Nothing has been found of record to show why Surgeon E. F. Sanger was relieved from duty in charge of prisoners of war at Elmira. . . .' F. C. Ainsworth, Adjutant-General, U.S.A. Neither is there anything to show that he was ever assigned to any other position under the Government." Holmes, *Elmira Prison Camp,* 121. James Robertson Jr., in his article published originally in 1962, states only that "Sanger abruptly left Elmira in December, 1864." Robertson, "Scourge of Elmira," 91. In a more recent article printed in 1985, J. Michael Horigan writes, "Dr. Sanger was mysteriously relieved of his duties." Horigan, "Elmira Prison Camp," 3453.

50. E. F. Sanger to J. K. Barnes, Sept. 16, 1864, Personal Papers of Eugene F. Sanger.

51. E. F. Sanger to J. K. Barnes, Sept. 16, 1864.

52. E. F. Sanger to J. K. Barnes, Nov. 30, 1864, Personal Papers of Eugene F. Sanger.

53. Post Returns at Elmira, New York, Dec. 1864.

54. A. E. Stocker to B. F. Tracy, Dec. 31, 1864. Stocker's improvements also included repairing conditions outside the workplace to create better facilities for his assistants. Perhaps he clarified why Elmira Prison lacked more qualified medical personnel: "If we consider the very low rate of compensation offered to these gentlemen for their professional services and the sacrifices necessarily made by them in discharging their duties in this camp, when equal compensation and better accommodations with more attractions are offered to them in the General Hospital in the large cities of the North, we can scarcely hope to retain them long in service here." Stocker had transferred from the Chesapeake General Hospital in Virginia, where he and his medical director had frequently squabbled over management issues. Anthony E. Stocker, Personal Papers of Medical Officers and Physicians.

55. E. F. Sanger to J. K. Barnes, Dec. 24, 1864, Personal Papers of Eugene F. Sanger.

56. A. B. Eaton to E. F. Sanger, Dec. 29, 1864, A. B. Eaton to E. F. Sanger, Feb. 6, 1865, vol. 54, entry 1, RG 192; E. F. Sanger to C. B. Penrose, Jan. 14, H. R. Sibley to A. E. Eaton, Jan. 27, 1865, Letters Received, box 231, entry 10.

57. E. F. Sanger to C. S. Tripler, Jan. 19, 1865, Personal Papers of Eugene F. Sanger.

58. Special Order No.25, Personal Papers of Eugene F. Sanger, Feb. 2, 1865.

59. C. S. Tripler to J. K. Barnes, Apr. 7, 1865, Personal Papers of Eugene F. Sanger.

60. C. S. Tripler to J. K. Barnes, Apr. 7, 1865.

61. E. F. Sanger to J. K. Barnes, Apr. 8, 1865, Personal Papers of Eugene F. Sanger.

62. E. F. Sanger to J. K. Barnes, Apr. 8, 1865.

63. E. F. Sanger to J. K. Barnes, May 6, June 30, July 9, 1865, Personal Papers of Eugene F. Sanger; Special Orders No. 173, Apr. 17, 1865, RG 94; "Military Order"; *History of Penobscot County*, 769–70.

64. "Military Order"; *History of Penobscot County*, 769–70.

65. Divorce from the Bonds of Matrimony, Eugene F. Sanger Pension File, State of Maine.

66. "Military Order."

67. Record of Death, Eugene F. Sanger Pension File, City of Bangor, State of Maine.

CHAPTER SIX

1. U.S. War Department, *Medical and Surgical History,* pt. 2, vol. 5:56.

2. *OR,* vol. 7:693, 786, 878, 918–19, 989.

3. Ibid., 918–19, 989–99. The prison fund had already covered previous bills to local lumber merchants for repairs and construction at the guard and prison camps. The bills included one in September from Spaulding and Haskell for about five thousand dollars in lumber, shingles, flooring, fixtures, and battens. Statement of the Prison Fund, Sept. 30, 1864, box 87, entry 11, RG 249.

4. *OR,* vol. 7, 918–19, 989–99; Report of Persons and Articles Hired, Oct–Dec. 1864; *New York Times,* Oct. 9, 1864. M. A. Bell was selected as the chief carpenter of the prison

camp and guard camps. He was paid an additional twelve dollars a month for his supervision. Statement of the Prison Fund, Oct.–Nov. 1864, box 87, entry 11.

5. *OR,* vol. 7:1003.

6. Horigan, "Elmira Prison Camp," 3454; *OR,* vol. 7:1092, 1003–4.

7. *OR,* vol. 7:1003–4, 1042–43, 1146. Surveyor Daniel March was paid $10 for his services. Expenditures from the Prison Fund, Nov. 1864, box 89, entry 11, RG 249.

8. *OR,* vol. 7:1004, 1025, 1042–43.

9. Ibid., 1042–43; *Elmira (N.Y.) Daily Advertiser,* Aug. 7, 1865; Abstract of Articles, Aug. 1865, box 140, entry 11; Expenditures from the Prison Fund, Jan. 1865, box 142, entry 11, RG 249. The project earned Smith $156.15 for twenty-seven days of work. A few weeks after the work started the *Daily Advertiser* reported, "The needful authority has been granted to the quartermaster of this post to purchase as many tools as prisoners of war may need on their mechanical labor, the expense to be incurred by the prison fund. *Elmira (N.Y.) Daily Advertiser,* Nov. 16, 1864.

10. *Elmira (N.Y.) Daily Advertiser,* Oct. 21, 1864.

11. Ibid.

12. Ibid., Oct. 21, 1864; John J. Elwell pension file; *OR,* vol. 7:1104.

13. Spaulding and Haskell supplied 181,516 feet of hemlock, 2,733 feet of pine, 141,398 feet of box lumber, 43,545 feet of pine plank, 321 feet of shingles, 3,320 battens at 3 ft. x 12 in., 472 battens at 3 in. x 16 ft., 216 glazed window frames, 12,500 feet of lathe, and 16,100 feet of flooring; Hatch and Partridge provided 63,394 feet of hemlock, 1,790 feet of select plane, 7,240 feet of pine, 70,000 feet of hemlock timber, 250 feet of glazed sash, and 4,500 feet of pine ceiling. All told, in November some 1,059,625 feet of lumber were required at Elmira Prison and Camp Chemung for barracks, hospitals, medical offices, and privies. On December 1, Cook and Covell charged $5,664.51 for 63,125 feet of felt gravel roof and 1,868 tin roof for use at the pen. They also furnished doorknobs, nails, gutters, hinges, screws, springs, glass, ventilators, tar, bolts, staples, rivets, and solder. In October, the firm had sold $4,174.64 worth of goods for the pen. Other items beside building materials included mops, pipe, utensils, washtubs and boards, wheelbarrows, lamps, plates, and other tools, fixtures, and equipment. Cook and Covell became a primary provider to the prison and guard camps. Statement of the Prison Fund, Nov. 18, 20, 30, Dec. 1, 1864, box 142; Expenditures on Prisoners of War, Oct.–Nov. 1864, boxes 85, 87, entry 11; J. J. Elwell to W. Hoffman, Nov. 4, 1864, Letters Received, box 87, entry 11; H. Colt to B. F. Tracy, Nov. 14, 1864, Letters Received, box 87, entry 11; *OR,* vol. 7:1050, 1136, 1146; J. J. Elwell to W. Hoffman, Jan. 10, 1865, Letters Received, box 561, entry 225, RG 92; Wilkeson, *Recollections,* 227.

14. *OR,* vol. 7:1136.

15. Ibid., 1027, 1050, 1173, 1237.

16. Ibid., 1213.

17. J. J. Elwell to M. C. Meigs, Dec. 16, 1864, Letters Received, box 561, entry 225, RG 92; Statement of the Prison Fund, Dec. 31, 1864, box 142.

18. John J. Elwell pension file; *Elmira (N.Y.) Daily Advertiser,* Jan. 12, 1865.

19. *Elmira (N.Y.) Daily Advertiser,* Jan. 31, 1865.

20. *OR,* vol. 7:1272.

21. Holmes, *Elmira Prison Camp,* 67.

22. Ibid., 332, 334, 345–46. Wood inspectors supervised the quality and quantity of the wood, which could be turned away if inferior. Wood suppliers got away at times with selling poor supplies and on occasion Commandant Tracy had to reprimand inspectors, who took for granted the honesty of some wood salesmen. After wood was unloaded, seemingly helpful contractors might assist inspectors by holding one end of the tape measure so the load's value could be assessed. As the inspector moved down the pile and unraveled the tape measure, the contractor would begin rolling it up around his finger, thus giving a false reading of the actual supply. A. S. Diven to B. F. Tracy, Nov. 15, 1864, Letters Received, vol. 88, entries 854, 856, RG 393; Holmes, *Elmira Prison Camp,* 345–46.

23. Marvin backed his contract with a $10,000 bond. For 2,000 cords of dry hardwood he was paid $7.50 a cord; for 1,000 cords of green hardwood, $7.25 per cord; and for 1,000 cords of softwood, $6 per cord. Textual Records of the Quartermaster General, vol. 16, entry 1238, vol. 1., entry 1252.

24. J. D. Baldwin supplied the prison with coal. Grambling diary, Dec. 25, 1864; *OR,* vol. 7:1201, 1237; N. J. Sappington to A. B. Eaton, March 8, 1865, Letters Received, box 9, entry 17; Statement of the Prison Fund, Dec. 31, 1864, Mar. 31, 1865, boxes 2, 142.

25. *OR,* vol. 7:919, vol. 8:39; U.S. War Department, *Medical and Surgical History,* pt. 2, vol. 5:56–57; King, *My Experience,* 36, 39; Stewart, "Reminiscences," 2; Holmes, *Elmira Prison Camp,* 208, 334–35. The completion of buildings at Barracks Number 3 was very costly, as indicated in the December figures for prison fund expenditures. Spaulding and Haskell billed $13,551.37 for lumber, Hatch and Partridge, $4,523.47, and Henry Baker and Co., $600. Statement of the Prison Fund, Dec. 21, 31, 1864, box 142.

26. Tracy temporarily reported to a new chief, Henry W. Wessells, who sent Medical Inspector Thomas Getty to Elmira at the end of November because "unfavorable reports are continually received at this office, and it is desirable to correct existing evils." Getty recommended that the prison use coal stoves and better insulate the hospitals, which Wessells approved. *OR,* vol. 7:1157, 1173, 1201, 1237, vol. 8:3–4.

27. Ibid., vol. 8:3–4.

28. Hunter, "Warden for the Union," 177.

29. Leon, *Diary of a Tarheel,* 67.

30. Holmes, *Elmira Prison Camp,* 68–69.

31. Wade, "Getting Out of Prison," 379.

32. *Elmira (N.Y.) Daily Advertiser,* Feb. 11, 1865; Holmes, *Elmira Prison Camp,* 69.

33. Keiley, *In Vinculis,* 129.

34. King, *My Experience,* 38; Toney, *Privations,* 104. On the last day of December, Dr. Stocker warned Colonel Tracy that "the buildings already erected and in use for the accommodation of prisoners are too crowded, needing more light and ventilation if practicable. The present effects of too crowded buildings are to produce in their occupants a low form of Pneumonia or Inflammation of the Lungs, a form of disease greatly on the increase, and to propagate contagious and infectious diseases, especially of Small-Pox, now also on the increase." A. Stocker to B. F. Tracy, Dec. 31, 1864, Letters Received, box 140, entry 11.

35. Opie, *Rebel Cavalryman,* 318.

36. Wade, "Getting Out of Prison," 379; Toney, *Privations*, 103; King, *My Experience*, 39.

37. Toney, *Privations*, 103–4.

38. King, *My Experience*, 34.

39. Toney, *Privations*, 104; King, *My Experience*, 34; Grambling diary, Oct. 1, Dec. 11, 1864.

40. Jan. 16, 1865, William Campbell Papers, Special Collections, Duke University Library, Durham, N.C. (hereafter cited as Duke University).

41. King, *My Experience*, 38–39, Toney, *Privations*, 104–5.

42. Toney, *Privations*, 105.

43. King, *My Experience*, 38–39; Wilkeson, *Recollections*, 226; Grambling diary, Dec. 20, 1864, Wade, "Getting Out of Prison," 379; U.S. War Department, *Medical and Surgical History*, pt. 2, vol. 5:56.

44. Grambling diary, Oct. 1, 1864.

45. *OR*, vol. 7:466.

46. *New York Evening Post*, Aug. 17, 1864.

47. U.S. War Department, *Medical and Surgical History*, pt.2, vol. 5:57; Wilkeson, *Recollections*, 225–26; *Elmira (N.Y.) Daily Advertiser*, July 27, 1865; *OR*, vol. 7:1136, 1167; King, *My Experience*, 38.

48. King, *My Experience*, 33.

49. *OR*, vol. 7:1065.

50. Ibid., 1167.

51. Toney, *Privations*, 112.

52. King, *My Experience*, 38. See also Stamp, "Ten Months," 497, and Leon, *Diary of a Tarheel*, 69.

53. *OR*, vol. 7:1184–85.

54. Ibid., 1184–85, 1213, 1240 1272; *Elmira (N.Y.) Daily Advertiser*, July 27, 1865.

55. *OR*, vol. 7:573, 584. To his credit, Hoffman tried providing rejected uniforms and government blankets at his prisons whenever available, a matter not as urgent in warmer southern compounds. Inmates on both sides tried to make up for necessities not provided by captors—whether food, clothing, or other goods—by making written requests. For more information on regulations regarding articles that could be sent to inmates, see Hesseltine, *Civil War Prisons*, 42–43, 45–46

56. Oct. 17, 1864, D. Bruin Papers, Special Collections, University of North Carolina, Chapel Hill. Many times clothing was permitted after a written request was made to the commissary general of prisons. For example, E. B. Nicholas wrote to Hoffman in September: "Sir, Most respectfully I make an application to you for a permit, to send a box of warm clothing containing a coarse heavy over-coat & flannel shirts to my brother in law, Robert W. Drewry—a Rebel prisoner at Elmira, N.Y. . . . I beg that the favor may be granted for the sake of humanity as my brother in law is not strong & entirely unaccustomed to the severity of a Northern climate, & without these comforts must suffer very keenly." Hoffman approved the application. E. B. Nicholas to W. Hoffman, Sept. 22, 1864, Letters Received, box 140, entry 12, RG 249.

57. W. Campbell to Z. Campbell, Jan. 24, 1865, Letters, Duke University.

58. James Hardaway to E. G. Booth, Nov. 1, 1864, Elmira Prison File, Chemung County Historical Society, Elmira, N.Y.

59. Grambling diary, Feb. 2, 1865; James P. Jones and Edward F. Keuchel, eds., "A Rebel's Diary of Elmira Prison Camp," *Chemung Historical Journal* 20.4 (Mar. 1975): 2457, 2463. The Floridian never admitted, at least in his diary, that he wore the underwear.

60. Jefferson Davis, "Andersonville and Other War Prisons," *Confederate Veteran* 15 (1907): 164.

61. *Elmira (N.Y.) Daily Advertiser,* Dec. 2, 19, 1864.

62. Holmes, *Elmira Prison Camp,* 76–78.

63. Stephen Moore Pension File, NA; *Elmira (N.Y.) Daily Advertiser,* Jan. 13, 1865.

64. *OR,* vol. 7:1063, 1101, 1117–18, 1148–49, 1230.

65. Dec. 15, 1864, William N. R. Beall Collection, Prisoner of War series, Eleanor S. Brockenbrough Library, Museum of the Confederacy, Richmond, Va; *Elmira (N.Y.) Daily Advertiser,* Feb. 9, 1865; *OR,* vol. 8:67–68, 77, 23–24.

66. *OR,* vol. 8:90.

67. Ibid., 105–6, 137, 195–96.

68. *Elmira (N.Y.) Daily Advertiser,* Feb. 9, 10, 11, 13, 16, July 27, 1865; Feb. 15, 1865, Beall Collection.

69. Feb. 12, 15, 28, 1865, Beall Collection; Inspection Reports, Mar. 1865, box 30, entry 199, RG 109.

70. Feb. 12, 1865, Beall Collection. The only other evidence that locals provided additional clothing for inmates were twenty-five pairs of mittens bought from Baldwin and Reynolds for twenty-five dollars and perhaps used by prisoners on work duty. Statement of the Prison Fund, Feb. 11, 1865, box 142.

71. Feb. 28, Mar. 4, 25, 1865, Beall Collection.

72. Inspection Reports, Mar. 4, 1865.

73. Mar. 6, 7, May 16, 1865, Beall Collection.

74. Mar. 12, Apr. 14, May 16, 1865, Beall Collection.

75. Inspection Reports, Mar. 12, 1865.

76. Invoice for Clothing, Mar. 24, 25, 1865, Beall Collection.

77. Apr. 12, 1865, Beall Collection.

78. Inspection Reports, May 20, 1865.

79. *OR,* vol. 8:182.

80. Ibid.

81. Ibid., 231–32; *Elmira (N.Y.) Daily Advertiser,* Feb. 14, 1865. The paper also reported: "There were many stout, healthy looking ones among the entire number, but, as a general thing the sick and complaining who were able to be moved or travel were selected for the first five hundred exchanged."

82. *OR,* vol. 8:231–32.

83. Ibid., 232.

84. Ibid.

85. Howard claimed that "from fifteen to thirty-five of our men were buried every day while small pox raged in our camp." Howard, "Short Sketch," 15; King, *My Experiences,* 40; Addison, "Recollections," 8.

86. *OR,* vol. 7:1065, 1240, 1272–73, vol. 8:3.

87. Ibid., vol. 7:1272–73, vol. 8:24–25, 39; U.S. War Department, *Medical and Surgical History,* pt. 2, vol. 5:57.

88. *OR,* vol. 8:39.

89. U.S. War Department, *Medical and Surgical History,* pt. 2, vol. 5:57; Inspection Reports, Jan. 29, 1865.

90. Addison, "Recollections," 9.

91. Grambling diary, Dec. 26, 1864.

92. Stamp, "Ten Months," 497–98.

93. Opie, *Rebel Cavalryman,* 320–21.

94. "Statement of a United States Medical Officer," 296. Complaints about poor vaccinations at the Confederate prison in Andersonville, Georgia, may have led to postwar accusations about similar problems in Elmira.

95. U.S. War Department, *Medical and Surgical History,* pt.2, vol. 5:57; Dawn P. Dawson, ed., *Magill's Medical Guide: Health and Illness* (Englewood Cliffs, N.J.: Salem Press, 1995), 3:717; Toney, *Privations,* 110–11.

96. Toney, *Privations,* 110–11.

97. Sherrill, *Soldier's Story,* 12; Toney, *Privations,* 111.

98. Sherrill, *Soldier's Story,* 12–13.

99. Toney, *Privations,* 112.

100. Ibid.; Toney, "Prison Life," 278–79. Toney offered other comments about his experience in the smallpox ward: "I never spent a more wretched week than while there. Both of my bedfellows died, and their bodies were prepared for their rude coffins in front of my tent.

101. Sherrill, *Soldier's Story,* 13; Toney, *Privations,* 112.

102. Toney, *Privations,* 112.

103. Stewart, "Reminiscences," 2–3.

104. "Statement of a United States Medical Officer," 296.

105. Addison, "Recollections," 8; Toney, *Privations,* 112; Sherrill, *Soldier's Story,* 13–14.

106. Sherrill, *Soldier's Story,* 13–14.

107. Ibid.

108. List of Articles for Smallpox Patients, Beall Collection.

109. Holmes, *Elmira Prison Camp,* 123, 295; Barrack Inventory; Mar. 7, 1865, Beall Collection; *OR,* vol. 8:419–420.

CHAPTER SEVEN

1. *Elmira (N.Y.) Daily Advertiser,* Sept. 19, 1864.

2. Benson, *Civil War Book,* 135.

3. *New York Times,* Oct. 16, 1864; Benson, *Civil War Book,* 133; King, *My Experience,* 30.

4. Howard, "Short Sketch," 15; Benson, *Civil War Book,* 133

5. Benson, *Civil War Book,* 133.

6. Huffman, *Ups and Downs,* 97.

7. King, *My Experience,* 45.

8. Benson, *Civil War Book,* 133—34; Stamp, "Ten Months," 494; King, *My Experience,* 45; Toney, *Privations,* 101.

9. Opie, *Rebel Cavalryman,* 322.

10. Toney, *Privations,* 97, 120.

11. Opie, *Rebel Cavalryman,* 322.

12. King, *My Experience,* 45.

13. *OR,* vol. 7:75; Opie, Rebel *Cavalryman,* 322; Benson, *Civil War Book,* 133; Toney, *Privations,* 96; Howard, "Short Sketch," 14–15; *Elmira (N.Y.) Daily Advertiser,* Sept. 8, 1864.

14. Albert A. Banks to Edwin G. Booth, Nov. 1, 1864, Elmira Prison File.

15. James S. Montgomery to F. J. Fergeson, Oct. 19, 1864, Elmira Prison File.

16. Toney, *Privations,* 96.

17. Holmes, *Elmira Prison Camp,* 38.

18. Opie, *Rebel Cavalryman,* 322; Toney, *Privations,* 96; King, *My Experience,* 49.

19. King, *My Experience,* 49.

20. Toney, *Privations,* 96; Keiley, *In Vinculis,* 159–60.

21. Keiley, *In Vinculis,* 159–60.

22. Holmes, *Elmira Prison Camp,* 24, 265–66.

23. T. C. Davis, captured at Fort Fisher, did not like the procedure: "We were halted in an old warehouse and robbed of all valuables by Lieut. Groves and an unknown Sergeant Major." T. C. Davis, "Mark Charley Herbst's Grave," *Confederate Veteran* 7.1 (1899): 65; *New York Post,* Aug. 17, 1964; "Records of the Adjutant General, Letters Received," box 131, entry 199; Sutler Records, box 131, entry 199; King, *My Experience,* 37–38, 45; Huffman, *Ups and Downs,* 97.

24. Howard, "Short Sketch," 14.

25. Stamp, "Ten Months," 494.

26. King, *My Experience,* 37.

27. Ibid., 37–38; Grambling diary, July 1864–Mar. 1865.

28. *New York Evening Post,* Aug. 17, 1864.

29. *OR,* vol. 7:74–75; Sutler Records; Prisoners of War, vol. 233, roll 71, microcopy No. 598, NA.

30. Huffman, *Ups and Downs,* 94, 97.

31. Ibid., 97.

32. Ibid., 97–100.

33. Ibid., 100.

34. King, *My Experience,* 41; Toney, *Privations,* 109. The prisoners especially targeted horses that pulled supplies into the prison. Toney added: "Finally the horses were about to lose their hair appendages, and a guard was sent with each wagon." In another instance, an assistant provost marshal general came into the pen on a "handsome and favorite white horse of his, much of whose beauty consisted in a flowing mane and especially profuse

tail." After hitching his ride to a post and leaving it unattended, he commenced business without a second thought. Returning some time after, he discovered that his "white beauty" had lost its most distinguished features, with hardly anything remaining on the tail and mane. It was long remembered how a number of rings, chains, and broaches took on a decidedly white hue after that officer left. Towner, *History of Chemung County,* 272.

35. Toney, *Privations,* 108; Huffman, *Ups and Downs,* 100; Sherrill, *Soldier's Story,* 17.

36. Sherrill, *Soldier's Story,* 17.

37. Huffman, *Ups and Downs,* 100.

38. Ibid.; Toney, *Privations,* 108–9; King, *My Experience,* 41; Holmes, *Elmira Prison Camp,* 92. One method of depositing money in the prisoners' account was by mailing it to the treasurer. The partner working with inmates specified the name of the manufacturer, his residence, the item, its cost, and the purchaser. The following correspondence by J. W. Merriam, an assistant surgeon employed in the hospital, indicates exactly how the system worked: "Lieut Groves, I send you two dolls & twenty five cts ($2.25) please place one dollar to the credit of Seth Warton Priv E 1st N.C. Ward 26 for 3 rings—and $1.25 to the credit of W. G. Hammond Priv C 20 N.C. Ward 27 for one fan, are bought by Madam Varian. Please note receipt on envelop, return by bearer. Very Respectfully, Your Obt Servt, J. W. Merriam. J. W. Merriam to J. Groves, May 27, 1865, box 131, entry 199, RG 109.

39. Holmes, *Elmira Prison Camp,* 296.

40. King, *My Experience,* 41.

41. Ibid.

42. Ibid., 22–23; J. Kidder to H. Kidder, May 14, July 28, 1864, The Family Papers of John S. Kidder, MS, Sharon Springs, N.Y. (hereafter cited as Kidder Papers).

43. McPherson, *Battle Cry,* 728–31; J. S. Kidder to H. Kidder, May 14, 19, 30, 1864, Kidder Papers; John S. Kidder Pension File, NA.

44. J. S. Kidder to H. Kidder, June 6, 1864, Kidder Papers.

45. J. S. Kidder to H. Kidder, June 21, 24, 30, July 28, 1864, Kidder Papers.

46. J. S. Kidder to H. Kidder, July 21, Sept, 9, 10, 1864, J. S. Kidder to L. Thomas, Aug. 12, 1864, J.S. Kidder to D. Vanburen, Sept, 9, 1864, Kidder Papers.

47. J. S. Kidder to H. Kidder, Sept. 25, 1864, Kidder Papers.

48. J. S. Kidder to H. Kidder, Oct. 1, 1864, Kidder Papers.

49. J. S. Kidder to H. Kidder, Dec. 30, 1864, Jan. 30, Mar. 30, Apr. 19, 1865, Kidder Papers. Kidder claimed that he earned $672 in the "Special War Tax" of 1864. It was highly unlikely that his income tax form included earnings from the Elmira Prison ring trade. *Elmira (N.Y.) Daily Advertiser,* Apr. 24, 1865.

50. J. A. Evans to J. S. Kidder, Sept. 5, Apr. 25, 1865, Kidder Papers.

51. Keiley, *In Vinculis,* 133.

52. Ibid., 172.

53. Ibid.,133.

54. Holmes, *Elmira Prison Camp,* 91–92.

55. Ibid., 163–65.

56. Ibid., 352; Trinket Blotter, Joseph Groves, box 131, entry 199.

57. Holmes, *Elmira Prison Camp*, 296, 298.

58. Sherrill, *Soldier's Story*, 10.

59. Holmes, *Elmira Prison Camp*, 335.

60. Trinket Blotter; Toney, *Privations*, 108; Grambling diary, Feb. 5, 1865; King, *My Experience*, 41–42.

61. Trinket Blotter; King, *My Experience*, 41–42. King also remembered seeing Captain Peck with a parasol in hand. "I suppose he found a purchaser for it," wrote King.

62. Holmes, *Elmira Prison Camp*, 313.

63. If one wanted to witness the engine work, a cracker had to be paid to the inventor. Grambling diary, July 29, 1864; King, *My Experience*, 43.

64. *Elmira (N.Y.) Daily Advertiser*, July 25, 1864.

65. J. S. Kidder to H. Kidder, Nov. 13, Dec. 13, 1864, Kidder Papers.

66. Lieutenants John McConnell and Isaac B. Richmond headed the general labor detail. Capt. George Whiton was in charge of commissary detail. Doctors Sanger and Stocker, respectively, presided over the hospital department; and C. C. Barton and H. H. Mott headed the Adjutant's Office. Every ten days, each departmental head had to document the number of workers under his charge and list how many days each worker was employed so the men could be paid. The prison fund, which increased as more employment was offered at the pen, provided the earnings for men employed on public works. In October, for example, $316.45 was paid to inmates; in November, $455.20. By April 1865, $1,429.80 had been doled out, and in May, $1,016.30. Statements of Prison Funds and Certification of Prisoners Engaged in Public Works, box 142, entry 11; Statements of Prison Funds and Certification of Prisoners Engaged in Public Works, box 87, entry 11; Keiley, *In Vinculis*, 152; *New York Times*, Oct. 9, 1864; *Elmira (N.Y.) Daily Advertiser*, Aug. 25, 1864, Jan. 13, 1865; Holmes, *Elmira Prison Camp*, 318.

67. King, *My Experiences*, 44.

68. Holmes, *Elmira Prison Camp*, 334.

69. Stamp, "Ten Months," 495–96; Holmes, *Elmira Prison Camp*, 323, 267; Opie, *Rebel Cavalryman*, 319; Howard, "Short Sketch," 13–14.

70. Holmes, *Elmira Prison Camp*, 322–23, 278; Letters Received, Collection of Confederate Records, Feb. 21, 25, Mar. 15, June 27, 1865, box 131, entry 199, RG 109; Keiley, *In Vinculis*, 150–51.

71. Keiley, *In Vinculis*, 150–53, 180–82, 184, 188.

72. Holmes, *Elmira Prison Camp*, 309–13.

73. W. Campbell to Z. Campbell, Feb. 1, Jan. 16, Mar. 13, 1865, Letters, Duke University.

74. Major Beall relieved Campbell because Campbell would not testify in a court martial against Asst. Surg. P. C. Pease, whom Campbell had befriended in prison, and because Campbell was caught in the aforementioned mail scandal, which also involved three Union soldiers. The letters that Campbell later wrote to his brother, James, exceeded the standard regulation size of one page, but found another outlet that enabled him to continue sending his extended correspondence out of Elmira Prison. Campbell revealed to his brother at least one reason for his vigorous pen. "Dear James . . . I will show you the

extensively written letters that I have from some of the first ladies of the North: truly, it is flattering to my pride. I am carrying about ½ dozen flirtations; but no serious intentions are entertained." W. Campbell to Z. Campbell, Feb. 1, Mar. 13, 1865; Mar. 15, 18, Apr. 1, 1865, Letter Book, entry 854, 856, RG 393.

75. *New York Times,* Oct. 9, 1864; *New York Post,* Aug. 17, 1864; Howard, "Short Sketch," 13–16; Towner, *History of Chemung County,* 271; Holmes, *Elmira Prison Camp,* 317–18, 171, 283, 56; Inspection Reports, Jan. 29, Mar. 4, Apr. 15, 1865; Grambling diary, Jan. 18, 1865; King, *My Experience,* 36; Keiley, *In Vinculis,* 174. A Union guard commented about the importance of public works at Elmira: "I have seen prisoners display as much eagerness to secure this employment, as free men would to secure remunerative positions of trust. And they worked faithfully and honestly, and earned their scanty pay." Wilkeson, *Recollections,* 227.

76. Grambling diary, July 26, 31, Oct. 1, Nov. 19, 1864, Feb. 9, 1865.

77. Holmes, *Elmira Prison Camp,* 332–33.

78. *Elmira (N. Y.) Daily Advertiser,* Aug. 30, 1864; Wade, "Getting Out of Prison," 379; Grambling diary, Jan. 12, 18, 25, 1865.

79. Howard, "Short Sketch," 16.

80. Grambling diary, Jan. 12, 1865.

81. Wade, "Getting Out of Prison"; 379; Prisoners sometimes weighed themselves on the cookhouse scales. Toney, *Privations,* 102.

CHAPTER EIGHT

1. Ottman, "History of Elmira," 162–65; A. G. Steen, "Recollections of Elmira in Civil War Days," TS, Chemung County Historical Society 1–4; *Elmira (N. Y.) Star-Gazette,* May 17, 1993.

2. Ottman, "History of Elmira," 170.

3. *Elmira (N. Y.) Star-Gazette,* May 17, 1993; Ottman, "History of Elmira," 165–71; Annual Report of Captain S. P. Suydam, A.Q.M., to the Quartermaster General, 1865, box 18, entry 225, RG 92. Horses sold for about $155 apiece, and 15,725 were purchased by war's end, which cost the government millions of dollars. Annual Report of Captain J. J. Elwell to the Quartermaster General, 1864, 1865, box 6, entry 225, RG 92.

4. Ottman, "History of Elmira," 200; Horigan, "Elmira Prison Camp," 3450; *Elmira (N. Y.) Daily Advertiser,* Aug. 9, Sept. 15, 20, 1864; *Elmira (N. Y.) Star-Gazette,* May 17, 1993; Towner, *History of the Chemung County,* 259; Elwell's Annual Report, 1865, box 6, entry 225, RG 92; Suydam's Annual Report, 1865, box 18, entry 225, RG 92.

5. *Elmira (N. Y.) Daily Advertiser,* Nov. 18, 1864.

6. Ibid., Aug. 8, 1865.

7. Ibid., July 15, 1864.

8. Ibid., Aug. 9, 1864.

9. Ibid., Aug. 11, 1864.

10. Ibid., Oct. 19, 1864.

11. *New York Evening Post,* Aug. 17, 1864.

12. Ibid.

13. *New York Evening Express,* Oct. 10, 1864.

14. E. Monell to E. M. Stanton, Oct. 24, 1864, Letters Received, box 561, entry 225, RG 92.

15. M. C. Meigs to E. M. Stanton, Nov. 5, 1864, Letters Received, box 561.

16. S. P. Suydam to J. J. Elwell, Oct. 24, 31 1864, Letters Received, box 561.

17. Statement of the Prison Fund, 1864, box 1, entry 16, 77.

18. Record of Contracts, Dec. 13, 1864, box 9, entry 77, RG 192.

19. B. F. Tracy to A. B. Eaton, Feb. 28, 1865, General Correspondence, box 10, entry 17, RG 192.

20. B. F. Tracy to A. B. Eaton, Feb. 28, 1865.

21. Record of Contracts, Jan. 1, 1865, box 12, entry 77, RG 192.

22. N. J. Sappington to A. B. Eaton, Feb. 2, 1865, Letters Received, box 231, entry 17, RG 192. Other items on contract with the Commissary Department included 198 bushels of white beans to James Hotchkip at $2.25 per bushel; salt to George McGrath and V. B. Read, 250 bushels each at 53 cents per bushel. N. J. Sappington to A. B. Eaton, April 6, 1865, Letters Received, box 9, entry 17; Record of Contracts, June 23, 1865, box 11, entry 77.

23. N. J. Sappington to A. B. Eaton, Aug. 23, 1865, General Correspondence, box 10, entry 17, entry 192.

24. Record of Contracts, Feb. 2, 1865, box 12, entry 77, RG 192; N. J. Sappington to A. B. Eaton, Feb. 6, 1865, Letters Received, box 9, entry 17, RG 192; Record of Contracts, Mar. 3, 1865, box 12.

25. Record of Contracts, Apr. 29, 1865, box 11; N. J. Sappington to A. B. Eaton Apr. 24, 1865, Letters Received, box 232, entry 17, RG 192; Cooling, *Tracy,* 7. Throughout 1865 the prison fund also paid locals a significant amount of money to feed inmates, particularly sick ones. In March, the fund paid J. H. Loring and Co. $568.06 for 218 bushels of onions and Andrew Hawthorn $890.43 for 302 bushels of onions; Levi Coke received $575.95 for 575 onions and J. A. Bundy got $173.69 for potatoes. In April, William Ryan was paid $38.70 for about 60 pounds of potatoes, J. A. Bundy $12 for potatoes, and Andrew Hawthorn $661.85 for 189 bushels of onions. In May, the fund paid Levi Coke $463.83 for 337 bushels of potatoes, J. H. Loring and Co. $1,012.47 for 291 bushels of onions, Loremore Brothers $68.75 for 25 gallons of whiskey, and M. P. Fitch $168.59 for 269 bushels of potatoes. Abstract of Disbursements On Account of the Prison Fund, Mar.–May, 1865, box 142, entry 11, RG 249; Statement of the Prison Fund, Feb.–May, 1865, box 142.

26. Holmes, *Elmira Prison Camp,* 340.

27. Toney, *Privations,* 98. The Tennessean added, "We had the same kind of scandal in the corned beef business during the Spanish-American War; we would nowadays call them grafters."

28. Holmes, *Elmira Prison Camp,* 340.

29. Towner, *History of Chemung County,* 273; undated newspaper clipping, Prison File, Chemung County Historical Society, Elmira, N.Y.; Holmes, *Elmira Prison Camp,* 92.

30. Report of Persons and Articles Hired.

31. J. J. Elwell to M. C. Meigs, Aug. 14, Sept. 9, 1864, Letters Received, box 561, entry 225, RG 92.

32. Report of Persons and Articles Hired. In October, the prison fund expended $230.02 to pay citizens and soldiers who worked inside the prison. In November, $199.05 was paid to "Clerks, Orderlies, Mechanics, & Laborers in Military Prison." In April 1865, the free-labor force earned $703.51, and in May $431.85. Abstract of Disbursements, Oct., Nov. 1864, Apr., May, 1865, box 142.

33. *Elmira (N.Y.) Daily Advertiser,* Aug. 12, 1864; Holmes, *Elmira Prison Camp,* 343–45. William Merwin charged $112 for four single sets of cart harnesses at $28 apiece. Palmer and Knowl repaired prison carts at a fee of about $20. Statement of the Prison Fund, Apr. 30, May 19, 1865, box 142; Abstract of Disbursements, May, 1865, box 142.

34. Report of Persons and Articles Hired.

35. It might take as many as 12 grosses of matches, 2 grosses of lamp wicks, and from 250 to more than 500 gallons of kerosene oil to keep the prison illuminated for a month. Cook and Covell charged 75 cents a gallon for the oil. List of Quartermaster Stores, Nov. 1864, Jan., Feb., Apr., 1865, boxes 85, 136, 138, entry 11; Statement of the Prison Fund, Mar. 31, Apr. 29, 1865, box 142.

36. List of Quartermaster Stores, Jan. 1865, box 135; Statement of the Prison Fund, Jan. 31, Mar. 31, 1865, box 135. In addition to expenses for building material, Russell and French charged from $2.25 to $3.50 a day for their work as masons. The cost per barrel of lime was $1.75, and the camp could average from thirty to sixty barrels a month to disinfect privies. Cook and Covell also supplied lime. List of Quartermaster Stores, Nov. 1864, Jan., Feb., Apr. 1865, box 135.

37. In July 1864, Presnick and Dudley sold $145.91 in supplies, and in August, September, and December, $117.58, $93.91, and $270.45, respectively. In January 1865, the company sold $113.97, and in February and March, $165.97 and $181.25, respectively. In addition, Hall Brothers sold more than $400 worth of goods to the prison. Statement of the Prison Fund, July 19, 31, 1864, Aug. 29, 30, Sept. 30, Dec. 31, Feb. 28, Mar. 31, 1865, boxes 87, 142; Abstract of Disbursements, Oct. 1864, Apr., May, 1865, boxes 87, 142.

38. In February 1865, George McGrath supplied the hospital with 5,800 pounds of hay for $87; in March, 13,900 pounds for $208.50; and in April, 8,112 pounds for $109.51. R. Simmons provided 4,150 pounds of hay for $51.87. From March through May 1865, D. D. Reynolds and Co., J. G. Widing, George McGrath, W. T. Post, and J. A. Sly all furnished straw that totaled around $200. Statement of Prison Fund, Feb. 28, Mar. 31, Apr. 11, 30, 1865, box 142, entry 11; Abstract of Disbursements, Mar.–May, 1865, box 142.

39. The costly medicines included opium, ammonia, mustard, acetic acid, chalk, morphine, quinine, and Juniper berries, all of which the prison fund purchased. John K. Perry and Son also sold provisions, and in September 1864 Dr. Sanger approved an expenditure of $63.15 from the Perrys' store. In February 1865, Cook and Covell sold $92 worth of drugs to the pen. From February through April, Ingraham and Robinson sold $500 in medicine to the prison hospital. Statement of the Prison Fund, Sept. 13, 1864, Feb. 20, 28, 1865, Mar. 20, Apr. 8, 20, boxes 87, 142.

40. Holmes, *Elmira Prison Camp,* 131, 140–43, 145–46; *OR,* vol. 7:506; Burial Report to the Quartermaster General, Sept. 23, 1874, box 25, entry 576, RG 92.

41. *New York Sun,* Aug. 13, 1880.

42. Jones bore responsibility for "interring the remains, setting headboards and recording deaths." Receipt of Rolls of Employees paid by the Prison Fund, 1864–65 boxes 87, 142, entry 11, RG 249; Ledgers of Deceased Prisoners of War, Elmira, N.Y., Eleanor S. Brockenbrough Library; Lease Agreement at Woodlawn, Jan. 1, 1865, box 25, entry 576; Veterans Administration Pamphlet, Woodlawn National Cemetery, Elmira, N.Y.; Burial Report.

43. Receipt of Rolls of Employees paid by Prison Fund 1865, box 142. Palmer and Knowl were responsible for repairing the hearse. In January, March, and April 1865, they rendered their services, which totaled $24.25. Lumber for construction of coffins was more expensive: 35 cents for every 10 feet. In January 1865, 18,000 feet of lumber were required. In February and April, 24,000 and 10,000 feet, respectively, were "used in the construction of coffins for deceased prisoners." In March, when the number of deaths was highest, Spaulding and Haskell received $770 for supplying 22,000 feet of "coffin lumber," while Hatch and Partridge provided 10,000 feet for $350. List of Quartermaster Stores, Jan., Feb., Apr., 1865 boxes 135, 136, 138; Statement of the Prison Fund, Jan. 31, Mar. 31, Apr. 30, 1865, box 142.

44. List of buildings at Elmira, N.Y.; Toney, *Privations,* 109–10; King, *My Experience,* 40; Holmes, *Elmira Prison Camp,* 129; *Elmira (N.Y.) Daily Advertiser,* Aug. 25, 1864; Howard, "Short Sketch," 16.

45. Toney, *Privations,* 109–10.

46. Holmes, *Elmira Prison Camp,* 129–30; "Woodlawn National Cemetery Pamphlet;" *New York Sun,* Aug. 13, 1880; *OR,* vol. 8:1001.

47. Report of Persons and Articles Hired; Holmes, *Elmira Prison Camp,* 130; Susie Gentry, "Confederate Dead at Elmira Prison," *Confederate Veteran* 22 (1914): 396; List of Quartermaster Stores, Apr. 1864, box 138. Cook and Covell supplied the paint for writing identifications on the headboards. In April 1865, for example, the task required one hundred pounds of powdered white lead paint, which cost the prison fund eighteen dollars. Statement of the Prison Fund, Apr. 30, 1865, box 142.

48. Holmes, *Elmira Prison Camp,* 130–31.

49. Ibid. Census records state that Jones was a forty-seven-year-old mulatto, that he had a framed house estimated to be worth two thousand dollars, that he could vote, and that he owned land. John W. Jones, Ward 1, New York State census for Elmira, 1865, Steele Memorial Library, Elmira, N.Y. Clay Holmes wrote that, after retirement, Jones "lived quietly on his little farm, working if he liked, spending much time in doing little acts of kindness to others." Holmes, *Elmira Prison Camp,* 150.

50. *Elmira (N.Y.) Daily Advertiser,* Dec. 2, Sept. 21, 23, 1864, June 30, 1865; *Elmira (N.Y.) Star-Gazette,* May 17, 1993.

51. Report of Persons and Articles Hired.

52. *Elmira (N.Y.) Daily Advertiser,* Nov. 16, 1864.

53. Ibid., Aug. 29, 1864.

54. Charles Petrillo, *The Junction Canal (1855–1871) Elmira, New York, to Athens, Pennsylvania* (Easton, Pa.: Canal History and Technology Press, 1991), 201–2; Thomas E. Byrne,

Chemung County, 16; *Elmira (N. Y.) Sun Telegram,* Aug. 25, 1940; Arthur Keifer, "Junction Canal: Elmira to Athens," *Chemung Historical Journal* 38.1 (Sept. 1992): 4173.

55. *Elmira (N. Y.) Daily Advertiser,* Nov. 18, 1864.

56. Coal cost $10.92½ per ton. In February, J. D. Baldwin provided the prison with 848,620 pounds of coal for $4,635.58. In March, he furnished 379 tons for $4,145.81, and in April, just 69,591 for $380.15. Statement of the Prison Fund, Feb. 28, Mar. 31, Apr. 30, 1865, box 142; Petrillo, *Junction Canal,* 201–2; Keifer, "Junction Canal," 4173.

57. Suydam's Annual Report, 1865; R. Burdell to E. M. Stanton, May 25, 1866, Consolidated Correspondence Erie Railroad, box 566, entry 225, RG 92.

58. M. C. Meigs to E. M. Stanton, June 4, 1866, Consolidated Correspondence Erie Railroad.

59. Hatch and Partridge to M. C. Meigs, Mar. 14, 1865, Letters Received, box 561.

60. Hatch and Partridge to M. C. Meigs, Mar. 14, 1865.

61. N. J. Sappington to A. B. Eaton, Mar. 1, 1865, Letters Received, box 231, entry 10, RG 192.

62. Records of the Commissary General of Prisons, Expenditures, box 1, entry 16, 77, RG 249; Abstract of Disbursements, Mar. 1865, box 142; Statement of the Prison Fund, Mar. 31, 1865, box 142.

63. *Elmira (N. Y.) Daily Advertiser,* May 1, 1865.

64. Ibid.

65. It was wishful thinking for the paper to speculate that the government might make the military depot "a permanent affair." Ibid.

66. Ibid., Nov. 16, 1864.

67. Ibid., Feb. 23, 1865.

68. Ibid., May 10, 1865.

69. Ibid. Some workers at the prison were fortunate to work through May. Among these were George Mathews, Lochmon May, and Horace Little, clerks who earned one hundred dollars a month, and Harrison Hart, Darwin Rudd, Henry Osborn, and Robert Even, all of whom except Even were also clerks, and all of whom earned forty cents daily. Sexton John Jones and hearse driver John Donohoe also remained on the payroll. Receipt Roll, Apr.–May, 1865, box 142, entry 11, RG 249.

70. *Elmira (N. Y.) Daily Advertiser,* July 14, 1865.

71. Abstract of Articles, July 1865. Only four local businesses were on the July account: Hall Brothers, Spaulding and Haskell, Cook and Covell, and Loremore Brothers, which altogether accumulated a bill of $724.80.

72. *Elmira (N. Y.) Daily Advertiser,* Aug. 4, 1865.

73. Records of the Commissary General of Prisons, Expenditures; Report of Persons and Articles Hired.

74. J. J. Elwell to J. D. Bingham, Nov. 14, 20, 1865, Letters Received, box 561.

75. Holmes, *Elmira Prison Camp,* 276; Consolidated Report of Prison Funds, box 1, entries 16, 77, RG 249; N. J. Sappington to A. B. Eaton, Sept. 7, 1865, Letters Received, box 233, entry 17.

76. Remarks on the Influence of War, New York State census for Elmira, N.Y., 1865.

77. Ottman, "History of Elmira," 170.

78. *Elmira (N.Y.) Daily Advertiser,* June 20, 1865.

79. N. J. Sappington to A. B. Eaton, June 28, 1865.

80. Samuel M. Guthe, New York State census for Elmira, N.Y., 1865.

81. D. T. Billings, New York State census for Elmira, N.Y., 1865.

82. Edwin Munson, New York State census for Elmira, N.Y., 1865.

83. Records of the Commissary General of Prisons Expenditures; U.S. War Department, *Medical and Surgical History,* pt. 2, vol. 5:50–63; Thompson, *Photographic History,* vol. 4:44, 54, 56, 69.

84. Munson, New York State census for Elmira, N.Y., 1865.

85. Records of the Commissary General of Prisons Expenditures; Levy, *Camp Douglas,* 7, 9.

CHAPTER NINE

1. *Elmira (N.Y.) Daily Advertiser,* July 6, 1864; Porter, "Nine Months," 160; *New York Post,* Aug. 24, 1864; Keiley, *In Vinculis,* 154–55; Toney, *Privations,* 10; *OR,* vol. 4:67–69; List of Buildings at Elmira, N.Y.

2. Huffman, *Ups and Downs,* 101.

3. Ibid.

4. Porter, "Nine Months," 160.

5. Huffman, *Ups and Downs,* 101.

6. Ibid.; Benson, *Civil War Book,* 143; Huffman, *Ups and Downs,* 101; Holmes, *Elmira Prison Camp,* 38.

7. Keiley, *In Vinculis,* 165, 169. Keiley explained that the bulletin board used to post letters was stolen one day. When officials notified the prisoners that their mail would not be handed out until the board was returned, it reappeared the next day, its back neatly reconfigured into checkerboard.

8. *New York Post,* Aug. 24, 1864; Holmes, *Elmira Prison Camp,* 113, 272.

9. Keiley, *In Vinculis,* 168–69, 176; *Elmira (N.Y.) Daily Advertiser,* Sept. 6, 1864; Grambling diary, Oct. 23, 1864.

10. *Elmira (N.Y.) Daily Advertiser,* July 18, 1864.

11. Keiley, *In Vinculis,* 173; Holmes, *Elmira Prison Camp,* 267.

12. Grambling diary, Dec. 20, 1864. Prisoner Louis Leon said of their dances, "We have a jolly good time." Leon, *Diary of a Tarheel,* 68.

13. King, *My Experience,* 43–44; Robertson, "Scourge of Elmira," 94. Other notable guests who visited the prison camp included Elmira's mayor, John Arnot. Keiley, *In Vinculis,* 167.

14. King, *My Experience,* 43–44; Benson, *Civil War Book,* 135. Prisoner R. B. Ewan asserted that "Buttons" had removed his charms from the jackets of dead Union soldiers laying on the field. Holmes, *Elmira Prison Camp,* 306.

15. King, *My Experience,* 49; Benson, *Civil War Book,* 135.

16. Benson, *Civil War Book,* 135.

17. Stewart, "Reminiscences," 2.

18. Sherrill, *Soldier's Story,* 11.

19. Ibid. See also Keiley, *In Vinculis,* 145, 147.

20. Toney, *Privations,* 103.

21. Holmes, *Elmira Prison Camp,* 338. Stolen rations were frequently sold at the market. Howard, "Short Sketch," 13.

22. Benson, *Civil War Book,* 133; Toney, *Privations,* 100. For more examples of wood stealing and forging sutler's orders, see Holmes, *Elmira Prison Camp,* 154, 317.

23. *Elmira (N.Y.) Daily Advertiser,* Aug. 19, 1864.

24. Holmes, *Elmira Prison Camp,* 71.

25. *New York Post,* Aug. 17, 1864.

26. Charles W. Rhodes, an enlisted soldier, was hired to examine letters for Elmira prisoners. Prison authorities also employed E. M. Mitchell as a mail carrier; each man was remitted forty cents per day for his services. Charles R. Abbott sold cloth mailbags to the prison camp at four dollars per bag. Statement of the Prison Fund, Aug. 31, 1864, Jan. 31, Apr.–May, 1865, boxes 46, 142; *Elmira (N.Y.) Star-Gazette,* Feb. 18, 1914; *Elmira (N.Y.) Daily Advertiser,* July 6, 1864; Keiley, *In Vinculis,* 170; *New York Post,* Aug. 17, 1864; Holmes, *Elmira Prison Camp,* 260; King, *My Experience,* 38.

27. *Elmira (N.Y.) Daily Advertiser,* July 29, 1864.

28. Ibid., Aug. 17, Oct. 3, 1864, Feb. 2, 1865; Holmes, *Elmira Prison Camp,* 262; Walter T. Pawtak, "The Many Addresses of Elmira's Post Offices," *Chemung Historical Journal* 16.2 (Dec. 1970): 1976; *New York Post,* Aug. 17, 1864.

29. Grambling diary, Dec. 25, 1864, Jan. 12, 16, Mar. 3, 12, 1865.

30. W. Campbell to Z. Campbell, Jan. 22, Mar. 3, 1865, Letters, Duke University.

31. Wilkeson, *Recollections,* 225–26. A reporter from the *Elmira Advertiser* also recognized that "we think home sickness is the prevailing disease though the Doctors have all sorts of names in describing the diseases of prisoners." *Elmira (N.Y.) Daily Advertiser,* Dec., 2, 1864.

32. Benson, *Civil War Book,* 135.

33. Toney, *Privations,* 104.

34. Huffman, *Ups and Downs,* 96.

35. Sherrill, *Soldier's Story,* 11, 12.

36. Thomas C. Jones, June 26, 1904, Elmira Prison File.

37. King, *My Experience,* 40; Barrack Inventory.

38. *New York Post,* Aug. 24, 1864; Keiley, *In Vinculis,* 159, 166; *Elmira (N.Y.) Daily Advertiser,* July 21, 1864; Holmes, *Elmira Prison Camp,* 39–40, 320.

39. Holmes, *Elmira Prison Camp,* 39.

40. Prisoner L. B. Jones wrote of the religious services: "We enjoyed those meetings. Never shall we forget them." Holmes, *Elmira Prison Camp,* 39.

41. *New York Post,* Aug. 24, 1864; Benson, *Civil War Book,* 136. Benson noted that there were "constant prayer meetings in various parts of the camp."

42. *New York Post,* Aug. 24, 1864.

43. Holmes, *Elmira Prison Camp,* 41–42.

44. Keiley, *In Vinculis,* 173.

45. Holmes, *Elmira Prison Camp,* 41–42.

46. Keiley, *In Vinculis,* 159.

47. *New York Post,* Aug. 24, 1864; Keiley, *In Vinculis,* 159; Holmes, *Elmira Prison Camp,* 42, 320.

48. Huffman, *Ups and Downs,* 105.

49. Keiley, *In Vinculis,* 166.

50. Ibid., 166–67.

51. *Elmira (N.Y.) Daily Advertiser,* Aug. 17, 1864.

52. Keiley, *In Vinculis,* 166–67.

53. *New York Post,* Aug. 24, 1864; *Elmira (N.Y.) Daily Advertiser,* July 21, 22, Sept. 6, 1864.

54. In the survey, seventy prisoners did not reveal their faith. *Elmira (N.Y.) Daily Advertiser,* Feb. 7, 1865.

55. *New York Post,* Aug. 24, 1864.

56. Among other significant Northern prisons—those that confined about five thousand men from July, 1864 to July, 1865—only two pens had escape records better than Elmira: Camp Chase in Ohio, with two; and Point Lookout, Maryland, with ten. The remaining prisons and the number of prisoners who escaped were Fort Delaware (twenty-five); Rock Island, Illinois (thirty-five); Camp Douglas, Illinois (thirty-eight); and Camp Morton, Indiana (forty-nine). *OR,* vol. 8:997–1003.

57. Ibid., 997–1003; *Elmira (N.Y.) Daily Advertiser,* July 12, 1864; Holmes, *Elmira Prison Camp,* 151, 162–67. Official tallies indicate that a second Elmira prisoner absconded in December 1864, but no account of his method or whereabouts could be ascertained.

58. Holmes, *Elmira Prison Camp,* 337–38.

59. Ibid., 151–53, 158.

60. Joseph Womack, "My Escape," *Nineteenth Century* (May 1870): 971–72.

61. Ibid., 972–73.

62. Ibid., 974–76.

63. Holmes, *Elmira Prison Camp,* 163–65.

64. Wade, "Getting Out of Prison," 380.

65. Ibid.; Robertson, "Scourge of Elmira," 92–93; Holmes, *Elmira Prison Camp,* 160–62.

66. Holmes, *Elmira Prison Camp,* 162.

67. Ibid., 166.

68. Ibid., 161; Robert H. Moore II, ed., "Break Out!" *Civil War Times Illustrated* 30.5 (Nov./Dec. 1991): 56. The latter source is the published memoir of Washington B. Traweek, a prisoner at Elmira.

69. Benson, *Civil War Book,* 64–65, 80–83, 90, 95, 119–25. The old Capitol, former home to the U.S. Congress, was privately owned until the government again utilized the two-story facility during the war, this time for Rebel prisoners. Francis T. Miller, *The Photographic History of the Civil War,* vol. 4, *Prisons and Hospitals,* ed. Holland Thompson (New York: Review of Reviews, 1911) 67.

70. Benson, *Civil War Book,* 126–32, 141.

71. Ibid., 128–32; Holmes, *Elmira Prison Camp*, 161–62. After the hospital tunnels were discovered, Benson wrote: "The commandant is reported to have said: 'I must keep those fellows close, or they'll get away yet. If I hadn't caught them, they'd be halfway to Dixie by now. Well, I feel sorry for them, they deserved to succeed.' This made us feel kindly toward him, realizing he did not punish the men from cruelty, but merely to restrain them from repetition." Benson, *Civil War Book*, 131–32.

72. Benson, *Civil War Book*, 136–38.

73. Moore, "Break Out!" 26; Benson, *Civil War Book*, 137.

74. Benson, *Civil War Book*, 137–38, 146; Moore, "Break Out!" 52–53.

75. Benson, *Civil War Book*, 137–38; Moore, "Break Out!" 52–53.

76. Benson, *Civil War Book*, 138–39; Moore, "Break Out!" 52–53. Traweek wrote that he wore a large gray overcoat, customized with pockets in its tails, which held two sacks on each side. To conceal the limpness that weighed the coat down as the Alabaman walked to the pond, he shifted back and forth to make the tails wag. Inmates referred to Traweek as the "dude" because of his pretentious steps.

77. Benson, *Civil War Book*, 139–40.

78. Ibid., 140–41, 145–46; Moore, "Break Out!" 53.

79. Benson, *Civil War Book*, 140–41.

80. Ibid.

81. Moore, "Break Out!" 54, 59.

82. Ibid., 54; Benson, *Civil War Book*, 144; Holmes, *Elmira Prison Camp*, 162, 195.

83. Moore, "Break Out!" 54.

84. Ibid.; Benson, *Civil War Book*, 144; Holmes, *Elmira Prison Camp*, 162, 195.

85. Benson, *Civil War Book*, 145; Holmes, *Elmira Prison Camp*, 174.

86. Benson, *Civil War Book*, 141–43; Holmes, *Elmira Prison Camp*, 176.

87. Benson, *Civil War Book*, 145–46; Holmes, *Elmira Prison Camp*, 176; Moore, "Break Out!" 59.

88. Moore, "Break Out!" 59.

89. Benson, *Civil War Book*, 141, 146; Moore, "Break Out!" 59; Holmes, *Elmira Prison Camp*, 177, 184, 196.

90. Benson, *Civil War Book*, 147–48.

91. Ibid., 148; Moore, "Break Out!" 59; Holmes, *Elmira Prison Camp*, 177–78, 202–6.

92. Benson, *Civil War Book*, 148–50; Holmes, *Elmira Prison Camp*, 178–79, 186, 208.

93. "Use every effort to secure their arrest" was the telegraphic plea by District Commander Alexander Diven to the various provost marshals, who received word as far away as Troy, New York, and Williamsport, Pennsylvania. Records of the Provost Marshal General, Oct. 7, 1864, vol. 88, entries 854, 856; Moore, "Break Out!" 59.

94. Benson, *Civil War Book*, 153–63; Moore, "Break Out!" 59–61; Holmes, *Elmira Prison Camp*, 179, 182, 189–93.

95. Holmes, *Elmira Prison Camp*, 204. A military commission headed by Cols. J. Adams and John Wilson investigated the tunnel escape. Their findings concluded that the prisoners removed dirt up to the pond, that at some points their burrowing was three feet from the

surface, and that only a single man could fit through the tunnel at a time. J. Adams and J. Wilson to W. Hoffman, Letters Received, Nov. 2, 1864, box 87, entry 11.

CHAPTER TEN

1. Barrack Inventory; Moore, "Break Out!" 54, 56; Toncy, *Privations,* 105; Keiley, *In Vinculis,* 147.

2. Moore, "Break Out!" 54; Toney, *Privations,* 105; Grambling diary, Dec. 13, 1864.

3. Benson, *Civil War Book,* 132; Stewart, "Reminiscences," 2; King, *My Experience,* 48.

4. King, *My Experience,* 48; Toney, *Privations,* 100; Addison, "Recollections," 9–10; Stamp, "Ten Months," 495; Stewart, "Reminiscences," 2; Wade, "Getting Out of Prison," 379.

5. Toney, *Privations,* 100. Sometimes an inmate found guilty of a crime could escape the barrel shirt if willing to cut wood. King, *My Experience,* 48.

6. Keiley, *In Vinculis,* 147; Addison, "Recollections," 9; Porter, "Nine Months," 160; Moore, "Break Out!" 54.

7. Moore, "Break Out!" 54.

8. Keiley, *In Vinculis,* 135; Stamp, "Ten Months," 495.

9. Stamp, "Ten Months," 495.

10. Keiley, *In Vinculis,* 135; King, *My Experience,* 42; Stewart, "Reminiscences," 2; Toney, *Privations,* 116.

11. Toney, *Privations,* 116.

12. Keiley, *In Vinculis,* 135–36.

13. Taylor, "Prison Experience in Elmira, N.Y.," 327. Holmes conceded that "there is no doubt that some of the officers were brutal." Holmes, *Elmira Prison Camp,* 290.

14. Stamp, "Ten Months," 497.

15. Sherrill, *Soldier's Story,* 9.

16. Stamp, "Ten Months," 497.

17. Ibid., 497; Addison, "Recollections," 7; Porter, "Nine Months," 160.

18. Keiley, *In Vinculis,* 134.

19. Ibid.

20. Holmes, *Elmira Prison Camp,* 305. McConnell and Richmond were in charge of prisoners who were employed to keep grounds at the prison. Richmond was especially fastidious, which Marcus Toney realized, when he was sentenced to the guardhouse by the lieutenant for "throwing water on the street." When Toney told Major Colt, "It was not dirty water, but from the dipper, as I saw some sediment previous to drinking," the commandant released him. Toney, *Privations,* 105.

21. Keiley, *In Vinculis,* 134.

22. Ibid.

23. Ibid., 134–35.

24. Holmes, *Elmira Prison Camp,* 316–17.

25. Ibid., 283–84.

26. Ibid., 305, 309.

27. Keiley, *In Vinculis,* 133.

28. Holmes, *Elmira Prison Camp*, 285–86, 324.

29. Ibid., 286–87; Keiley, *In Vinculis*, 145. Mutual feelings of respect between employer and employee were noted at the hospital under the auspices of Dr. Stocker. He wrote his five inmate clerks, "Having the opportunity of expressing to them my entire satisfaction with the faithful and creditable manner in which each discharges his duty, . . . I do not permit any difference in our political views to prejudice me against you, as honorable prisoners, as soldiers, and as gentlemen. . . . I am each day trying to promote your comfort—I am sincerely your friend and well wisher, Anthony E. Stocker., M.D." A. E. Stocker to Prison Hospital, Jan 18, 1865, Beall Collection.

30. Keiley, *In Vinculis*, 195. Other Elmira officers were described in similar terms. G. W. D. Porter stated that "Lieutenant Groves, the cashier of the prison bank, was, in every respect, a gentleman, and, for his kindness and humanity, his name is gratefully remembered by every inmate of the Elmira Prison who come in contact with him." Porter, "Nine Months," 161. Even the highly critical Walter Addison admitted, "I will say in justice to two officers, Captains Whiton and Munger, that they did what they could to alleviate the suffering of prisoners." Addison, "Recollections," 8–9. Depending on the individual circumstances, some inmates considered prison officers their friends, at least after the war, due to kind treatment. See Holmes, *Elmira Prison Camp*, 307–8.

31. Post Returns at Elmira, N.Y.; *New York Times*, Oct. 9, 1864.

32. Moore, "Break Out!" 52; Holmes, *Elmira Prison Camp*, 84; *New York Post*, Aug. 17, 1864; *Rochester Union*, Sept. 13, 1864; Toney, *Privations*, 93–94; Wilkeson, *Recollections*, 221.

33. J. Requa to M. Requa, Sept. 2, 21, 1864, Requa Letters, U.S. Military History Institute, Carlisle Barracks, Carlisle, Pa. (hereafter USAMHI). In addition to guarding Rebel prisoners at Elmira, Requa had helped the Union earlier in the war by inventing a gun that bears his name. Better known as the "Covered Bridge Gun," it was manufactured at his home town, Rochester, N.Y., by the Billinghurst Company.

34. *New York Times*, Oct. 9, 1864.

35. J. J. Elwell to M. C. Meigs, Dec. 20, 1864, Jan. 2, 1865, Letters Received, box 561; *New York Times*, Oct. 9, 1864; J. Requa to M. Requa, Sept. 2, 8, 1864, Letters, Museum of the Confederacy; *Rochester (N.Y.) Union*, Aug. 17, Sept. 13, 1864.

36. *New York Times*, Oct. 9, 1864.

37. J. J. Elwell to M. C. Meigs, Jan. 2, 1865.

38. Wilkeson, *Recollections*, 225.

39. William L. Perry Letters, Feb. 18, 1865, Letters, USAMHI.

40. *Rochester (N.Y.) Union*, Sept. 13, 1864.

41. J. J. Elwell to M. C. Meigs Dec. 16, 20, 1864, Jan. 6, 1865. After the new year, a large portion of the prison fund was expended not only on building for prisoners, but also on supporting their keepers. In January, 1865, Spaulding and Haskell billed $8,482.27 for lumber. Their competitors, Hatch and Partridge, charged $8,909.11 for lumber. Meanwhile, Cook and Covell sold $5,837.43 in hardware to the prison. In February, Spaulding and Haskell, Hatch and Partridge, and Cook and Covel sent invoices for lumber that totaled $4,877.88, $1,191.76, and $3,322.68, respectively. List of Quartermaster Stores, Jan., Feb., 1865, boxes 135, 136; Statement of the Prison Fund, Jan.–Feb. 1865, box 142.

42. *Elmira (N.Y.) Daily Advertiser,* July 14, 1865.

43. Barrack Inventory; List of Buildings at Elmira, N.Y; Abstract of Articles, Aug. 1865.

44. Bruce Catton, *Bruce Catton's Civil War Book* (New York: Fairfax Press, 1984), 544; *Elmira (N.Y.) Daily Advertiser,* Aug. 25, 1864, Jan. 13, 1865.

45. *Elmira (N.Y.) Daily Advertiser,* Aug. 3, 1864.

46. Stewart, "Reminiscences," 2. Most prisoners protested being guarded by U.S. Colored Troops, but a less biased John King wrote about one "negro who stood guard sometimes in our pen. He behaved like a gentlemen." King, *My Experience,* 43.

47. *Rochester (N.Y.) Union,* Aug. 6, 1864. Southerners were not alone in their prejudice toward black prison keepers. According to the *Rochester Union,* "Negroes do it well and are just fitted to do that duty—the drudgery of camp. . . . 'Put a negro where you will, He'll be a negro still.'" *Rochester (N.Y.) Union,* Aug. 6, 1864.

48. Ibid., Sept. 16, 1864.

49. *New York Times,* Oct. 9, 1864; Post Returns at Elmira, N.Y.; *Elmira (N.Y.) Daily Advertiser,* Aug. 2, 1864, Jan. 13, 1865.

50. Post Returns at Elmira, N.Y.; *(Port Jervis, N.Y.) Tri-States Union,* Aug. 12, 1864; *Elmira (N.Y.) Daily Advertiser,* Sept, 1, Oct. 14, 1864, Jan. 30, 1865; William Perry Letters, Feb. 18, 1865.

51. *Elmira (N.Y.) Daily Advertiser,* Sept. 1, Oct. 17, 1864; J. Requa to M. Requa, Oct. 16, 1864, Letters, Museum of the Confederacy.

52. *Rochester (N.Y.) Union,* Aug. 6, 17, 1864.

53. *Elmira (N.Y.) Daily Advertiser,* Oct. 19, 1864.

54. Ibid., Sept. 20, Oct. 17, 28, 1864, May 25, 1865; *Rochester (N.Y.) Union,* Nov. 4, 1864.

55. *Elmira (N.Y.) Daily Advertiser,* Oct. 14, 18, Nov. 24, 1864, Jan. 9, 10, 18, July 18, 1865. The Ladies Hospital Aid Society also held holiday dinners for the officers at Camp Chemung. Ibid., Nov. 28, 1864.

56. Ibid., Oct. 14, 1864.

57. Ibid.

58. Ibid., Jan. 9, 10, July 18, 1865; *Rochester (N.Y.) Union,* Oct. 18, 1864.

59. *Elmira (N.Y.) Daily Advertiser,* Oct. 14, 1864.

60. *Elmira (N.Y.) Daily Advertiser,* Sept. 6, 9, 12, 1864. It might be worth mentioning that Captain Barton, from Rochester, umpired the game.

61. J. Requa to M. Requa, Sept. 2, 8, 1864, Letters, Museum of the Confederacy.

62. J. Requa to M. Requa, Oct. 24, 1864, Letters, Museum of the Confederacy.

63. J. Kidder to H. Kidder, Nov. 10, 1864, Kidder Papers.

64. J. Kidder to H. Kidder, Sept. 25, 1864, Kidder Papers.

65. J. Requa to M. Requa, Sept. 8, Oct. 16, 1864; Civil War Diary of John Holland, March—December, 1865, TS, University of Missouri, Western Historical Manuscript Collection, Rolla, Mo., Sept. 12, 1865.

66. New York State Census for Elmira, N.Y., July 10, 1865, Steele Memorial Library, Elmira, New York.

67. William Perry Letters, Feb. 18, Mar. 9, 1865.

68. William Perry Letters, Feb. 24, June 11, 1865.

69. William Perry Letters, Feb. 18, 1865.

70. Holland diary, Aug. 5, 1865.

71. Holland diary, Aug. 27, 28, 1865.

72. Holland diary, July 28, Dec. 2, 1865.

73. Holland diary, Oct. 20, 1865.

74. Holland diary, Oct. 22, 27, 28, Nov. 3, Dec. 25, 1865.

75. General and Special Orders, Military Court Cases, Elmira, New York, part 3, entry 853, RG 393.

76. General and Special Orders, Military Court Cases, Elmira, New York, part 3.

77. General and Special Orders, Military Court Cases, Elmira, New York, part 3.

78. *Elmira (N.Y.) Daily Advertiser,* Nov. 14, 1864, July 14, 1865; Holland diary, Oct. 17, 1865.

79. *Elmira (N.Y.) Daily Advertiser,* Aug. 3, 1864.

80. Ibid., Sept. 21, 23, Nov. 15, 1864, Feb. 20, 1865; Holland diary, Aug. 25, 1865.

81. J. Requa to M. Requa, Sept. 21, 1864.

82. Holland diary, Aug. 11, Sept. 26, Oct. 5, 1865.

83. *Elmira (N.Y.) Daily Advertiser,* Sept. 21, 1864, Jan. 3, Apr. 15, July 14, 1865; Holland diary, Aug. 13, 29, Oct. 17, 1865; A. G. Steen, "Recollections of Elmira in Civil War Days," 4. Steen also wrote in his account about the period in which "saloons did a big business." Ibid., 3.

84. *Elmira (N.Y.) Daily Advertiser,* Jan. 10, 1865. Other breweries included Manders, Gerbers, and Briggs. Steen, "Recollections," 4.

85. *Elmira (N.Y.) Daily Advertiser,* July 14, 1865.

86. Ibid.

87. The women's college also helped Elmira gain a reputation for containing attractive ladies. Thomas E. Byrne, *Chemung County 1890–1975,* 6. Prisoners and guards both took notice. Prisoner Wilbur Grambling stated that "Elmira is noted for pretty women and a good many of them." Grambling diary, July 25, 1864. Guard John Holland noticed while in town that "there was quite a number of young ladies very good looking." Holland diary," Sept. 14, 1865.

88. Keiley, *In Vinculis,* 168–69.

89. *Elmira (N.Y.) Daily Advertiser,* Feb. 11, Mar. 30, Apr. 10, 1865.

90. Ibid., May 11, 1865.

91. Ibid., Jan. 20, 21, 1865.

92. Ibid., Apr. 10, 24, 1865.

93. Ibid., Apr. 15, June 5, 1865.

94. Ibid., June 5, 1865.

95. Ibid., Aug. 31, 1864.

96. Ibid., Sept. 17, 19, 1864.

97. Ibid., Aug. 25, 1864.

98. Ibid., Sept. 24, 1864. Diven wrote that the order "does not apply to men in detachments under charge of a commissioned officer or sergeant under orders of a commanding officer or men in the execution of orders." A. S. Diven, Sept. 23, 1864, General and Special Orders, Elmira, New York, part 3.

99. *Elmira (N.Y.) Daily Advertiser,* Aug. 14, 1864, Apr. 15, 1865; Holland diary, Aug. 13, 1865. The fine for selling alcohol on Sundays was $10. Eleven days after reinforcing General Orders Number 2, on September 23, an irked General Diven informed Colonel Tracy that "in coming to my office this morning two carriages for soldiers and as many prostitutes passed me. I stopped them and examined the passes of the soldiers. They were leaves to pass in and out of Barracks at pleasure." He had the men arrested, then had three guards "take the girls to the recorders office. I rode to the office and found but 2 of the girls there. The guard must be held responsible for neglect of duty. You will see that they are properly punished." A. S. Diven to B. F. Tracy, Oct. 4, 1865, General and Special Orders, Elmira, New York, vol. 88, entries 854, 856.

100. *Elmira (N.Y.) Daily Advertiser,* Jan. 3, 1865.

101. Ibid., Jan. 20, 1865.

102. Ibid., Feb. 18, 1865.

103. Ibid., Aug. 25, 1864, May 25, 1865.

104. General and Special Orders, Military Court Cases, Elmira, New York, part 3.

105. General and Special Orders, Military Court Cases, Elmira, New York, part 3.

106. General and Special Orders, Military Court Cases, Elmira, New York, part 3.

107. General and Special Orders, Military Court Cases, Elmira, New York, part 3.

108. *Elmira (N.Y.) Daily Advertiser,* Mar. 22, 1865; "Chemung's First Cain," Jan. 28, 1887, Civil War File, Chemung Historical Society.

109. *Elmira (N.Y.) Daily Advertiser,* Mar. 22, 1865; "Chemung's First Cain"; General and Special Orders, Military Court Cases, Elmira, New York, part 3.

110. "Chemung's First Cain."

111. "Chemung's First Cain."

112. "Chemung's First Cain."

113. "Chemung's First Cain." Clay Holmes discovered little regarding any hanging: "Mr. Thad Moore [Commandant. Moore's son] states that, in the barn used by his father while commandant, there was a gallows erected, presumably for a hanging, but no one was ever hung. . . . The fact remains that a gallows was erected, but for what purpose no one seems to know." Holmes, *Elmira Prison Camp,* 351–52. Although Holmes devoted many pages to civilian doctor William C. Wey, further inquiry into Wey's life might have assisted the author. The corpse of Gardner already taken, Dr. Wey retained the imperfect head of Amasa Mulock for his medical study.

CHAPTER ELEVEN

1. B. F. Tracy to H. Wessells, Jan. 9, 1865, Letters Received, box 140, entry 11.

2. A. E. Stocker to B. F. Tracy, Dec. 31, 1864.

3. Undated newspaper clipping written by George S. Crandall, in prison file, Chemung Historical Society; *OR,* vol. 8:419–20; Inspection Reports, Mar. 20, 1865; Holmes, *Elmira Prison Camp,* 123–24.

4. *Elmira (N.Y.) Daily Advertiser,* Mar. 17, 1865; Inspection Reports, Mar. 20, 1865; Holmes, *Elmira Prison Camp,* 122–24; Crandall newspaper clipping. The *Elmira Daily Advertiser* alerted its readers that "Several tents and the flooring of the board barracks occupied

last winter, for the rebels having small pox, passed down the river yesterday, and everybody therefore along the river looking after flood wood and refuse should handle these articles gingerly." *Elmira (N.Y.) Daily Advertiser*, Mar. 17, 1865.

5. King, *My Experience*, 47.

6. Ibid., 47; Holmes, *Elmira Prison Camp*, 124; Crandall newspaper clipping; Huffman, *Ups and Downs*, 103–4.

7. Holmes, *Elmira Prison Camp*, 339.

8. King, *My Experience*, 47.

9. Ibid.

10. Holmes, *Elmira Prison Camp*, 339.

11. Towner, *History of the Chemung County*, 275; *Elmira (N.Y.) Daily Advertiser*, Mar. 17, 1865; Crandall newspaper clipping; *OR*, vol. 8:419–20.

12. Inspection Reports, Mar. 20, 1865, box 130, entry 199; Holmes, *Elmira Prison Camp*, 124–25; King, *My Experience*, 47.

13. Huffman, *Ups and Downs*, 104.

14. Inspection Reports, Mar. 20, 1865.

15. *OR*, vol. 8:419–20. James Huffman had a hand in this: "As soon as the water began to fall and before it left the cookhouses, some of the boys waded in and got some choice hams intended for Yankee officers, but we feasted on them all the same. They tasted 'Moreish.'" Huffman, *Ups and Downs*, 104.

16. *OR*, vol. 8:420; *Elmira (N.Y.) Daily Advertiser*, Mar. 23, 31, 1865.

17. *OR*, vol. 8:420.

18. Inspection Reports, Mar. 20, 1865.

19. Huffman, *Ups and Downs*, 103.

20. King, *My Experience*, 47.

21. Holmes, *Elmira Prison Camp*, 295.

22. Towner, *History of the Chemung County*, 275.

23. *OR*, vol. 8:997–1003; Towner, *History of the Chemung County*, 275.

24. *OR*, vol. 8:419–20.

25. Huffman, *Ups and Downs*, 104.

26. *OR*, vol. 8:997–1003; *Elmira (N.Y.) Daily Advertiser*, Mar. 3, 11, 14, 27, 1865. After sick and wounded prisoners were exchanged, officials gave preference to prisoners from states under Union control. Wilbur Grambling commented there was "an unfair way of sending them off. Just whoever has money to buy his way out can go." Grambling diary, Feb. 28, 1865. His accusation seemed warranted. F. S. Wade, from McNeill's Texas Scouts, for example, wrote that "an order was issued for all prisoners from the subjugated States of Missouri, Kentucky, West Virginia, and Louisiana to report to parole." The Texan approached a parole officer and said "I will give you $10 to erase Texas and substitute Louisiana," and the reply was, "Show me the money." "Then he made the change, and I walked out with my parole." Wade, "Getting Out of Prison," 380. Faced with the same opportunity, Georgian H. T. Davenport "resorted to the making of rings, which he exchanged for tobacco and then the tobacco for money; and when he had ten dollars he bribed the clerk of an officer for parole, and reached home about two weeks before General Lee surrendered." Davenport concluded that bribing

his way to the head of the list "was the best purchase I ever made." H. T. Davenport, "New Commander Georgia Division," *Confederate Veteran* 20 (1912): 454.

27. Some 8,000 feet of pine lumber, 8,400 feet of flooring, 5,864 feet of hemlock, 600 feet of box pine, 450 feet of oak, and 108 feet of pine timber, plus battens, windows, and hardware were required for constructing additional privies, fixing barracks, hospitals, laundry and mess rooms, along with the stockade wall. In March and April, Spaulding and Haskell provided $7,161.82 worth of lumber, while Cook and Covell supplied $3,371.59 worth of hinges, nails, screws, bolts, nuts, lime for privies, door locks, tools, and other accessories. The $487.85 in lumber that Hatch and Partridge supplied was used for coffins. Quartermaster Stores Expended On Prisoners of War, Apr. 1865, box 158, entry 11; Abstract of Disbursements, Mar.–May 1865, box 142; Statement of the Prison Fund, Mar. 31, Apr. 29, 30, 1865, box 142; Inspection Reports, Apr. 11, 1865.

28. Inspection Reports, Apr. 11, 1865.

29. *Elmira (N.Y.) Daily Advertiser,* Apr. 4, 1865.

30. Ibid.

31. Ibid.

32. Ibid.

33. Ibid.

34. Leon, *Diary of a Tarheel,* 69.

35. King, *My Experience,* 48; Toney, *Privations,* 113–14.

36. Grambling diary, Apr. 13, 1865.

37. Toney, *Privations,* 114; Howard, "Short Sketch," 16.

38. Holmes, *Elmira Prison Camp,* 320.

39. Ibid.

40. Toney, *Privations,* 115–16.

41. Ibid. See also *Elmira (N.Y.) Daily Advertiser,* Apr. 4, 1865.

42. Toney, *Privations,* 116; Inspection Reports, Apr. 15, 1865.

43. Huffman, *Ups and Downs,* 106.

44. Toney, *Privations,* 116-17; Holmes, *Elmira Prison Camp,* 320.

45. William A. Tidwell, James O. Hall, and David W. Gaddy, *Come Retribution: The Confederate Secret Service and the Assassination of Lincoln* (Jackson: Univ. Press of Mississippi, 1988), 203, 280, 430. Arch Merrill, a local historian, alleged that Surratt gained access to the prison: "On the arrival in Elmira on April 12, Surratt registered at the Brainard House as 'John Harrison' and mingled freely with the many Union officers who were his fellow guests. By bribing one of them, he got into the prison camp, made his sketches and gathered his data." However, Merrill did not find any evidence that Surratt was actually inside the pen, which undermines the foundation of the story. Merrill wrote: "The Brainard House register he had signed was mysteriously missing" and "sketches he made of Elmira Prison were never found." Merrill's article was based on "the patient research of a Rochester housewife, Margaret Kahler Bearden. Arch Merrill, "John Surratt—Confederate spy incident" in "Southerner Tier," vol. 2, Elmira Prison File.

46. *Elmira (N.Y.) Daily Advertiser,* Apr. 21, 19, 1865. The document was destroyed in 1890 when Tracy's Washington D.C., home was damaged by fire. Holmes, *Elmira Prison*

Camp, 351. Lincoln built a reputation for his pardons. For example, a Virginia prisoner injured in the Shohola train wreck, was released after an old Northern schoolmate made a personal appeal to Lincoln with an endorsement from Pennsylvania governor Andrew Curtin. *Wayne (Pa.) Independent,* Feb. 11, 1914. Lincoln did not limit his pardon to prisoners. Buck Armstrong, an Elmira guard whose family had befriended Lincoln back in Illinois, was allowed to leave military service to help his widowed mother at home. *Elmira (N.Y.) Telegram,* Feb. 11, 1948.

47. A large number of inmates were employed on public works after the flood to assist in the spring cleanup and they earned substantial sums of money. In March, the prison fund expended $2,653.20 "For Prisoners of War Working as Mechanics and Laborers"; in April and May, $1,986.40 and $1,260.90 were paid out from the fund to captives. Abstract of Disbursements, Mar.–May 1865, box 142; Inspections, Apr. 15, 23, May 6, 13, 1865, box 130, entry 199; Towner, *History of the Chemung County,* 271; Holmes, *Elmira Prison Camp,* 24, 272, 274.

48. Holmes, *Elmira Prison Camp,* 274; *Elmira (N.Y.) Daily Advertiser,* Apr. 26, 1865.

49. *Elmira (N.Y.) Daily Advertiser,* Apr. 26, 1865.

50. Ibid., Apr. 25, 1865.

51. L. Thomas to J. Hooker, Aug. 17, 1865, Letters Received, box 561; *Elmira (N.Y.) Daily Advertiser,* May 29, 1865.

52. Elmira (N.Y.) Daily Advertiser, May 29, 1865.

53. Toney, *Privations,* 117–18.

54. Grambling diary, Apr. 24, 26, 1865.

55. Leon, *Diary of a Tarheel,* 69–70.

56. *OR,* vol. 8:1001. Point Lookout came closest with 203 deaths for the month of April.

57. W. Campbell to Z. Campbell, May 9, 1865, Letters, Duke University.

58. Toney, *Privations,* 118.

59. Holmes, *Elmira Prison Camp,* 259.

60. *Elmira (N.Y.) Daily Advertiser,* May 18, 1865.

61. *OR,* vol. 8:1002.

62. Ibid.; *Elmira (N.Y.) Daily Advertiser,* June 3, 1865.

63. Toney, *Privations,* 118.

64. King, *My Experience,* 49–50.

65. *OR,* vol. 8:579.

66. King, *My Experience,* 50. King continued: "As I write today the memories of that prison, our suffering, many old comrades I knew well, all rush to my memory so vividly that I seem to live it all over again. It brings sadness to my heart that I can hardly shake off at times."

67. *Elmira (N.Y.) Daily Advertiser,* Oct. 11, 1864; *OR,* vol. 8:641; King, *My Experience,* 50; Toney, *Privations,* 120. James Marion Howard, employed in burying the dead, wrote, "When we got the dead buried we were permitted to talk to the citizens. . . . To them we could sell finger rings and watch chains. . . . I remember that I had $64.00 when I was discharged." Howard, "Short Sketch," 16.

68. Toney, *Privations,* 149–50.

69. Ibid.; *Elmira (N.Y.) Star-Gazette,* Feb. 18, 1914; Holmes, *Elmira Prison Camp,* 373; *OR,* vol. 8:1002.

70. *Elmira (N.Y.) Daily Advertiser,* June 20, 1865; Cooling, *Tracy,* 35–36.

71. Inspection Reports, July 1, 1865.

72. *Elmira (N.Y.) Daily Advertiser,* July 10, 15, 17, 1865; Holmes, *Elmira Prison Camp,* 260; *OR,* vol. 8:689.

73. *Elmira (N.Y.) Daily Advertiser,* July 11, 1865.

74. Holmes, *Elmira Prison Camp,* 278–79; Grambling diary, Mar. 30, 1865.

75. *Elmira (N.Y.) Daily Advertiser,* Aug. 7, 1865.

76. Ibid.; Account Sales of Articles of Prison Fund Property, Elmira, New York, box 140, entry 11, RG 249. Among the numerous buyers were T. C. Lowell, who bought 8,640 pounds of worn stove pipe for $90.80; E. A. Parker who bought 32 wood stoves for $57.60; Jerry Liddy who purchased 44 coal stoves for $211.20. Meanwhile, Cook and Covell repurchased many of their goods at reduced rates, including wood and coal stoves at $4.50 per unit, and bought the 117 prison camp reflectors for $21 apiece.

77. *Elmira (N.Y.) Telegram,* Feb. 8, 1925, Feb. 8, 1940; Holmes, *Elmira Prison Camp,* 276, 374; *Elmira (N.Y.) Star-Gazette,* Jan. 7, 1987.

78. *Elmira (N.Y.) Daily Advertiser,* Aug. 15, 1865.

79. Ibid. The newspaper did not detail where the prisoners came from, but simply reported that "600 rebel prisoners from various parts of the South were brought to Elmira last Wednesday and consigned to Barracks No 3. for future disposal."

80. Account Sales of Articles of Prison Fund Property, Elmira, New York; L. Thomas to J. Hooker, Aug. 17, 1865, Letters Received; *OR,* vol. 8:700–701; Holmes, *Elmira Prison Camp,* 275–76.

CHAPTER TWELVE

1. *Elmira (N.Y.) Star-Gazette,* Feb. 18, 1914.

2. Memos and Reports of Prisoners of War, Elmira N.Y., United States Military Prison, entry 105, RG 249; U.S. War Department, *Medical and Surgical History,* pt. 2, vol. 5:63. The exact number that died at Elmira will probably never be known. The *Elmira Daily Advertiser* set the number as low as 2,933; Clay Holmes estimated a middling figure of 2,963; and Ausburn Towner believed it was as high as 2,994. *Elmira (N.Y.) Daily Advertiser,* July 27, 1865; Holmes, *Elmira Prison Camp,* 255; Towner, *History of the Chemung County,* 274. With inexact record keeping and uncertainty of every fatality, numbers could be higher than that indicated in the *Official Records.*

3. *OR,* vol. 8:997–1003.

4. Ibid., 986–1003; U.S. War Department, *Medical and Surgical History,* pt. 2, vol. 5:63.

5. George Levy, *To Die in Chicago: Confederate Prisoners At Camp Douglas 1862–1865* (Evanstown, Ill.: Evanstown Publishing, 1994), 273. For a comprehensive look into this Union prison see ibid.

6. U.S. War Department, *Medical and Surgical History,* pt. 2, vol. 5:63.

7. U.S. War Department, *Medical and Surgical History*, pt. 2, vol. 3; 37–38.

8. Ibid., 5:61–63.

9. Ibid., 63.

10. David S. Muzzey, *James G. Blaine: A Political Idol of Other Days* (New York: Dodd, Mead and Co., 1935), 62, 76–78; Haywood J. Pearce, *Benjamin H. Hill: Secession and Reconstruction* (Chicago: Univ. of Chicago Press, 1928), 265–66.

11. *Congressional Record,* 44th Cong., 1st sess., 1876, 4, pt. 1:323–45. For a detailed account of Andersonville, see *Andersonville: The Last Depot* (Chapel Hill, North Carolina: The University of North Carolina Press, 1994) by William Marvel. Marvel finds the deaths at Andersonville more attributable to dearths of food, medicine, and shelter—all of which augmented sickness—than to actions of the camp's commandant, Henry Wirz. Marvel is sympathetic toward Wirz's plight, which ultimately led to his execution, but less lenient with the federal government's refusal to reinstate the prisoner exchange system.

12. *Congressional Record,* 44th Cong., 1st sess., 1876, 4, pt. 1: 323–45. Libby Prison gained enough repute that the building was disassembled and carted off to Chicago for an upcoming world's fair.

13. Ibid.

14. Ibid.

15. Representative Preston Brooks's violent caning of Massachusetts senator Charles Sumner in Congress before the war was praised in the same manner as Hill's verbal assault on Blaine after the conflict. Pearce, *Benjamin H. Hill,* 62, 265, 279–81, 303; McPherson, *Battle Cry,* 150–51.

16. *Congressional Record,* 44th Cong., 1st sess., 1876, 4, pt. 1:345.

17. Ibid., 345–49.

18. Ibid., 347–48. The author, who wrote that he "served as one of the medical officers for many months" at Elmira Prison, only identified himself at the end of the letter as an "Ex-Medical Officer United States Army." See "Statement of a United States Medical Officer," 296–98.

19. *Congressional Record,* 44th Cong., 1st sess., 1876, 4, pt. 1:348.

20. Cooling, *Tracy,* 40–41; Harold F. Gosnell, *Boss Platt and His New York Machine* (Chicago: Univ. of Chicago Press, 1924), 20–23; *Congressional Record,* 348.

21. *Congressional Record,* 44th Cong., 1st sess., 1876, 4, pt. 1:348.

22. Ibid. At Andersonville, about 13,000 of the prison's 45,000 inmates perished, which translates into a mortality rate of 28.8 percent—a rate fairly comparable to Elmira's 24.3 percent. McPherson, *Battle Cry,* 796–97.

23. Tracy, *Cooling,* 8, 32, 40–41.

24. *Congressional Record,* 44th Cong., 1st sess., 1876, 4, pt. 1:385.

25. Ibid.

26. Holmes, *Elmira Prison Camp,* 282.

27. *Elmira (N.Y.) Daily Advertiser,* Jan. 17, 1876.

28. Ibid., Jan. 19, 1876.

29. *Portland (Maine) Daily Press,* Jan. 24, 1876.

30. Ibid., Jan. 24, 1876.

31. Ibid.

32. Ibid.

33. Hunter, "Warden for the Union," 2, 29, 159.

34. Ibid., 161, 227. Hunter added, "Most damning was the fact most of the fund remained unused. Large sums were not expended for the purpose they were intended, providing for the needs of prisoners" (p. 161). Hunter also asserted that "being thrifty, the Colonel even deleted the word 'Respectfully' from his signature in telegrams to General Grant, apparently to save the cost of a word" (p. 158–59). Remember that Depot Commander Eastman tried to convince Hoffman that Barracks Number 3 could only support half the number proposed by the prison commissary. See *OR*, vol. 7:152, 157, 394.

35. Expenditures.

36. Burial Records in the Office of the Quartermaster General, Elmira, New York, Sept. 23, 1874, box 25, entry 576. RG 92; Statement by John W. Jones, Burial Records in the Office of the Quartermaster General, Elmira, New York, box 69, entry 576; Woodlawn National Cemetery Pamphlet," Elmira, N.Y.

37. Burial Records, Sept. 23, 1874, Feb. 1, 7, 1876, Nov. 24, 1876, box 25, entry 576.

38. Holmes, *Elmira Prison Camp*, 162–63.

39. Burial Records, Mar. 9, 1906, box 2158, entry 89.

40. William Elliot was appointed commissioner for marking Confederate graves and paid $2,500 annually for his services, plus travel expenses. Burial Records, Mar. 9, 1906.

41. Burial Records, boxes 2158, 561, 4, entries 89, 225, RG 92; Statement of Expenses incurred by William Elliot while traveling on official business with the marking of Confederate graves, entry 701, RG 92; Towner, *History of the Chemung County,* 274; Holmes, *Elmira Prison Camp,* 132–33.

42. Burial Records, May 17, 1909, Aug. 15, 1910, box 2158, entry 89; Statement of Expenses by William Elliot.

43. Records of the Quartermaster General Proposals for the Manufacture and Delivery of Markers For Confederate Graves, 1903–1910, Sept. 26, 1907, entry 701, RG 92. Altogether, twenty thousand headstones were placed on order from the Blue Ridge Marble Company. Burial Records, June 17, 1909, box 2158, entry 89.

44. Markers, Sept. 26, 1907, entry 701, RG 92.

45. Markers, Aug. 15, 1907.

46. Markers, Oct. 2, 1907.

47. Gentry, "Confederate Dead at Elmira Prison," 396.

48. Burial Records, May 17, 1909. To be fair, it was also noted that Mr. Vogt and his family members were some of the first people to help the injured after the collision. See Boyd, "Shohola Train Wreck," 1259–60.

49. Burial Records, May 17, 1909.

50. Burial Records, July 22, 1909, boxes 2157–58, entry 89.

51. Burial Records, July 28, Aug. 5, Sept. 14, 19, Oct. 8, 12, 17, 22, Dec. 13, 1910, boxes 2157–58, entry 89; Burial Records, Mar. 23, Apr. 8, Sept. 6, Oct. 14, 1911, box 7017, entry 89.

52. Burial Records, Apr. 8, 1911.

53. Burial Records, Sept. 2, 6, 9, 22, 1911, Oct. 12, 1910, box 7017, entry 89; Mott, *Story of Erie*, 442–43; *Pike County (N.Y.) Dispatch*, Mar. 7, 1974.

54. Burial Records, Sept. 6, 9, 22, Oct. 14, 1911, Oct. 12, 1910; Holmes, *Elmira Prison Camp*, 374–75; Boyd, "Shohola Train Wreck," 1256, 1260; S. A. Cunningham, ed., "Monument at Woodlawn, Elmira, N.Y.," *Confederate Veteran* 20 (1912): 312; Jack Jackson, "The Great Locomotive Wreck," *Civil War Times Illustrated* (Feb. 1995): 51, 53. Two Southerners, John and Michael Johnson, were taken back to Shohola, but subsequently died from their wounds. They were buried across the Delaware, at the Congregational church cemetery of Barryville, New York, and remain there to this day. On September 1, 1993, a state historical marker was dedicated to the accident victims and erected in Shohola rather than the wreck site for the convenience of sightseers; it is located near the Shohola Township Caboose Museum, off Route 434, not far from the Delaware River Bridge. "Unveiling and Dedication of the State Historical Marker Commemorating the Civil War Prison Train Wreck at Shohola Pennsylvania," Sept. 1, 1993.

55. *Elmira (N.Y.) Star-Gazette*, Aug. 6, 1914. The paper continued: "Burials were not known to have been made there to any extent but no doubt there are many other unmarked, unknown graves beneath the surface thereabouts, bodies of fathers, brothers, sons, and sweethearts of whom some brave Southern woman waited in vain for news." For more on unmarked graves, see also Holmes, *Elmira Prison Camp*, 138.

56. *Elmira (N.Y.) Telegram*, Feb. 8, 1925. The paper also commented about Guinnip's other building, which was "once offered to the city as a Civil War relic, to be moved to a city park. The city, however, did not take the suggestion and the subject was dropped."

57. Inscription on the Shohola Monument, Woodlawn National Cemetery, Elmira, N.Y.

58. *Elmira (N.Y.) Telegram*, Oct. 13, 1940.

59. Ibid., Jan. 16, 1955.

60. Ibid.

61. See *Chemung Historical Journal* 6.1 (Sept. 1960), 9.4, (June 1964), 10.1 (Sept. 1964), and Robertson, "Scourge of Elmira."

62. *Rochester (N.Y.) Democrat and Chronicle*, Aug. 19, 1984; *New York Times*, Aug. 12, 1984.

63. *New York Times*, Aug. 12, 1984.

64. *Rochester (N.Y.) Democrat and Chronicle*, Aug. 19, 1984.

65. Ibid.

66. Ibid.; *New York Times*, Aug. 12, 1984; Thomas E. Byrne, ed., "Memorial Honors the Blue and Grey," *Chemung Historical Journal* 31.1, (Sept. 1985) 3497–3500. Among the local contributors was the Elmira Water Board, which gave the property on which the monument is built; John Parks Williams and McDonald Excavating directed the construction; Dalrymple Gravel and Contracting gave thirty-five tons of cement; Elmira Quality Printers contributed the photographs; and citizens donated their time for tasks that ranged from historical research to arrangements for the monument's dedication day. The Chemung County Chamber of Commerce and the Chemung County Historical Society guided activities. Byrne, "Memorial Honors the Blue and Grey," 3497–3503.

67. Byrne, "Memorial Honors the Blue and Grey," 3497–3503.

68. Ibid.; "Elmira Civil War Monument Souvenir Program," Aug. 25, 1985.

69. Byrne, "Memorial Honors the Blue and Grey," 3497–3503; "Elmira Civil War Monument Souvenir Program," Aug. 25, 1985. More recently, a flag pole that stands on the property of Paul and Norma Searles on Winsor Avenue was authenticated as a part of the prison camp. City historian Carl Morrell directed movement of the flag pole and its stone foundation, which the Searles donated, down the street to the site of the monument. *Elmira (N.Y.) Star-Gazette,* Dec. 1, 1991, Feb. 4, 1992. Expenditures from prison camp records indicate that military officials did indeed purchase a "Flag Staff for Prison Camp" at a cost of $6.35. Abstract of Disbursements, May 1865, box 142.

Bibliography

UNPUBLISHED MATERIAL

Addison, Walter D. Recollections of a Confederate Soldier of the Prison Pens at Point Lookout, Md., and Elmira, New York. MS. Thomas Jefferson Green Papers, Southern Historical Collection, University of North Carolina, Chapel Hill.

Army and Continental Command. Record Group 393. National Archives.

Beall, William N. R. William N. R. Beall Collection. Prisoner of War Series, Eleanor S. Brockenbrough Library, Museum of the Confederacy, Richmond, Virginia.

Bruin, D. D. Bruin Papers. Special Collections, University of North Carolina, Chapel Hill.

Campbell, William. William L. Campbell Papers. Special Collections, Duke University.

Chemung County Historical Society. Miscellaneous Letters and Papers in the Prison and Civil War Files. MS, TS. Elmira, New York.

Colt, Henry V. Pension and Service Records. National Archives, Washington, D.C.

Elwell, John J. Pension and Service Records. National Archives, Washington, D.C.

Grambling, Wilbur. Diary and Account Book. Chemung County Historical Society, Elmira, New York.

Fluhr, George J. Miscellaneous Papers. Shohola Railroad and Historical Society, Shohola, Pennsylvania.

Holland, John. Civil War Diary of John Holland. TS. University of Missouri, Western Historical Manuscript Collection, Rolla.

Howard, James Marion. A Short Sketch of My Early Life. TS. Chemung County Historical Society, Elmira, New York.

Kidder, John S. Family Papers of John S. Kidder. MS. Sharon Historical Society, Sharon Springs, New York.

———. Pension and Service Records. National Archives, Washington, D.C.

Military Order of the Loyal Legion—Companion Eugene Francis Sanger. Bangor Historical Society, Bangor, Maine.

Office of the Adjutant General. Record Group 94. National Archives.

Office of the Commissary General of Subsistence. Record Group 192. National Archives.
Office of the Commissary General of Prisons. Record Group 249. National Archives.
Office of the Quartermaster General. Record Group 92. National Archives.
Perry, William L. William L. Perry Papers, 150th Pa. Infantry. United States Army Military
    Institute, Carlisle Barracks, Carlisle, Pennsylvania.
Requa, Josephus. Josephus Requa Papers, 54th N.Y.N.G. United States Army Military
    Institute, Carlisle Barracks, Carlisle, Pennsylvania.
Sanger, Eugene F. Pension and Service Records. National Archives, Washington, D.C.
Sappington, Nicholas J. Pension and Service Records. National Archives, Washington, D.C.
Snyder, Howard B. The Wreck Of The Prison Train: A Factual Narrative Based on
    Observations of Persons on the Scene at the Time. TS. Chemung Historical Society,
    Elmira, New York.
Steen, A. G. Recollections of Elmira in Civil War Days. TS. Chemung Historical Society,
    Elmira, New York.
Stewart, Tapley H. Reminiscences of Tapley H. Stewart, McGregor, Texas. MS. Special
    Collections, Emory University, Atlanta, Georgia.
War Departments Collection of Confederate Records. Record Group 109. National Archives.

PRINTED PRIMARY SOURCES

Benson, Susan W., ed. *Berry Benson's Civil War Book: Memoirs of a Confederate Scout and
    Sharpshooter*. Athens, Ga.: Univ. of Georgia Press, 1991.
Huffman, James. *Ups and Downs of a Confederate Soldier*. New York: William E. Rudge's
    Sons, 1940.
Jones, James P., and Edward F. Keuchel. "A Rebel's Diary of Elmira Prison Camp." *Che-
    mung Historical Journal* (Mar. 1975):2457–64.
Keiley, Anthony M. *In Vinculis; or, The Prisoner of War*. Petersburg, Va.: Daily Index
    Office, 1866.
King, John R. *My Experience in the Confederate Army and in Northern Prisons*. Clarksburg,
    W.V.: United Daughters of Confederacy, 1917.
Leon, Louis. *Diary of a Tarheel Confederate Soldier*. Charlotte, N.C.: Stone Publishing,
    1913.
Moore, Robert H., ed. "Break Out!" *Civil War Times Illustrated* 30.5 (Nov.–Dec. 1991):
    26, 52–61.
New York State census for Elmira, New York, 1865.
Opie, John N. *A Rebel Cavalryman With Lee, Stewart and Jackson*. Chicago: W. B. Conkey,
    1899.
Porter, G. W. D. "Nine Months In A Northern Prison." *Annals of the Army of the Ten-
    nessee* 1.4 (1878): 157–62.
Rifleman, A. *Prisoner of War or Five Months Among the Yankees*. Richmond, Va.: West
    and Johnston, 1865.
Sherrill, Miles O. *A Soldier's Story: Prison Life and Other Incidents in the War of 1861–65*.
    Raleigh, N.C.: Edward's and Broughton Printing, 1911.

Stamp, J. B. "Ten Months Experience in Northern Prisons." *Alabama Historical Quarterly* 18 (1956): 486–98.

Toney, Marcus B. *The Privations of a Private.* Nashville, Tenn.: Publishing House of the M. E. Church, South, Smith & Lamar, Agents, 1907.

U.S. census for Chemung County, Elmira, New York, 1850.

U.S. census for Chemung County, Elmira, New York, 1860.

U.S. Congressional Record. 44th Congress, 1st Session and Special Senate, 4.1, January 10–13, 1876, 323–45.

U.S. War Department. *The War of the Rebellion: A Compilation of the Official Records of the Union and Confederate Armies,* Series 2, Vols. 4, 6–8. *Prisoners of War.* Washington, D.C.: Government Printing Office, 1899.

———. *The Medical and Surgical History of the War of the Rebellion.* Part 2, Vols. 1, 3, 5, 8. *Medical History.* Washington, D.C.: Government Printing Office, 1879.

Wilkeson, Frank. *Recollections Of A Private Soldier In The Army Of The Potomac.* New York: G. P. Putnam's Sons, 1887.

Womack, Joseph. "My Escape." *Nineteenth Century* (May 1870): 967–76.

SECONDARY SOURCES

Boyd, Joseph C. "Shohola Train Wreck." *Chemung Historical Journal* (June 1964): 1253–60.

Byrne, Thomas E. *Chemung County 1890–1975.* Elmira, N.Y.: Chemung County Historical Society, 1976.

———, ed. *Chemung County . . . Its History.* Elmira, N.Y.: Chemung County Historical Society, 1961.

———. "Elmira's Civil War Prison Camp: 1864–65." *Chemung Historical Journal* 10.1 (Sept. 1964): 1279–300.

Catton, Bruce. *Bruce Catton's Civil War Book.* New York: Fairfax Press, 1984.

Cooling, Benjamin F. *Benjamin Franklin Tracy: Father of the Modern American Fighting Navy.* Hamden, Conn.: Archon Books, 1973.

Davis, William C., ed. *The Image of War.* Vol. 4, *Fighting for Time.* New York: Doubleday, 1983.

Dawson, Dawn P., ed. *Magill's Medical Guide: Health and Illness.* Vol. 3. Englewood Cliffs, N.J.: Salem Press, 1995.

Fluhr, George J. *Shohola—History of a Township.* Lackawaxen, Pa.: Alpha Publishing, 1992.

Gosnell, Harold F. *Boss Platt and His New York Machine.* Chicago: Univ. of Chicago Press, 1924.

Harvey, Oscar J. *History of Wilkes-Barre.* Wilkes-Barre, Pa.: Raeder Press, 1909.

Hesseltine, William B. *Civil War Prisons: A Study in War Psychology.* Columbus, Ohio: Ohio State Univ. Press, 1930.

———, ed. *Civil War Prisons.* Kent, Ohio: Kent State Univ. Press, 1972.

Holmes, Clay W. *The Elmira Prison Camp: A History of the Military Prison at Elmira, N.Y. July 6, 1864, to July 10, 1865.* New York: Knickerbocker Press, 1912.

Hunter, Leslie G. "Warden for the Union: General William Hoffman (1807–1884)." Ph.D. diss., Univ. of Arizona, 1971.

Jackson, Jack. "The Great Locomotive Wreck." *Civil War Times Illustrated* (Feb. 1995): 48–53.

Keifer, Arthur. "Junction Canal: Elmira to Athens." *Chemung Historical Journal* (Sept. 1992): 4169–75.

Klein, Philip S. and Ari Hoogenboom, *A History of Pennsylvania*. University Park: Pennsylvania State Univ. Press, 1980.

Levy, George. *To Die in Chicago: Confederate Prisoners at Camp Douglas 1862–1865*. Evanstown, Ill.: Evanstown Publishing, 1994.

McPherson, James M. *Battle Cry of Freedom: The Civil War Era*. New York: Oxford Univ. Press, 1988.

Marvel, William. *Andersonville: The Last Depot*. Chapel Hill: Univ. of North Carolina Press, 1994.

Miller, Francis T., ed. *The Photographic History of the Civil War*. Vol. 7, *Prisons and Hospitals*. Holland Thompson, ed. New York: Review of Reviews, 1911.

Miller, Zane L. *The Urbanization of Modern America: A Brief History*. New York: Harcourt Brace Jovanovich, 1973.

Horigan, J. Michael. "Elmira Prison Camp—A Second Opinion." *Chemung Historical Journal* 30.3 (Mar. 1985): 3449–57.

Morrell, Carl. "Elmira's Elusive Northside Civil War Barracks." *Chemung Historical Journal* 41.1 (Sept. 1996): 4557–59.

Mott, Edward H. *Between the Ocean and the Lakes: The Story of Erie*. New York: Tickner, 1899.

Muzzey, David S. *James G. Blaine: A Political Idol of Other Days*. New York: Dodd, Mead, 1935.

Ottman, Walter H. "A History of the City of Elmira, New York." Ph.D. diss., Cornell Univ., 1900.

Pawtak, Walter T. "The Many Addresses of Elmira's Post Offices," *Chemung Historical Journal* 16.2 (Dec. 1970): 1976.

Pearce, Haywood J. *Benjamin Hill: Secession And Reconstruction*. Chicago: Univ. of Chicago Press, 1928.

Petrillo, Charles. *The Junction Canal (1855–1871) Elmira, New York, to Athens, Pennsylvania*. Easton, Pa.: Canal History and Technology Press, 1991.

Sifakis, Stewart. *Who Was Who in the Civil War*. New York: Facts On File, 1988.

Strickland, G. Kent. "The Search For Thomas." *The State: Down Home in North Carolina*. 54.6 (Nov. 1986): 20–22, 36–37.

Tidwell, William A., James O. Hall, and David W. Gaddy. *Come Retribution: The Confederate Secret Service and the Assassination of Lincoln*. Jackson: Univ. Press of Mississippi, 1988.

Towner, Ausburn. *History of the Chemung County, New York*. Syracuse, N.Y.: D. Mason, 1892.

NEWSPAPERS

Albany Atlas & Argus
Bangor (Maine) Daily News
Binghamton (N.Y.) Times
Elmira Daily Advertiser
Elmira Star-Gazette
Elmira Sun-Telegram
Elmira Telegram
Elmira Weekly Advertiser
Honesdale (Pennsylvania) Republic
New York Evening Express
New York Evening Post
New York Herald
New York Sun
New York Times
New York World
Pike County Dispatch (Milford, Pennsylvania)
Portland (Maine) Daily Press
Rochester (New York) Democrat and Chronicle
Rochester (New York) Union & Advertiser
Port Jervis (New York) Tri-States Union
Wayne County Herald (Honesdale, Pennsylvania)
Wayne Independent (Honesdale, Pennsylvania)

JOURNALS

Chemung Historical Journal
Civil War History
Civil War Times Illustrated
Confederate Veteran
Southern Historical Society Papers

Index